James Buchanan

The Administration on the Eve of the Rebellion

A History of Four Years before the War

James Buchanan

The Administration on the Eve of the Rebellion
A History of Four Years before the War

ISBN/EAN: 9783337208783

Printed in Europe, USA, Canada, Australia, Japan

Cover: Foto ©ninafisch / pixelio.de

More available books at **www.hansebooks.com**

THE ADMINISTRATION

ON THE

EVE OF THE REBELLION:

History of Four Years before the War.

BY JAMES BUCHANAN,

EX-PRESIDENT OF THE UNITED STATES OF AMERICA.

LONDON:
SAMPSON LOW, SON, & MARSTON,
English, American, and Colonial Booksellers and Publishers,
59, LUDGATE HILL.

1865.

PREFACE.

THE following historical narrative of the events preceding the late rebellion was prepared soon after its outbreak, substantially in the present form. It may be asked, Why, then, was it not published at an earlier period? The answer is, that the publication was delayed to avoid the possible imputation, unjust as this would have been, that any portion of it was intended to embarrass Mr. Lincoln's administration in the vigorous prosecution of pending hostilities. The author deemed it far better to suffer temporary injustice than to expose himself to such a charge. He never doubted the successful event of the war, even during its most gloomy periods. Having drawn his first breath soon after the adoption of the Federal Constitution and the Union which it established, and having been an eye-witness of the blessed effects of these, in securing liberty and prosperity at home, and in presenting an example to the oppressed of other lands, he felt an abiding conviction that the American people would never suffer the Great Charter of their rights to be destroyed. To the Constitution, as interpreted by its framers, he has ever been devoted, believing that the specific powers which it confers on the Federal Government, notwithstanding the experience of the last dreary years, are sufficient for almost every possible emergency, whether in peace or in war. He, therefore, claims the merit—if merit it be simply to do one's duty—that whilst in the exercise of Executive functions, he never violated any of its provisions.

It may be observed that no extensive and formidable rebellion of an intelligent people against an established Government has ever arisen without a long train of previous and subsidiary causes. A principal object of the author, therefore, is to present to the reader a historical sketch of the antecedents ending in the late rebellion. In performing this task, the eye naturally fixes itself, as the starting point, upon the existence of domestic slavery in the South, recognized and protected as this was by the Constitution of the United States. We shall not inquire whether its patriotic and enlightened framers acted with wise foresight in yielding their sanction to an institution which is in itself a great social evil, though they considered this was necessary to avoid the still greater calamity of dissolving the Convention without the formation of our Federal Union.

The narrative will prove that the original and conspiring causes of all our future troubles are to be found in the long, active, and persistent hostility of the Northern Abolitionists, both in and out of Congress, against Southern slavery, until the final triumph of their cause in the election of President Lincoln; and on the other hand, the corresponding antagonism and violence with which the advocates of slavery resisted these efforts, and vindicated its preservation and extension up till the period of secession. So excited were the parties, that had they intended to furnish material to inflame the passions of the one against the other, they could not have more effectually succeeded than they did by their mutual criminations and recriminations. The struggle continued without intermission for more than the quarter of a century, except within the brief interval between the passage of the Compromise measures of 1850 and the repeal of the Missouri Compromise in 1854, during which the hostile feelings of the parties were greatly allayed, and hopes were entertained that the strife might finally subside. These peaceful prospects, it will appear, were soon blasted by the repeal of this Compromise, and the struggle was then renewed with more bitterness than ever until the final catastrophe. Many grievous errors were committed by both parties from the beginning, but the most fatal of them all was the secession of the cotton States.

The authorities cited in the work will show that Mr. Buchanan never failed, upon all suitable occasions, to warn his countrymen of the approaching danger, and to advise them of the proper means to avert it. Both before and after he became President he was an earnest advocate of compromise between the parties to save the Union, but Congress disregarded his recommendations. Even after he had, in his messages, exposed the dangerous condition of public affairs, and when it had become morally certain that all his efforts to avoid the civil war would be frustrated by agencies far beyond his control, they persistently refused to pass any measures enabling him or his successor to execute the laws against armed resistance, or to defend the country against approaching rebellion.

The book concludes by a notice of the successful domestic

and foreign policy of the administration. In the portion of it concerning our relations with the Mexican Republic, a history of the origin and nature of "the Monroe doctrine" is appropriately included.

It has been the author's intention, in the following pages, to verify every statement of fact by a documentary or other authentic reference, and thus save the reader, as far as may be possible, from reliance on individual memory. From the use of private correspondence he has resolutely abstained.

WHEATLAND, *September*, 1865.

CONTENTS.

CHAPTER I.

The rise and progress of Anti-Slavery agitation—The Higher Law—Anti-Slavery Societies—Their formation and proceedings—Their effect destructive of State Emancipation—The case in Virginia—Employment of the Post Office to circulate incendiary publications and pictures among the slaves—Message of General Jackson to prohibit this by law—His recommendation defeated—The Pulpit, the Press, and other agencies—Abolition Petitions—The rise of an extreme Southern Pro-Slavery party—The Fugitive Slave Law of 1793, and the case of Prigg *vs.* Pennsylvania, and its pernicious effects—The South threaten Secession—The course of Mr. Buchanan as Senator—The Wilmot Proviso and its consequences—The Union in serious danger at the meeting of Congress in December, 1849, ... 9

CHAPTER II.

Meeting of Congress in December, 1849—The five Acts constituting the Compromise of September, 1850—Effect of the Compromise in allaying excitement—Whig and Democratic Platforms indorse it—President Pierce's happy reference to it in his Message of December, 1853—The repeal of the Missouri Compromise reopens the slavery agitation—Its passage in March, 1820, and character—Its recognition by Congress in 1845, on the Annexation of Texas—The history of its repeal—This repeal gives rise to the Kansas troubles—Their nature and history—The Lecompton Constitution and proceedings of Congress upon it—The Republican party greatly strengthened—Decision of the Supreme Court in the Dred Scott case—Repudiated by the Republican party and by the Douglas Democracy—Sustained by the old Democracy—The Kansas and Nebraska Act—The policy and practice of Congress toward the Territories—Abuse of President Buchanan for not adhering to the Cincinnati Platform without foundation, ... 21

derson's removal from Fort Moultrie to Fort Sumter—The President's interview with the Commissioners, who demand a surrender of all the forts—His answer to this demand—Their insolent reply, and its return to them—Its presentation to the Senate by Mr. Davis—Secretary Floyd requested to resign—He resigns and becomes a secessionist—Fort Sumter threatened—The *Brooklyn* ordered to carry reënforcements to the fort—The *Star of the West* substituted at General Scott's instance—She is fired upon—Major Anderson demands of Governor Pickens a disavowal of the act—The Governor demands the surrender of the fort—The Major proposes to refer the question to Washington—The Governor accepts—The truce—Colonel Hayne and Lieutenant Hall arrive in Washington on the 13th January—Letter from Governor Pickens not delivered to the President until the 31st January—The answer to it—Colonel Hayne's insulting reply—It is returned to him—Virginia sends Mr. Tyler to the President with a view to avoid hostilities—His arrival in Washington and his proposals—Message of the President, ... 180

CHAPTER XI.

Fort Sumter again—An expedition prepared to relieve it—The expedition abandoned on account of a despatch from Major Anderson—Mr. Holt's letter to President Lincoln—Fort Pickens in Florida—Its danger from the rebels—The *Brooklyn* ordered to its relief—The means by which it was saved from capture approved by General Scott and Messrs. Holt and Toucey, with the rest of the Cabinet—Refutation of the charge that arms had been stolen—Report of the Committee on Military Affairs and other documentary evidence—The Southern and Southwestern States received less than their quota of arms—The Pittsburg cannon—General Scott's unfounded claim to the credit of preventing their shipment to the South—Removal of old muskets—Their value—Opinion of Mr. Holt in regard to the manner in which President Buchanan conducted the administration, ... 209

CHAPTER XII.

The reduction of the expenses of the Government under Mr. Buchanan's administration—The expedition to Utah—The Covode Committee, . . . 231

CHAPTER XIII.

The successful foreign policy of the administration with Spain, Great Britain, China, and Paraguay—Condition of the Mexican Republic; and the recommendations to Congress thereupon not regarded, and the effect—The treaty with Mexico not ratified by the Senate, and the consequences—The origin, history, and nature of the "Monroe Doctrine," 258

MR. BUCHANAN'S ADMINISTRATION.

CHAPTER I.

The rise and progress of Anti-Slavery agitation—The Higher Law—Anti-Slavery Societies—Their formation and proceedings—Their effect destructive of State Emancipation—The case in Virginia—Employment of the Post Office to circulate incendiary publications and pictures among the slaves—Message of General Jackson to prohibit this by law—His recommendation defeated—The Pulpit, the Press, and other agencies—Abolition Petitions—The rise of an extreme Southern Pro-Slavery party—The Fugitive Slave Law of 1793, and the case of Prigg *vs.* Pennsylvania, and its pernicious effects—The South threaten Secession—The course of Mr. Buchanan as Senator—The Wilmot Proviso and its consequences—The Union in serious danger at the meeting of Congress in December, 1849.

THAT the Constitution does not confer upon Congress power to interfere with slavery in the States, has been admitted by all parties and confirmed by all judicial decisions ever since the origin of the Federal Government. This doctrine was emphatically recognized by the House of Representatives in the days of Washington, during the first session of the first Congress,* and has never since been seriously called in question. Hence, it became necessary for the abolitionists, in order to furnish a pretext for their assaults on Southern slavery, to appeal to a law higher than the Constitution.

Slavery, according to them, was a grievous sin against God, and therefore no human Constitution could rightfully shield it from destruction. It was sinful to live in a political confederacy which tolerated slavery in any of the States composing it; and if this could not be eradicated, it would become a sacred

---

* Annals of Congress, vol. ii., p. 1474, Sept. 1, 1789–'90.

duty for the free States to separate from their guilty associates. This doctrine of the higher law was preached from the pulpits and disseminated in numerous publications throughout New England. At the first, it was regarded with contempt as the work of misguided fanatics. Ere long, however, it enlisted numerous and enthusiastic partisans. These were animated with indomitable zeal in a cause they deemed so holy. They constituted the movement party, and went ahead; because, whether from timidity or secret sympathy, the conservative masses failed in the beginning to resist its progress in an active and determined spirit.

The anti-slavery party in its career never stopped to reflect that slavery was a domestic institution, exclusively under the control of the sovereign States where it existed; and therefore, if sinful in itself, it was certainly not the sin of the people of New England. With equal justice might conscience have impelled citizens of Massachusetts to agitate for the suppression of slavery in Brazil as in South Carolina. In both cases they were destitute of all rightful power over the subject.

The Constitution having granted to Congress no power over slavery in the States, the abolitionists were obliged to resort to indirect means outside of the Constitution to accomplish their object. The most powerful of these was anti-slavery agitation: agitation for the double purpose of increasing the number of their partisans at home, and of exciting a spirit of discontent and resistance among the slaves of the South. This agitation was conducted by numerous anti-slavery societies scattered over the North. It was a new and important feature of their organization that women were admitted as members. Sensitive and enthusiastic in their nature against wrong, and believing slavery to be a mortal sin, they soon became public speakers, in spite of the injunctions of an inspired apostle; and their harangues were quite as violent and extreme as those of their fathers, husbands, and brothers. Their influence as mothers was thus secured and directed to the education of the rising generation in anti-slavery principles. Never was an organization planned and conducted with greater skill and foresight for the eventual accomplishment of its object.

The New England Anti-Slavery Society was organized in Boston on January 30th, 1832; that of New York in October, 1833; and the National Society was organized in Philadelphia in December, 1833. Affiliated societies soon became numerous.

After the formation of the New England society the agitation against Southern slavery proceeded with redoubled vigor, and this under the auspices of British emissaries. One of the first and most pernicious effects of these proceedings was to arrest the natural progress of emancipation under legitimate State authority.

When this agitation commenced, the subject of such emancipation was freely discussed in the South, and especially in the grain-growing border States, and had enlisted numerous and powerful advocates. In these States the institution had become unprofitable. According to the witty and eccentric Virginian, Mr. Randolph, if the slave did not soon run away from the master, the master would run away from the slave. Besides, at this period nobody loved slavery for its own sake.

Virginia, whose example has always exercised great influence on her sister States, was, in 1832, on the verge of emancipation.* The current was then running strong in its favor throughout the State. Many of the leading men, both the principal newspapers, and probably a majority of the people sustained the policy and justice of emancipation. Numerous petitions in its favor were presented to the General Assembly. Mr. Jefferson Randolph, a worthy grandson of President Jefferson, and a delegate from one of the largest slaveholding counties of the commonwealth (Albemarle), brought forward a bill in the House to accomplish the object. This was fully and freely discussed, and was advocated by many prominent members. Not a voice was raised throughout the debate in favor of slavery. Mr. Randolph, finding the Legislature not quite prepared for so decisive a measure, did not press it to a final vote; but yet the House resolved, by a majority of 65 to 58, "that they were profoundly sensible of the great evils arising from the condition of the colored population of the commonwealth, and were induced by policy

* Letter of Geo. W. Randolph to Nahum Capen, of 18th April, 1851.

as well as humanity to attempt the immediate removal of the free negroes; but that further action for the removal of the slaves should await a more definite development of public opinion."

Mr. Randolph's course was approved by his constituents, and at the next election he was returned by them as a member of the House of Delegates, on this very question. Unfortunately, at this moment the anti-slavery agitation in New England began to assume an alarming aspect for the peace and security of the Southern people. In consequence, they denounced it as a foreign and dangerous interference with rights which the Constitution had left exclusively under their own control. An immediate and powerful reaction against emancipation by State authority was the result, and this good cause, to which so many able and patriotic Southern men had been devoted, was sacrificed.

Mr. Randolph himself, a short time thereafter, expressed a confident belief to the author, that but for this interference, the General Assembly would, at no distant day, have passed a law for gradual emancipation. He added, so great had been the revulsion of public sentiment in Virginia, that no member of that body would now dare to propose such a measure.

The abolitionists became bolder and bolder as they advanced. They did not hesitate to pervert the Post Office Department of the Government to the advancement of their cause. Through its agency, at an early period, they scattered throughout the slaveholding States pamphlets, newspapers, and pictorial representations of an incendiary character, calculated to arouse the savage passions of the slaves to servile insurrection. So alarming had these efforts become to the domestic peace of the South, that General Jackson recommended they should be prohibited by law, under severe penalties. He said, in his annual message of 2d December, 1835: "I must also invite your attention to the painful excitement produced in the South by attempts to circulate, through the mails, inflammatory appeals addressed to the passions of the slaves, in prints, and in various sorts of publications, calculated to stimulate them to insurrection and to produce all the horrors of a servile war." * And he also commended to the special attention of Congress "the propriety of passing such a

* 2 Statesman's Manual, 1018.

law as will prohibit, under severe penalties, the circulation in the Southern States, through the mails, of incendiary publications intended to instigate the slaves to insurrection." *

A bill for this purpose was reported to the Senate, but after a long and animated debate, it was negatived, on the 8th of June, 1836, by a vote of 19 to 25.† It is worthy of remark, that even at this early period not a single Senator from New England, whether political friend or opponent of General Jackson, voted in favor of the measure he had so emphatically recommended. All the Senators from that portion of the Union, under the lead of Messrs. Webster and Davis, of Massachusetts, denied to Congress the Constitutional power of passing any law to prevent the abolitionists from using our own mails to circulate incendiary documents throughout the slaveholding States, even though these were manifestly intended to promote servile insurrection and civil war within their limits. The power and duty of Congress to pass the bill were earnestly urged by Mr. Buchanan, then a Senator from Pennsylvania, in opposition to the objections of Mr. Webster.

This anti-slavery agitation in New England was prosecuted by other and different agencies. The pulpit, the press, State Legislatures, State and county conventions, anti-slavery societies, and abolition lectures were all employed for this purpose. Prominent among them were what were called, in the language of the day, abolition petitions.

Throughout the session of 1835-'6, and for several succeeding sessions, these petitions incessantly poured in to Congress. They prayed for the abolition of slavery in the District of Columbia, and in the forts, magazines, arsenals, and dockyards of the United States within the slaveholding States. They also protested against the admission of any new slaveholding State into the Union, and some of them went even so far as to petition for a dissolution of the Union itself.

These petitions were signed by hundreds of thousands of men, women, and children. In them slavery was denounced as a national sin and a national disgrace. Every epithet was employed

* 2 Statesman's Manual, p. 1019.
† Senate Journal, June 2, 1836, pp. 399, 400, and Con. Globe of June 8, 1836.

calculated to arouse the indignation of the Southern people. The time of Congress was wasted in violent debates on the subject of slavery. In these it would be difficult to determine which of the opposing parties was guilty of the greatest excess. Whilst the South threatened disunion unless the agitation should cease, the North treated such threats with derision and defiance. It became manifest to every reflecting man that two geographical parties, the one embracing the people north and the other those south of Mason and Dixon's line, were in rapid process of formation—an event so much dreaded by the Father of his Country.

It is easy to imagine the effect of this agitation upon the proud, sensitive, and excitable people of the South. One extreme naturally begets another. Among the latter there sprung up a party as fanatical in advocating slavery as were the abolitionists of the North in denouncing it. At the first, and for a long time, this party was small in numbers, and found it difficult to excite the masses to support its extreme views. These Southern fanatics, instead of admitting slavery to be an evil in itself, pronounced it to be a great good. Instead of admitting that it had been reluctantly recognized by the Constitution as an overruling political necessity, they extolled it as the surest support of freedom among the white race. If the fanatics of the North denounced slavery as evil and only evil, and that continually, the fanatics of the South upheld it as fraught with blessings to the slave as well as to his master. Far different was the estimation in which it was held by Southern patriots and statesmen both before and for many years after the adoption of the Constitution. These looked forward hopefully to the day when, with safety both to the white and black race, it might be abolished by the people of the slaveholding States themselves, who alone possessed the power.

The late President, as a Senator of the United States, from December, 1834, until March, 1845, lost no opportunity of warning his countrymen of the danger to the Union from a persistence in this anti-slavery agitation, and of beseeching them to suffer the people of the South to manage their domestic affairs in their own way. All they desired, to employ their oft-repeated language, was "to be let alone." With a prophetic vision, at so early a period as the 9th March, 1836, he employed the following language in the Senate: "Sir," said Mr. B., "this question of domestic slavery is the weak point in our institutions. Tariffs may be raised almost to prohibition, and then they may be reduced so as to yield no adequate protection to the manufacturer; our Union is sufficiently strong to endure the shock. Fierce political storms may arise—the moral elements of the country may be convulsed by the struggles of ambitious men for the highest honors of the Government—the sunshine does not more certainly succeed the storm, than that all will again be peace. Touch this question of slavery seriously—let it once be made manifest to the people of the South that they cannot live with us, except in a state of continual apprehension and alarm for their wives and their children, for all that is near and dear to them upon the earth—and the Union is from that moment dissolved. It does not then become a question of expediency, but of self-preservation. It is a question brought home to the fireside, to the domestic circle of every white man in the Southern States. This day, this dark and gloomy day for the Republic, will, I most devoutly trust and believe, never arrive. Although, in Pennsylvania, we are all opposed to slavery in the abstract, yet we will never violate the Constitutional compact which we have made with our sister States. Their rights will be held sacred by us. Under the Constitution it is their own question, and there let it remain." *

A new source of anti-slavery agitation was about this time opened against the execution of the old Fugitive Slave Law, passed in February, 1793.

This was greatly increased by the decision of the Supreme Court of the United States, at the January term, 1842, in the case of Prigg vs. the Commonwealth of Pennsylvania. † It is true, the opinion of the Court, delivered by Mr. Justice Story, explicitly affirmed the Constitutional right of the master to recover his fugitive slave in any State to which he had fled. It even went so far as to clothe the master himself "with full

---

* Gales and Seaton's Register of Debates, vol. xii., part 1, 1835–'6, p. 781.
† 16 Peters, 539.

authority, in every State of the Union, to seize and recapture his slave, wherever he can do it without a breach of the peace. or any illegal violence." After these strong affirmations it becomes necessary to state the reason why this decision became the occasion of increased anti-slavery agitation.

The act of 1793 * authorized and required State judges and magistrates, in common with judges of the United States, to carry its provisions into effect. At the date of its passage no doubt was entertained of the power of Congress to direct this duty to be performed by appropriate State authorities. From the small number of Federal judges in each State, and their distance from each other, the masters, in almost every instance, resorted to the magistrate of the "county, city, or town corporate," where the slave had been arrested. Before him the necessary proof was made, and, upon being satisfied, he granted a certificate to the master, which was a sufficient warrant under the law "for removing the said fugitive from labor to the State or Territory from which he or she fled." These State magistrates were familiar to the people of the respective localities, and their duties were performed in a satisfactory manner, and with but little complaint or commotion. This continued to be the practice until the opinion of the Court in the case of Prigg was pronounced. In this it was decided that State magistrates were not bound to perform these duties; and the question whether they would do so or not, was left entirely to their own discretion.

It was thus rendered competent for State Legislatures to prohibit their own functionaries from aiding in the execution of the Fugitive Slave Act.

Then commenced a furious agitation against the execution of this so-called "sinful and inhuman" law. State magistrates were prevailed upon by the abolitionists to refuse their agency in carrying it into effect. The Legislatures of several States, in conformity with this decision, passed laws prohibiting these magistrates and other State officials from assisting in its execution. The use of the State jails was denied for the safe-keeping of the fugitives. Personal Liberty Bills were passed, inter-

* 1 U. S. L. 302.

posing insurmountable obstacles to the recovery of slaves. Every means which ingenuity could devise was put in operation to render the law a dead letter. Indeed, the excitement against it rose so high that the life and liberty of the master who pursued his fugitive slave into a free State were placed in imminent peril. For this he was often imprisoned, and, in some instances, murdered.

The Fugitive Slave Law, although passed under the administration of Washington for the purpose of carrying into effect a plain, clear, and mandatory provision of the Constitution, was set at naught. And this was done in the face of a well-known historical fact, that without such a provision the Constitution itself never could have existed. Without this law the slaveholder would have had no remedy to enforce his Constitutional right. There would have been no security for his property. If the slave, by simply escaping across a State line, could make himself free, the guarantees of the Constitution in favor of the master would be effectually abolished. These very guarantees were rendered practically of little or no avail, by the decision of the Court in the case of Prigg vs. Pennsylvania, declaring that the Congress of 1793 had violated the Constitution by requiring State magistrates to aid in executing the law.

We have no disposition to dispute the binding force of this decision, although made by a bare majority against the opinion of Chief-Justice Taney and three other judges. It was nevertheless pronounced by the Constitutional tribunal in the last resort, and therefore challenges the obedience, if not the approval, of every law-abiding citizen.

Mr. Justice Story himself seems to have clearly and complacently foreseen the injurious consequences to the rights of the slaveholder which would result from his decision. In his biography, written by his son (vol. ii., p. 392), it is stated: "But in establishing, contrary to the opinion of four of the judges, that the extradition of fugitive slaves is exclusively within the jurisdiction of the Federal Government, and that the State Legislatures are prohibited from interfering, even to *assist* in giving effect to the clause in the Constitution on this subject; he (Judge Story) considered that a great point had been gained for liberty;

so great a point, indeed, that, on his return from Washington, he repeatedly and earnestly spoke of it to his family and his intimate friends as being 'a triumph of freedom.'"

Again (page 394): "Nor were these views contradicted by subsequent experience. From the day of the decision of Prigg *vs.* the Commonwealth of Pennsylvania, the act of 1793 was," says his biographer, " a dead letter in the free States."

The slaveholders, thus deprived of their rights, began to threaten secession from the Union. They contended that, the people of the Northern States having violated the Constitution in a fundamental provision necessary to their peace and safety, they of the South, according to the settled rules governing the construction of all contracts, whether between States or individuals, had a right to rescind it altogether.

In 1846, in the midst of the agitation against the Fugitive Slave Law, came that on the Wilmot Proviso. This asserted it to be the right and duty of Congress to prohibit the people of the Southern States from emigrating with their slave property to the common territory of the United States, which might be acquired by the war with Mexico. Thus was raised anew the question in regard to slavery in the territories, which has since proved so fatal.

In May, 1846, the existence of war with Mexico, by the act of that Republic, was recognized by Congress, and measures were adopted for its prosecution.*

On the 4th of August, 1846, near the close of the session,† President Polk, desirous of restoring peace as speedily as possible, and of adjusting the boundaries between the two Republics in a satisfactory manner, asked Congress for a small contingent appropriation, to be applied to this purpose, which it might or might not become necessary to employ before their next meeting. Accordingly, on the 8th of August a bill was presented to the House granting the President $2,000,000.

To this bill Mr. Wilmot offered his proviso as an amendment. ‡ The proviso declared "That, as an express and fundamental condition to the acquisition of any territory from the

---

* Act of 13th May, 1846; 9 U. S. S. at Large, p. 9.   † 3 Statesman's Manual, 1610.
‡ Con. Globe, 1845-'6, p. 1217.

Republic of Mexico by the United States, by virtue of any treaty which may be negotiated between them, and to the use by the Executive of the moneys herein appropriated, neither slavery nor involuntary servitude shall ever exist in any part of said territory, except for crime, whereof the party shall first be duly convicted."

Had this proviso been never so proper in itself, it was both out of time and out of place. Out of time, because, whether any treaty could be made acquiring territory from Mexico, was future and contingent; and in fact that of Guadalupe Hidalgo, under which we acquired Upper California and New Mexico, was not concluded until almost eighteen months thereafter.* But Mr. Wilmot was so eager to introduce this new subject for anti-slavery agitation, that he could not await the regular course of events.

The proviso was also out of place in an appropriation bill confined to a single important object, because it was calculated to defeat, as it actually did defeat, the appropriation. It was a firebrand recklessly and prematurely cast among the free and slave States, at a moment when a foreign war was raging, in which all were gallantly fighting, side by side, to conquer an honorable peace. This was the moment selected, long in advance, to announce to the people of the slaveholding States that if we should acquire any new territory by our common blood and treasure, they should forever be prohibited from entering any portion of it with by far the most valuable part of their property.

The introduction of this proviso instantly caused the flames of fanaticism to burn with more intense ardor, both North and South, than they had ever done before. How wise is the Divine maxim, that "sufficient unto the day is the evil thereof"!

The new territory afterwards acquired from Mexico, being outside of the ancient province of Louisiana, was not embraced by the Missouri Compromise. The late President, then Secretary of State, strongly urged the extension of the line of 36° 30′ through this territory to the Pacific Ocean, as the best mode of adjustment. He believed that its division by this ancient line,

* Treaty, Feb. 2, 1848; 9 U. S. Statutes at Large, 922.

to which we had been long accustomed, would be more just in itself, and more acceptable to the people, both North and South, than any new plan which could be devised.*

This proposal was defeated by the Wilmot Proviso. That ill-starred measure continued to be forced upon the consideration of Congress, as well as of State Legislatures, session after session, in various forms. Whilst Northern Legislatures were passing resolutions instructing their Senators and requesting their Representatives to vote for the Wilmot Proviso, Southern Legislatures and conventions were passing resolutions pledging themselves to measures of resistance.

The interposition of the proviso, in season and out of season, and the violent and protracted debates to which it gave rise, defeated the establishment of territorial governments in California and New Mexico throughout the whole of the thirtieth Congress (1847–'8 and 1848–'9). Meanwhile it placed the two sections of the Union in hostile array against each other. The people of the one, instead of regarding those of the other as brethren, were converted into deadly enemies. At the meeting of the thirty-first Congress (December, 1849) serious apprehensions were everywhere entertained, among the most enlightened and purest patriots, for the safety of the Union. The necessity was admitted by all that measures should be adopted to ward off the impending danger.

* Letter to Berks County, Aug. 25, 1847.

CHAPTER II.

Meeting of Congress in December, 1849—The five Acts constituting the Compromise of September, 1850—Effect of the Compromise in allaying excitement—Whig and Democratic Platforms indorse it—President Pierce's happy reference to it in his Message of December, 1853—The repeal of the Missouri Compromise reopens the slavery agitation—Its passage in March, 1820, and character—Its recognition by Congress in 1845, on the Annexation of Texas—The history of its repeal—This repeal gives rise to the Kansas troubles—Their nature and history—The Lecompton Constitution and proceedings of Congress upon it—The Republican party greatly strengthened—Decision of the Supreme Court in the Dred Scott case—Repudiated by the Republican party and by the Douglas Democracy—Sustained by the old Democracy—The Kansas and Nebraska Act—The policy and practice of Congress toward the Territories—Abuse of President Buchanan for not adhering to the Cincinnati Platform without foundation.

THE thirty-first Congress assembled on the first Monday of December, 1849, and they happily succeeded in averting the present danger by the adoption of one of those wise compromises which had previously proved so beneficent to the country.

The first ray of light to penetrate the gloom emanated from the great and powerful State of Pennsylvania. Her House of Representatives refused to consider instructing resolutions in favor of the Wilmot Proviso. Soon thereafter, on the 4th of February, 1850, the House of Representatives at Washington, by a vote of 105 to 75, laid resolutions favoring this proviso upon the table.* The way was now opened for compromising all the existing questions in regard to slavery.

The bold, eloquent, and patriotic Clay, who, thirty years before, had contributed so much to the passage of the Mis-

---

* Con. Globe, 1849–'50, p. 276.

souri Compromise, was designated by the voice of the country as the leader in effecting this new Compromise. He did not, in his old age, shrink from the task. In this he was powerfully aided by several of our wisest and most conservative statesmen.

The necessary legislation for this purpose was accomplished in September, 1850, by the passage of five distinct acts of Congress. These were: 1. "An Act to amend and supplementary to" the old Fugitive Slave Law of the 12th of February, 1793.* This provided for the appointment of as many Commissioners by the Courts of the United States as the public convenience might require to supply the place of the State magistrates who had, as heretofore explained, been forbidden to carry into effect the mandate of the Constitution for the restoration of fugitive slaves. The chief object was to make the Federal Government independent of State assistance in the execution of the law.

2. An Act for the admission of California, *as a free State*, into the Union, embracing its entire territory, as well that south as north of the Missouri Compromise line.†

3 and 4. Acts for establishing Territorial Governments in New Mexico and Utah, under which both these Territories were to be admitted as States into the Union, "with or without slavery as their respective Constitutions might provide." ‡ From abundant but wise caution, the first of these Acts declared, in conformity with the Constitution, that "no citizen of the United States shall be deprived of his life, liberty, or property in said Territory, except by the judgment of his peers and the laws of the land." These two Acts, in addition to the old Missouri Compromise, embraced all our remaining Territories, whether derived from Mexico or France. They terminated the agitation on the Wilmot Proviso, by depriving it of any territory on which it could operate.

The Act establishing the Territory of New Mexico provided also for annexing to it all that portion of Texas lying

---

* 9 U. S. Laws, 462, Sept. 18.   † Ibid., 452, Sept. 9.
‡ Ibid. 446 and 453, Sept. 9.

north of 36° 30'; thus withdrawing it from the jurisdiction of a slave State.

5. An Act was passed to abolish the domestic slave trade within the District of Columbia.*

These five Acts constituted the famous Compromise of September, 1850. At the first, this Compromise was condemned both by extreme abolitionists at the North and by extreme secessionists in the South. By the abolitionists, because it tolerated slavery in New Mexico, and provided for the due execution of the Fugitive Slave Law; and by the secessionists, because it admitted the great State of California as a free State into the Union, and this notwithstanding a considerable part of it lies south of the Missouri line. Nevertheless, it gradually made its way to public favor, and was hailed by the conservative masses, both North and South, as a wise and judicious arrangement. So far had it enlisted the general approval, that in June, 1852, the National Conventions of both the Democratic and Whig parties bestowed upon it their approbation, and expressed their determination to maintain it. They both resolved, to employ the language of the Democratic platform, that they would "resist all attempts at renewing, in Congress or out of it, the slavery agitation, under whatever shape or color the attempt may be made."†

On this subject the Whig platform is specific and emphatic. Its eighth and last resolution is as follows:‡

"That the series of Acts of the thirty-second Congress, the Act known as the Fugitive Slave Law included, are received and acquiesced in by the Whig party of the United States as a settlement in principle and substance of the dangerous and exciting questions which they embrace; and, so far as they are concerned, we will maintain them and insist upon their strict enforcement, until time and experience shall demonstrate the necessity of further legislation to guard against the evasion of the laws on the one hand, and the abuse of their powers on the other —not impairing their present efficiency; and we deprecate all further agitation of the question thus settled, as dangerous to

---

* 9 U. S. Laws, 467, Sept. 20.   † Greeley's Political Text Book, 1860, p. 20.
‡ Ibid. p. 19.

our peace, and will discountenance all efforts to continue or renew such agitation, whenever, wherever, or however the attempt may be made; and we will maintain the system as essential to the nationality of the Whig party and the integrity of the Union."

When Congress assembled, after the election of President Pierce, on the first Monday of December, 1853, although the abolition fanatics had not ceased to agitate, crimination and recrimination between the sectional parties had greatly subsided, and a comparative political calm everywhere prevailed. President Pierce, in his annual message, felicitously referred to the "sense of repose and security to the public mind throughout the Confederacy," and pledged himself "that this repose should suffer no shock during his official term," if he had the power to avert it.

The Compromise of 1850 ought never to have been disturbed by Congress. After long years of agitation and alarm, the country, under its influence, had enjoyed a season of comparative repose, inspiring the people with bright hopes for the future.

But how short-lived and delusive was this calm! The very Congress which had commenced so auspiciously, by repealing the Missouri Compromise before the end of its first session, reopened the floodgates of sectional strife, which, it was fondly imagined, had been closed forever. This has ever since gone on increasing in violence and malignity, until it has involved the country in the greatest and most sanguinary civil war recorded in history.

And here it is necessary, for a correct understanding of the subject, to refer to the origin, the nature, and the repeal of this celebrated Compromise.

It was passed on the 6th of March, 1820, after a long and violent struggle in Congress between the friends and the opponents of what was then called the Missouri restriction.* This proposed to require from Missouri, as a condition precedent to her admission as a State, that she should "ordain and establish that there shall be neither slavery nor involuntary servitude" therein, except as a punishment for crime.

* 3 U. S. Laws, 545.

Under the Compromise as finally effected, whilst the restrictionists were obliged to submit to the existence of slavery in Missouri, they obtained, on their part, a guarantee for perpetual freedom throughout the vast remaining territory north of the parallel of 36° 30', which had been acquired from France under the Louisiana Treaty.* These were the equivalents reciprocally granted and accepted by the opposing parties.

This guarantee is to be found in the 8th section of the Act authorizing the people of the then Missouri Territory to form a Constitution and State Government, preparatory to admission as a State into the Union.† It is embraced in the following language: "That in all that territory ceded by France to the United States, under the name of Louisiana, which lies north of 36° 30' north latitude, not included within the limits of the State [Missouri] contemplated by this Act, slavery and involuntary servitude, otherwise than in the punishment of crimes, whereof the parties shall have been duly convicted, shall be, and is hereby, forever prohibited. Provided always: That any person escaping into the same, from whom labor or service is lawfully claimed in any State or Territory of the United States, such fugitive may be lawfully reclaimed and conveyed to the person claiming his or her labor or service as aforesaid."

The Missouri Compromise finally passed Congress by large majorities. On a test question in the Senate on the 2d March, 1820, the vote in its favor was 27 against 15; and in the House, on the same day, it was 134 against 42. Its wisdom and policy were recognized by Congress, a quarter of a century afterwards, in March, 1845, when Texas, being a slave State, was annexed to the Union. Acting on the presumption that several new States might be formed out of her territory, one of the express conditions of her annexation was, that in such of these States as might lie north of the Missouri Compromise line, slavery shall be prohibited.‡

The Missouri Compromise had remained inviolate for more than thirty-four years before its repeal. It was a covenant of peace between the free and the slaveholding States. Its authors

---

* For its history, vide Appendix to Con. Globe, 1st session 33d Congress, p. 226.
† 3 U. S. Laws, 545.   ‡ 5 U. S. Laws, 797.

were the wise and conservative statesmen of a former generation. Although it had not silenced anti-slavery discussion in other forms, yet it soon tranquillized the excitement which for some months previous to its passage had convulsed the country in regard to slavery in the Territories. It is true that the power of a future Congress to repeal any of the Acts of its predecessors, under which no private rights had been vested, cannot be denied; still the Missouri Compromise, being in the nature of a solemn compact between conflicting parties, whose object was to ward off great dangers from the Union, ought never to have been repealed by Congress.

The question of its constitutionality ought to have been left to the decision of the Supreme Court, without any legislative intervention. Had this been done, and the Court had decided it to be a violation of the Constitution, in a case arising before them in the regular course of judicial proceedings, the decision would have passed off in comparative silence, and produced no dangerous excitement among the people.

Let us briefly sketch the history of this repeal, which was the immediate cause of our present troubles.

Senator Douglas, on the 4th January, 1854, reported a bill from the Committee on Territories, to establish a Territorial Government in Nebraska.* This bill was silent in regard to the Missouri Compromise. It was nearly in the usual form, and would have doubtless passed, with but little, if any, opposition. Before it was reached in order, the Whig Senator Dixon, of Kentucky, on the 16th January, gave notice that when it should come before the Senate, he would move to add to it a section repealing the Missouri Compromise, not only in regard to Nebraska, but all other Territories of the United States.† A few days thereafter, on the 23d January, the Committee on Territories, through Mr. Douglas, their chairman, offered a substitute for the original bill. ‡ This, after dividing Nebraska into two Territories, the one still bearing that name, and the other the name of Kansas, proceeded to annul the Missouri Compromise in regard to these and all our other Territories. With this

---

* Con. Globe, 1853-'4, p. 115.   † Ibid, p. 175.   ‡ Ibid v. 222.

Mr. Dixon expressed himself "perfectly satisfied." * Such is the origin of what has since been familiarly called "the Kansas and Nebraska Bill."

On the question of repeal, a long and angry debate arose in both Houses of Congress. This consumed a large portion of the session, and exasperated the contending parties to a degree never before witnessed. The opponents of the bill openly and violently predicted imminent danger to the peace of the Union from its passage, whilst its advocates treated any such danger with proud and indignant disdain.

The bill finally passed both Houses on the 25th, and was approved by President Pierce on the 30th May, 1854.

It was ominous of evil that every Southern Senator present, whether Whig or Democrat, without regard to past political distinctions, voted for the repeal, with the exception of Mr. Bell, of Tennessee, and Mr. Clayton, of Delaware, who voted against it; and that every Northern Democratic Senator present, uniting with the South, also voted for the repeal, with the exception of Messrs. Allen and James, of Rhode Island, and Mr. Walker, of Wisconsin, who voted against it.†

The repeal was accomplished in the following manner: The 14th section of this bill, whilst extending the laws of the United States over Kansas and Nebraska, excepts therefrom "the 8th section of the Act preparatory to the admission of Missouri into the Union, approved March sixth, eighteen hundred and twenty, which, being inconsistent with the principle of non-intervention by Congress with slavery in the States and Territories, as recognized by the legislation of 1850, commonly called the Compromise measures, is hereby declared inoperative and void; it being the true intent and meaning of this Act not to legislate slavery into any Territory or State, nor to exclude it therefrom, but to leave the people thereof perfectly free to form and regulate their domestic institutions in their own way, subject only to the Constitution of the United States."

It is impossible to conceive how it could be inferred that the Compromise of 1850, on the question of slavery in the territories, would be inconsistent with the long previous Missouri Compromise

* P. 239.   † Con. Globe, 1853–'4, p. 1321.

of 1820; because each applied to distinct and separate portions of our territorial domain. Whilst the Missouri Compromise was confined to the territory acquired from France under the Louisiana purchase, that of 1850 provided only for the new territory long afterwards acquired from Mexico under the treaty of Guadalupe Hidalgo. The Compromise measures of 1850 contain no words to repeal or invalidate the Missouri Compromise. On the contrary, they expressly recognize it, as we have already seen, in the Act providing for the cession of a portion of Texas to New Mexico.

After a careful review of the history of the anti-slavery party, from its origin, the candid inquirer must admit that up till this period it had acted on the aggressive against the South. From the beginning it had kept the citizens of the slaveholding States in constant irritation, as well as serious apprehension for their domestic peace and security. They were the assailed party, and had been far more sinned against than sinning. It is true, they had denounced their assailants with extreme rancor and many threats; but had done nothing more. In sustaining the repeal of the Missouri Compromise, however, the Senators and Representatives of the Southern States became the aggressors themselves, and thereby placed the country in an alarming and dangerous condition from which it has never since been rescued.

The repeal of the Missouri Compromise having entirely removed the interdict against slavery in all our territories north of 36° 30′, the struggle immediately commenced in Kansas between the anti-slavery and pro-slavery parties. On this theatre the extreme men of both sections were brought into mortal conflict. Each party hurried emigrants to the Territory;—the one intent upon making it a free, the other, though in violation of the laws of climate, upon making it a slave State. The one strenuously contended that slavery, under the Constitution, was local in its character and confined to the States where it existed; and, therefore, if an emigrant passed into the Territory with his slaves, these became instantly free. The other maintained, with equal zeal, that slaves were recognized as property by the Constitution, and consequently their masters had a right to take them to Kansas and hold them there, under its guarantees, like any other property. Besides, the South insisted that without this right the equality of the States within their common territory was destroyed, and they would be degraded from the rank of equals to that of inferiors.

It was not long until a fierce and vindictive war arose in Kansas between the opposing parties. In this, scenes of bloodshed and rapine were enacted by both parties, disgraceful to the American character. It is not our purpose to recapitulate these sad events.

Whilst the pro-slavery party in the Territory sustained the Government in all its branches which had been established over it by Congress, the anti-slavery party repudiated it. They contended that frauds and violence had been committed in the election of members to the Territorial Legislature sufficient to render its enactments a nullity. For this reason they had held a Convention at Topeka, had framed a State Constitution, had elected their own Governor and Legislature to take the place of those in the actual administration of the Territorial Government, and had applied to Congress for admission into the Union.

Such were the first bitter fruits of repealing the Missouri interdict against slavery north of 36° 30′, and thus opening the Territory of Kansas to the admission of slaves.

It cannot be doubted that frauds and violence had been committed in this election; but whether sufficient to render it a nullity was a question for Congress to decide. After a long and violent struggle, Congress had decided this question by finally rejecting the application for the admission of Kansas as a State into the Union under the Topeka Constitution, and by recognizing the authority of the Territorial Government.

Such was the condition of Kansas when Mr. Buchanan entered upon the duties of the Presidential office. All these proceedings had taken place during the session of Congress (1856–'7) which terminated immediately before his inauguration. It will be admitted that he possessed no power to go behind the action of Congress and adjudge it to be null and void. In fact, he had no alternative but to sustain the Territorial Government.

A new era was now commencing with the accession of President Buchanan, and he indulged the hope that the anti-slavery party would abandon their hostility to the Territorial Government and obey the laws. In this he was encouraged by the fact, that the Supreme Court had just decided that slavery existed in Kansas under the Constitution of the United States, and consequently the people of that Territory could only relieve themselves from it by electing anti-slavery delegates to the approaching Lecompton Convention, in sufficient number to frame a free State Constitution preparatory to admission into the Union. They could no longer expect ever to be admitted as a State under the Topeka Constitution. The thirty-fourth Congress had just expired, having recognized the legal existence of the Territorial Legislature in a variety of forms which need not be enumerated.* The Delegate elected under a Territorial law to the House of Representatives had been admitted to his seat, and had completed his term of service on the day previous to Mr. Buchanan's inauguration.

In this reasonable hope the President was destined to disappointment. The anti-slavery party, during a period of ten months, from the 4th of March, 1857, until the first Monday of January, 1858, continued to defy the Territorial Government and to cling to their Topeka organization. The first symptom of yielding was not until the latter day, when a large portion of them voted for State officials and a member of Congress under the Lecompton Constitution. Meanwhile, although actual war was suspended between the parties, yet the peace was only maintained by the agency of United States troops. "The opposing parties still stood in hostile array against each other, and any accident might have relighted the flames of civil war. Besides, at this critical moment, Kansas was left without a Governor, by the resignation of Governor Geary."†

Soon after the inauguration an occasion offered to Mr. Buchanan to define the policy he intended to pursue in relation to Kansas. This was in answer to a memorial presented to him by forty-three distinguished citizens of Connecticut, a number of them being eminent divines. The following we extract from his letter dated at Washington, August 15, 1857:

---

* Message to Congress transmitting the Constitution of Kansas.
† Message of December, 1857, p. 18.

"When I entered upon the duties of the Presidential office, on the fourth of March last, what was the condition of Kansas? This Territory had been organized under the Act of Congress of 30th May, 1854, and the government in all its branches was in full operation. A governor, secretary of the Territory, chief justice, two associate justices, a marshal, and district attorney had been appointed by my predecessor, by and with the advice and consent of the Senate, and were all engaged in discharging their respective duties. A code of laws had been enacted by the Territorial Legislature; and the judiciary were employed in expounding and carrying these laws into effect. It is quite true that a controversy had previously arisen respecting the validity of the election of members of the Territorial Legislature and of the laws passed by them; but at the time I entered upon my official duties Congress had recognized this Legislature in different forms and by different enactments. The delegate elected to the House of Representatives, under a Territorial law, had just completed his term of service on the day previous to my inauguration. In fact, I found the government of Kansas as well established as that of any other Territory. Under these circumstances, what was my duty? Was it not to sustain this government? to protect it from the violence of lawless men, who were determined either to rule or ruin? to prevent it from being overturned by force? in the language of the Constitution, to 'take care that the laws be faithfully executed'? It was for this purpose, and this alone, that I ordered a military force to Kansas to act as a posse comitatus in aiding the civil magistrate to carry the laws into execution. The condition of the Territory at the time, which I need not portray, rendered this precaution absolutely necessary. In this state of affairs, would I not have been justly condemned had I left the marshal and other officers of a like character impotent to execute the process and judgments of courts of justice established by Congress, or by the Territorial Legislature under its express authority, and thus have suffered the government itself to become an object of contempt in the eyes of the people? And yet this is what you designate as forcing 'the people of Kansas to obey laws not their own, nor of the United States;' and for doing which you have denounced me as having violated my solemn oath. I ask, what else could I have done, or ought I to have done? Would you have desired that I should abandon the Territorial government, sanctioned as it had been by Congress, to illegal violence, and thus renew the scenes of civil war and bloodshed which every patriot in the country had deplored? This would, indeed, have been to violate my oath of office, and to fix a damning blot on the character of my administration.

"I most cheerfully admit that the necessity for sending a military force to Kansas to aid in the execution of the civil law, reflects no credit upon the character of our country. But let the blame fall upon the heads of the guilty. Whence did this necessity arise? A portion of the people of Kansas, unwilling to trust to the ballot-box—the certain American remedy for the redress of all grievances—undertook to create an independent government for themselves. Had this attempt proved successful, it would of course have subverted the existing government, prescribed and recognized by Congress, and substituted a revolutionary government in its stead. This was a usurpation of the same character as it would be for a portion of the people of Connecticut to undertake to establish a separate government within its chartered limits for the purpose of redressing any grievance, real or imaginary, of which they might have complained against the legitimate State government. Such a principle, if carried into execution, would destroy all lawful authority and produce universal anarchy."

And again: "I thank you for the assurances that you will 'not refrain from the prayer that Almighty God will make my administration an example of justice and beneficence.' You can greatly aid me in arriving at this blessed consummation, by exerting your influence in allaying the existing sectional excitement on the subject of slavery, which has been productive of much evil and no good, and which, if it could succeed in attaining its object, would ruin the slave as well as his master. This would be a work of genuine philanthropy. Every day of my life I feel how inadequate I am to perform the duties of my high station without the continued support of Divine Providence yet, placing my trust in Him and in Him alone, I entertain a good hope that He will enable me to do equal justice to all portions of the Union, and thus render me an humble instrument in restoring peace and harmony among the people of the several States."

This answer, at the time, appeared to give general satisfaction.

Soon after the 4th of March, 1857, Mr. Robert J. Walker was appointed Governor, and Mr. Frederick P. Stanton Secretary of the Territory of Kansas. The great object in view was to prevail upon the Anti-Slavery party to unite with their opponents in framing a State Constitution for Kansas, leaving the question to be decided at the ballot-box whether it should enter the Union as a free or as a slave State. Accordingly the Governor was instructed to take care that the election for delegates to the convention should be held and conducted with perfect fairness to both parties, so that the genuine voice of the people might be truly heard and obeyed. This duty he performed with fidelity and ability, but unfortunately without success.

The laws which had been passed by the Territorial Legislature providing for this election are liable to no just exception. The President, speaking on this subject in his message of 2d of February, 1858, transmitting the Kansas Constitution to Congress, employs the following language:—"It is impossible that any people could have proceeded with more regularity in the formation of a constitution than the people of Kansas have done. It was necessary, first, to ascertain whether it was the desire of the people to be relieved from their territorial dependence and establish a State government. For this purpose the Territorial Legislature, in 1855, passed a law 'for taking the sense of the people of this Territory upon the expediency of calling a convention to form a State constitution' at the general election to be held in October, 1856. The 'sense of the people' was accordingly taken, and they decided in favor of a convention. It is true that at this election the enemies of the territorial government did not vote, because they were then engaged at Topeka, without the slightest pretext of lawful authority, in framing a constitution of their own for the purpose of subverting the territorial government.

"In pursuance of this decision of the people in favor of a convention, the Territorial Legislature, on the 27th day of February, 1857, passed an act for the election of delegates on the third Monday of June, 1857, to frame a State constitution. This law is as fair in its provisions as any that ever passed a legislative body for a similar purpose. The right of suffrage at this election is clearly and justly defined. 'Every *bonâ fide* inhabitant of the Territory of Kansas' on the third Monday of June, the day of the election, who was a citizen of the United States, above the age of twenty-one, and had resided therein for three months previous to that date, was entitled to vote. In order to avoid all interference from neighboring States or Territories with the freedom and fairness of the election, provision was made for the registry of the qualified voters; and in pursuance thereof nine thousand two hundred and fifty-one voters were registered."

The great object was to convince these 9,251 qualified electors that they ought to vote in the choice of delegates to the convention, and thus terminate the controversy by the will of the majority.

The Governor urged them to exercise their right of suffrage; but in vain. In his Inaugural Address of the 27th of May, 1857, he informed them that, "Under our practice, the preliminary act of framing a State constitution is uniformly performed through the instrumentality of a convention of delegates chosen by the people themselves. That convention is now about to be elected by you under the call of the Territorial Legislature, created and still recognized by the authority of Congress, and clothed by it, in the comprehensive language of the organic law, with full power to make such an enactment. The Territorial Legislature, then, in assembling this convention, were fully sustained by the Act of Congress, and the authority of the convention is distinctly recognized in my instructions from the President of the United States." The Governor proceeded to warn them, clearly and distinctly, what would be the consequences, if they should not participate in the election. "The people of Kansas, then," he says, "are invited by the highest authority known to the Constitution, to participate, freely and fairly, in the election of delegates to frame a Constitution and State Government. The law has performed its entire appropriate function when it extends to the people the right of suffrage, but cannot compel the performance of that duty. Throughout our whole Union, however, and wherever free government prevails, those who abstain from the exercise of the right of suffrage authorize those who do vote to act for them in that contingency; and the absentees are as much bound, under the law and Constitution, where there is no fraud or violence, by the act of the majority of those who do vote, as if all had participated in the election. Otherwise, as voting must be voluntary, self-government would be impracticable, and monarchy or despotism would remain as the only alternative."

"This was the propitious moment," said the President, "for settling all difficulties in Kansas. This was the time for abandoning the revolutionary Topeka organization, and for the enemies of the existing government to conform to the laws, and to unite with its friends in framing a State Constitution. But this they refused to do, and the consequences of their refusal to submit to lawful authority and vote at the election of delegates may yet prove to be of a most deplorable character. Would that the respect for the laws of the land which so eminently distinguished the men of the past generation could be revived! It is a disregard and violation of law which have for years kept the Territory of Kansas in a state of almost open rebellion against its government. It is the same spirit which has produced actual rebellion in Utah. Our only safety consists in obedience and conformity to law. Should a general spirit against its enforcement prevail, this will prove fatal to us as a nation. We acknowledge no master but the law; and should we cut loose from its restraints, and every one do what seemeth good in his own eyes, our case will indeed be hopeless.

"The enemies of the territorial government determined still to resist the authority of Congress. They refused to vote for delegates to the convention, not because, from circumstances which I need not detail, there was an omission to register the comparatively few voters who were inhabitants of certain counties of Kansas in the early spring of 1857, but because they had predetermined, at all hazards, to adhere to their revolutionary organization, and defeat the establishment of any other constitution than that which they had framed at Topeka. The election was, therefore, suffered to pass by default; but of this result the qualified electors who refused to vote can never justly complain."

A large majority, therefore, of Pro-Slavery delegates were elected members of the convention.

"From this review, it is manifest that the Lecompton Convention, notwithstanding the refusal of the Anti-Slavery party to vote, was legally constituted and was invested with power to frame a constitution."

It has been urged that these proceedings were in violation of the sacred principle of popular sovereignty. "But in what manner," said the President, "is popular sovereignty to be exercised in this country, if not through the instrumentality of established law? In certain small republics of ancient times the people did assemble in primary meetings, passed laws, and directed public affairs. In our country this is manifestly impossible. Popular sovereignty can be exercised here only through the ballot-box; and if the people will refuse to exercise it in this manner, as they have done in Kansas at the election of delegates, it is not for them to complain that their rights have been violated."

Throughout the intervening period, and for some time thereafter, Kansas was in a dreadful condition. To illustrate this, we shall transcribe several paragraphs from the President's Message.* He says, that "A great delusion seems to pervade the public mind in relation to the condition of parties in Kansas. This arises from the difficulty of inducing the American people to realize the fact that any portion of them should be in a state of rebellion against the Government under which they live. When we speak of the affairs of Kansas, we are apt to refer merely to the existence of two violent political parties in that Territory, divided on the question of slavery, just as we speak of such parties in the States. This presents no adequate idea of

* Page 1.

the true state of the case. The dividing line there is not between two political parties, both acknowledging the lawful existence of the government, but between those who are loyal to this government, and those who have endeavored to destroy its existence by force and by usurpation—between those who sustain and those who have done all in their power to overthrow the territorial government established by Congress. This government they would long since have subverted, had it not been protected from their assaults by the troops of the United States. Such has been the condition of affairs since my inauguration. Ever since that period a large portion of the people of Kansas have been in a state of rebellion against the government, with a military leader at their head of a most turbulent and dangerous character. They have never acknowledged, but have constantly renounced and defied the government to which they owe allegiance, and have been all the time in a state of resistance against its authority. They have all the time been endeavoring to subvert it, and to establish a revolutionary government, under the so-called Topeka Constitution, in its stead. Even at this very moment the Topeka Legislature is in session. Whoever has read the correspondence of Governor Walker with the State Department, recently communicated to the Senate, will be convinced that this picture is not overdrawn. He always protested against the withdrawal of any portion of the military force of the United States from the Territory, deeming its presence absolutely necessary for the preservation of the regular government and the execution of the laws. In his very first despatch to the Secretary of State, dated June 2, 1857, he says: 'The most alarming movement, however, proceeds from the assembling on the 9th of June of the so-called Topeka Legislature, with a view to the enactment of an entire code of laws. Of course it will be my endeavor to prevent such a result, as it would lead to inevitable and disastrous collision, and, in fact, renew the civil war in Kansas.' This was with difficulty prevented by the efforts of Governor Walker; but soon thereafter, on the 14th of July, we find him requesting General Harney to furnish him a regiment of dragoons to proceed to the city of Lawrence, and this for the reason that he had received authentic intelligence, verified by his own actual observation, that a dangerous rebellion had occurred, 'involving an open defiance of the laws and the establishment of an insurgent government in that city.'

"In the Governor's despatch of July 15, he informs the Secretary of State 'that this movement at Lawrence was the beginning of a plan, originating in that city, to organize insurrection throughout the Territory; and especially in all towns, cities, or counties where the Republican party have a majority. Lawrence is the hot-bed of all the abolition movements in this Territory. It is the town established by the abolition societies of the east; and whilst there are respectable people there, it is filled by a considerable number of mercenaries who are paid by abolition societies to perpetuate and diffuse agitation throughout Kansas, and prevent a peaceful settlement of this question. Having failed in inducing their own so-called Topeka State Legislature to organize this insurrection, Lawrence has commenced it herself, and, if not arrested, the rebellion will extend throughout the Territory.'

"And again: 'In order to send this communication immediately by mail, I must close by assuring you that the spirit of rebellion pervades the great mass of the Republican party of this Territory, instigated, as I entertain no doubt they are, by eastern societies, having in view results most disastrous to the Government and to the Union; and that the continued presence of General Harney here is indispensable, as originally stipulated by me, with a large body of dragoons and several batteries.'

"On the 20th July, 1857, General Lane, under the authority of the Topeka Convention, undertook, as Governor Walker informs us, 'to organize the whole so-called free State party into volunteers, and to take the names of all who refuse enrolment. The professed object is to protect the polls, at the election in August, of the new insurgent Topeka State Legislature. The object of taking the names of all who refuse enrolment is to terrify the free State conservatives into submission. This is proved by recent atrocities committed on such men by Topekaites. The speedy location of large bodies of regular troops here, with two batteries, is necessary. The Lawrence insurgents await the development of this new revolutionary military organization,' etc., etc.

"In the Governor's despatch of July 27th, he says that 'General Lane and his staff everywhere deny the authority of the territorial laws, and counsel a total disregard of these enactments.'

"Without making further quotations of a similar character from other despatches of Governor Walker, it appears by a reference to Mr. Stanton's communication to General Cass, of the 9th of December last, that the 'important step of calling the [Territorial] Legislature together was taken after I [he] had become satisfied that the election ordered by the Convention on the 21st instant [December] could not be conducted without collision and bloodshed.' So intense was the disloyal feeling among the enemies of the government established by Congress, that an election which afforded them an opportunity, if in the majority, of making Kansas a free State, according to their own professed desire, could not be conducted without collision and bloodshed!

"The truth is, that, up till the present moment, the enemies of the existing government still adhere to their Topeka revolutionary constitution and government. The very first paragraph of the message of Governor Robinson, dated on the 7th of December, to the Topeka Legislature, now assembled at Lawrence, contains an open defiance of the Constitution and laws of the United States. The Governor says: 'The Convention which framed the constitution at Topeka originated with the people of Kansas Territory. They have adopted and ratified the same twice by a direct vote, and also indirectly through two elections of State officers and members of the State Legislature. Yet it has pleased the administration to regard the whole proceeding as revolutionary.'

"The Topeka government, adhered to with such treasonable pertinacity, is a government in direct opposition to the existing government prescribed and recognized by Congress. It is a usurpation of the same character as it would be for a portion of the people of any State of the Union to undertake to establish a separate government, within its limits, for the purpose of redressing any grievance, real or imaginary, of which they might complain against the legitimate State Government. Such a principle, if carried into execution, would destroy all lawful authority and produce universal anarchy.

"From this statement of facts, the reason becomes palpable why the enemies of the government authorized by Congress have refused to vote for delegates to the Kansas Constitutional Convention, and, also, afterwards on the question of slavery submitted by it to the people. It is because they have ever refused to sanction or recognize any other constitution than that framed at Topeka."

The Convention, thus lawfully constituted, met for the second time on the 4th of September, and proceeded to frame a constitution, and finally adjourned on the 7th day of November, 1857.* A large majority of its members, in consequence of the refusal of the Anti-Slavery electors to vote for delegates, were in favor of establishing slavery. The Convention having refused to submit the whole constitution to the people, in opposition to the desire of the President, determined finally to submit to them only the all-important question whether slavery should or should not exist in the new State. This they were required to do under the true construction of the Kansas and Nebraska Act, and without this the constitution would have encountered his decided opposition. It was not, however, until the last moment, and this after an angry and excited debate, that the Convention, by a majority of only three, determined to submit this question to a popular vote. Acting on the authority of former precedents, and considering that all other parts of the constitution had been finally adopted, they therefore submitted the question of slavery alone to the people, at an election to be held on the 21st December, 1857. For this purpose they provided that, before the constitution adopted by the Convention " shall be sent to Congress asking for admission into the Union as a State," an election shall be held to decide this question, at which all the white male inhabitants of the Territory should be entitled to vote. They were to vote by ballot; and "the bal-

* Senate Documents, 1857-'58, vol. vii., No. 21.

lots cast at said election shall be indorsed 'Constitution with Slavery,' and 'Constitution with no Slavery.'"

"Here, again," says the President, "a fair opportunity was presented to the adherents of the Topeka Constitution, if they were the majority, to decide this exciting question 'in their own way,' and thus restore peace to the distracted Territory; but they again refused to exercise their right of popular sovereignty, and again suffered the election to pass by default." In consequence, the result, according to the report of J. Calhoun, the President of the Convention, was 6,226 votes in favor of slavery, and but 569 against it.

The constitution thus adopted had provided for holding an election on the first Monday of January, 1858, for "a Governor, Lieutenant-Governor, Secretary of State, State Treasurer, and members of the Legislature, and also a member of Congress." The election was peaceably conducted under the instructions of the President. A better spirit now prevailed among the opponents of the Lecompton Constitution, and they no longer refrained from voting. A large majority of them, by a strange but happy inconsistency, recognized its existence by voting under its provisions.*

This election was warmly contested by the two political parties in Kansas, and a greater vote was polled than at any previous election. A large majority of the members of the Legislature elect belonged to that party which had previously refused to vote. The Anti-Slavery party were thus placed in the ascendant, and the political power of the State was in their hands.

The President hailed this evidence of returning reason as an auspicious event. It had been his constant effort from the beginning to induce the Anti-Slavery party to vote. Now that this had been accomplished, he knew that all revolutionary troubles in Kansas would speedily terminate. A resort to the ballot box, instead of force, was the most effectual means of restoring peace and tranquillity.

It was after all these events had transpired, that the Presi-

* Message Dec. 6, 1858.

dent, on the 30th January, 1858, received the Lecompton Constitution, with a request from the President of the Convention that it might be submitted to the consideration of Congress. This was done by the message of the 2d February, 1858, from which we have already made several extracts. In this the President recommended the admission of Kansas as a State under the Lecompton Constitution. He says: " The people of Kansas have, then, ' in their own way,' and in strict accordance with the organic act, framed a constitution and State Government; have submitted the all-important question of slavery to the people, and have elected a governor, a member to represent them in Congress, members of the State Legislature, and other State officers. They now ask admission into the Union under this constitution, which is republican in its form. It is for Congress to decide whether they will admit or reject the State which has thus been created. For my own part, I am decidedly in favor of its admission, and thus terminating the Kansas question. This will carry out the great principle of non-intervention recognized and sanctioned by the organic act, which declares in express language in favor of 'non-intervention by Congress with slavery in the States or Territories,' leaving 'the people thereof perfectly free to form and regulate their domestic institutions in their own way, subject only to the Constitution of the United States.' In this manner, by localizing the question of slavery and confining it to the people whom it immediately concerned, every patriot anxiously expected that this question would be banished from the halls of Congress, where it has always exerted a baneful influence throughout the whole country."

"If Congress, for the sake of those men who refused to vote for delegates to the convention when they might have excluded slavery from the constitution, and who afterwards refused to vote on the 21st December last, when they might, as they claim, have stricken slavery from the constitution, should now reject the State because slavery remains in the constitution, it is manifest that the agitation on this dangerous subject will be renewed in a more alarming form than it has ever yet assumed."

. "As a question of expediency, after the right [of admission] has been maintained, it may be wise to reflect upon the benefits

to Kansas and to the whole country which would result from its
immediate admission into the Union, as well as the disasters
which may follow its rejection. Domestic peace will be the
happy consequence of its admission, and that fine Territory,
which has hitherto been torn by dissensions, will rapidly increase in population and wealth, and speedily realize the blessings and the comforts which follow in the train of agricultural
and mechanical industry. The people will then be sovereign,
and can regulate their own affairs in their own way. If a majority of them desire to abolish domestic slavery within the State,
there is no other possible mode by which this can be effected so
speedily as by prompt admission. The will of the majority is
supreme and irresistible when expressed in an orderly and lawful manner. They can make and unmake constitutions at
pleasure. It would be absurd to say that they can impose
fetters upon their own power which they cannot afterwards
remove. If they could do this, they might tie their own hands
for a hundred as well as for ten years. These are fundamental
principles of American freedom, and are recognized, I believe,
in some form or other, by every State constitution; and if Congress, in the act of admission, should think proper to recognize
them, I can perceive no objection to such a course. This has
been done emphatically in the constitution of Kansas. It declares in the bill of rights that 'all political power is inherent
in the people, and all free governments are founded on their authority and instituted for their benefit, and therefore they have
at all times an inalienable and indefeasible right to alter, reform,
or abolish their form of government in such manner as they
may think proper.' The great State of New York is at this
moment governed under a constitution framed and established in
direct opposition to the mode prescribed by the previous constitution. If, therefore, the provision changing the Kansas constitution after the year one thousand eight hundred and sixty-four,
could by possibility be construed into a prohibition to make
such a change previous to that period, this prohibition would
be wholly unavailing. The Legislature already elected may, at
its very first session, submit the question to a vote of the people
whether they will or will not have a convention to amend their

constitution, and adopt all necessary means for giving effect to the popular will."

"Every patriot in the country had indulged the hope that the Kansas and Nebraska Act would put a final end to the slavery agitation, at least in Congress, which had for more than twenty years convulsed the country and endangered the Union. This act involved great and fundamental principles, and if fairly carried into effect will settle the question. Should the agitation be again revived, should the people of the sister States be again estranged from each other with more than their former bitterness, this will arise from a cause, so far as the interests of Kansas are concerned, more trifling and insignificant than has ever stirred the elements of a great people into commotion. To the people of Kansas, the only practical difference between admission or rejection depends simply upon the fact whether they can themselves more speedily change the present constitution if it does not accord with the will of the majority, or frame a second constitution to be submitted to Congress hereafter. Even if this were a question of mere expediency, and not of right, the small difference of time, one way or the other, is of not the least importance, when contrasted with the evils which must necessarily result to the whole country from a revival of the slavery agitation.

"In considering this question, it should never be forgotten that, in proportion to its insignificance, let the decision be what it may, so far as it may affect the few thousand inhabitants of Kansas who have from the beginning resisted the constitution and the laws, for this very reason the rejection of the constitution will be so much the more keenly felt by the people of fourteen of the States of this Union, where slavery is recognized under the Constitution of the United States.

"Again: The speedy admission of Kansas into the Union would restore peace and quiet to the whole country. Already the affairs of this Territory have engrossed an undue proportion of public attention. They have sadly affected the friendly relations of the people of the States with each other, and alarmed the fears of patriots for the safety of the Union. Kansas once admitted into the Union, the excitement becomes localized, and will soon die away for want of outside aliment. Then every difficulty will be settled at the ballot box."

"I have thus performed my duty on this important question, under a deep sense of responsibility to God and my country. My public life will terminate within a brief period; and I have no other object of earthly ambition than to leave my country in a peaceful and prosperous condition, and to live in the affections and respect of my countrymen. The dark and ominous clouds which now appear to be impending over the Union, I conscientiously believe may be dissipated with honor to every portion of it by the admission of Kansas during the present session of Congress; whereas, if she should be rejected, I greatly fear these clouds will become darker and more ominous than any which have ever yet threatened the Constitution and the Union."

This Message gave rise to a long, exciting, and occasionally violent debate in both Houses of Congress, between the Anti-Slavery members and their opponents, which lasted for nearly three months. In the course of it slavery was denounced in every form which could exasperate the Southern people and render it odious to the people of the North; whilst, on the other hand, many of the speeches of Southern members displayed characteristic violence. Thus two sessions of Congress in succession had been in a great degree occupied with the same inflammatory topics, in discussing the affairs of Kansas.

The debate was finally concluded by the passage of the "Act for the admission of the State of Kansas into the Union," of the 4th May, 1858.* This act, which had been reported by a Committee of Conference of both Houses, was passed in the Senate by a vote of 31 to 22, and in the House by a vote of 112 to 103.† This was strictly a party vote in both Houses, with the exception of Mr. Douglas, in the Senate, who voted with the minority, and a few so-called Anti-Lecompton Democrats who voted with the minority in the House. This act explicitly recognizes the validity of the proceedings in Kansas which had given birth to the Lecompton Constitution. The preamble recites that—

---

* 11 U. S. Laws, p. 269.
† Con. Globe, 1857-'8, pp. 1899 and 1905.

"*Whereas*, The people of the Territory of Kansas did, by a Convention of Delegates assembled at Lecompton, on the seventh day of November, one thousand eight hundred and fifty-seven, for that purpose, form for themselves a Constitution and State Government, which Constitution is republican," etc.; and it then proceeds to enact, "That the State of Kansas be, and is hereby, admitted into the Union on an equal footing with the original States in all respects whatever, but upon this fundamental condition precedent," etc.

The necessity for this condition precedent arose from the fact that the ordinance of the Convention accompanying the constitution, claimed for the State a cession of the public lands more than six times the quantity which had been granted to other States when entering the Union.* The estimated amount was more than twenty-three million five hundred thousand acres. To such an exaction Congress could not yield. In lieu of this ordinance, therefore, they proposed to submit to a vote of the people of Kansas a proposition reducing the number of acres to be ceded, to that which had been granted to other States. Should this proposition be accepted by the people, then the fact was to be announced by the proclamation of the President; and "thereafter, and without any further proceedings on the part of Congress, the admission of the State of Kansas into the Union, upon an equal footing with the original States in all respects whatever, shall be complete and absolute."

Such was the condition precedent, which was never fulfilled, because the people by their votes on the 2d of August, 1858, rejected the proposition of Congress, and therefore Kansas was not admitted into the Union under the Lecompton Constitution. Notwithstanding this, the recognition by Congress of the regularity of the proceedings in forming the Lecompton Constitution did much good, at least for a season. It diverted the attention of the people from fighting to voting, a most salutary change. The President, in referring to this subject in his next annual Message of December 6, 1858, uses the following language: " When we compare the condition of the country at the present

---

* Con. Globe, 1857–'8, p. 1766.

day with what it was one year ago, at the meeting of Congress, we have much reason for gratitude to that Almighty Providence which has never failed to interpose for our relief at the most critical periods of our history. One year ago the sectional strife between the North and the South on the dangerous subject of slavery had again become so intense as to threaten the peace and perpetuity of the confederacy. The application for the admission of Kansas as a State into the Union fostered this unhappy agitation, and brought the whole subject once more before Congress. It was the desire of every patriot that such measures of legislation might be adopted as would remove the excitement from the States and confine it to the Territory where it legitimately belonged. Much has been done, I am happy to say, towards the accomplishment of this object during the last session of Congress.

" The Supreme Court of the United States had previously decided that all American citizens have an equal right to take into the Territories whatever is held as property under the laws of any of the States, and to hold such property there under the guardianship of the Federal Constitution, so long as the territorial condition shall remain. This is now a well-established position, and the proceedings of the last session were alone wanting to give it practical effect.

"The principle has been recognized, in some form or other, by an almost unanimous vote of both Houses of Congress, that a Territory has a right to come into the Union either as a free or a slave State, according to the will of a majority of its people. The just equality of all the States has thus been vindicated, and a fruitful source of dangerous dissension among them has been removed.

" While such has been the beneficial tendency of your legislative proceedings outside of Kansas, their influence has nowhere been so happy as within that Territory itself. Left to manage and control its own affairs in its own way, without the pressure of external influence, the revolutionary Topeka organization, and all resistance to the territorial government established by Congress, have been finally abandoned. As a natural consequence, that fine Territory now appears to be tranquil and prosperous, and is attracting increasing thousands of immigrants to make it their happy home.

"The past unfortunate experience of Kansas has enforced the lesson, so often already taught, that resistance to lawful authority, under our form of government, cannot fail in the end to prove disastrous to its authors."

It is unnecessary to pursue this subject further than to state that Kansas was finally admitted into the Union on the 29th January, 1861.

The series of events already enumerated had greatly strengthened and extended the Anti-Slavery party. It soon drew within its vortex all other political organizations in the free States, except that of the old Democratic party, and consolidated them under the name of the Republican party. This thenceforward became purely sectional, and was confined to the States north of Mason and Dixon's line.

The Kansas and Nebraska Act had referred all constitutional questions respecting slavery in the Territories, to the Supreme Court of the United States. It accordingly furnished the necessary facilities for bringing cases "involving title to slaves," or the "question of personal freedom," before that tribunal.

At the period of Mr. Buchanan's inauguration a case was pending before that Court (Dred Scott *v.* Sandford, 19 Howard's Reports, p. 393) involving all the contested questions in regard to slavery. This, at the time, presented to him a cheerful but delusive prospect. He confidently expected that the decision of the Court would settle all these questions and eventually restore harmony among the States. Accordingly, in his Inaugural Address, he had declared that to this decision, whatever it might be, he should, in common with all good citizens, cheerfully submit. This was his imperative duty. Our free form of government must soon be destroyed, should the Executive set, up his judgment against that of the coördinate judicial branch, on a question clearly within its constitutional jurisdiction.

Two days after the inauguration, on the 6th March, 1857, the Supreme Court pronounced its judgment. This was delivered by Chief Justice Taney, and embraced all the points in controversy. It establishes the following propositions:

1. Congress has power to acquire territory, "to be held by the United States until it is in a suitable condition to become a State upon an equal footing with the other States."

2. This territory is "acquired by the General Government, as the representative and trustee of the people of the United States, and it must therefore be held in that character for their common and equal benefit; for it was the people of the several States, acting through their agent and representative, the Federal Government, who in fact acquired the territory in question, and the Government holds it for their common use, until it shall be associated with the other States as a member of the confederacy."

3. Until that time should arrive, it was the duty of Congress to establish a government over the Territory, "best suited for the protection and security of the citizens of the United States, and other inhabitants who might be authorized to take up their abode there."

4. But "the territory being a part of the United States, the Government and the citizen both enter it under the authority of the Constitution, with their respective rights defined and marked out; and the Federal Government can exercise no power over his person or property beyond what that instrument confers, nor lawfully deny any right which it has reserved."

5. The Federal Government possesses no power to violate the rights of property within such Territory, because these "are united with the rights of persons, and placed on the same ground by the fifth amendment to the Constitution, which provides that no person shall be deprived of life, liberty, or property, without due process of law." "And the powers over persons and property of which we speak, are not only not granted to Congress, but are in express terms denied, and they are forbidden to exercise them. And this prohibition is not confined to the States, but the words are general, and extend to the whole Territory over which the Constitution gives it power to legislate, including those portions of it remaining under Territorial Government, as well as that covered by States. It is a total absence of power everywhere within the dominion of the United States, and places the citizens of a Territory, as far as these rights are concerned,

on the same footing with citizens of the States, and guards them as firmly and plainly against any inroads which the General Government might attempt, under the plea of implied or incidental powers. And if Congress itself cannot do this—if it is beyond the powers conferred on the Federal Government—it will be admitted, we presume, that it could not authorize a territorial Government to exercise them. It could confer no power on any local Government, established by its authority, to violate the provisions of the Constitution."

6. "It seems, however, to be supposed, that there is a difference between property in a slave and other property, and that different rules may be applied to it in expounding the Constitution of the United States." "Now, as we have already said in an earlier part of this opinion, on a different point, the right of property in a slave is distinctly and expressly affirmed in the Constitution. The right to traffic in it, like an ordinary article of merchandise and property, was guaranteed to the citizens of the United States, in every State that might desire it, for twenty years. And the Government in express terms is pledged to protect it in all future time, if the slave escapes from his owner. This is done in plain words—too plain to be misunderstood. And no word can be found in the Constitution which gives Congress a greater power over slave property, or which entitles property of that kind to less protection than property of any other description. The only power conferred is the power coupled with the duty of guarding and protecting the owner in his rights."

"Upon these considerations it is the opinion of the Court that the Act of Congress which prohibited a citizen from holding and owning property of this kind in the territory of the United States north of the line therein mentioned [the Missouri Compromise line], is not warranted by the Constitution, and is therefore void."

This decision, so full and explicit, established the right of the master to take his slaves into the Territories and hold them there in despite of all conflicting Congressional or Territorial legislation, until the Territories should be prepared to assume the position of States.

It might have been expected that this decision would have superseded all opposing political platforms, and ended the controversy in regard to slavery in the Territories. This expectation, notwithstanding, soon proved to be a delusion. Instead of yielding it obedience, its correctness and binding effect were instantly resisted by the Republican party. They denounced and repudiated it in every possible form from the first moment, and continued to maintain, in opposition to its express terms, that it was not only the right but the duty of Congress to abolish slavery in all the Territories. This became a cardinal principle in the Chicago platform on which Mr. Lincoln was nominated and elected, and to which his Inaugural proves he had determined to adhere. The agitation continued for years, just as though the Supreme Court had never decided the question, until at length Congress passed an Act, on the 19th June, 1862,* declaring that from and after its passage, "there shall be neither slavery nor involuntary servitude in any of the Territories of the United States now existing, or which may at any time hereafter be formed or acquired by the United States, otherwise than in punishment of crimes whereof the party shall have been duly convicted."

This Act stands upon the Statute Book in direct conflict with the Constitution as expounded by the Supreme Coördinate Judicial Tribunal, and is therefore, according to the theory of our Government, a mere nullity.

On the other hand, a large and respectable portion of the old Democratic party of the North, best known as the Douglas Democracy, equally disregarded the decision of the Supreme Court. For some years before it was pronounced, this party, whilst admitting that the Constitution authorizes the migration of slaves from the States into the Territories, had maintained that after their arrival it was competent for the Territorial Legislature to impair or destroy the rights of the master. They claimed this power by virtue of a supposed inherent attribute of popular sovereignty alleged to belong to the first settlers of a Territory, just as it exists in the people of one of the States. This doctrine

* Pamph. Laws, 1861-'62, p. 432.

was appropriately, though not in good taste, called "squatter sovereignty." It involved, at least in appearance, an extension of popular rights, and was therefore well calculated to enlist public sympathy in its favor. It was presented and enforced by its advocates in such captivating colors, that before the date of the decision it had secured many enthusiastic adherents in the North, whilst it was utterly repudiated in the South. The Douglas Democracy contended that this their favorite theory had been recognized in May, 1854, by the Kansas and Nebraska Act, declaring it to be " the true intent and meaning of this Act not to legislate slavery into any Territory or State, nor to exclude it therefrom; but to leave the people thereof free to form and regulate their domestic institutions in their own way, subject only to the Constitution of the United States."

They ought to have reflected that even if this provision had in plain language conferred upon the first settlers the power to abolish slavery, still, according to its very terms, it was "subject to the Constitution of the United States," and like all other laws it would be void if in conflict with this Constitution. What tribunal was to decide this question? Certainly the Supreme Court. Indeed the law itself had, in express terms, recognized this, by prescribing the appropriate method of bringing the question before that Court. After the Court, therefore, in March, 1857, had decided the question against their ideas of Territorial sovereignty, they ought to have yielded. They ought to have acquiesced in the doctrine that property, including that in slaves, as well in the Territories as in the States, is placed under the protection of the Constitution, and that neither a Territorial Legislature nor Congress possesses the power to impair or destroy it.

This decision ought surely to have ended the question; but not so. Instead of this, the Douglas Democracy disregarded the decision altogether. They treated it as though it had never been made, and still continued to agitate without intermission, and with powerful effect, until the very day of President Lincoln's election. Absolute non-interference with slavery in the Territories, on the part of any human power outside of them, was their watchword; thus leaving the people thereof entirely free to regulate or destroy it according to their own discretion.

On the other hand, the old Democracy, true to its ancient and time-honored principles in support of law and order, at once yielded a willing obedience to the decision of the Supreme Court. Whatever differences of opinion previously existed among them in regard to the correctness of the decision, at once disappeared. Without being the advocates of domestic slavery, they held themselves bound by the compromises made and recorded in the Constitution by its illustrious authors, and sustained the decision from an imperious sense of public duty. It did not require the authority of the Supreme Court to convince a large majority of them that a Territorial Legislature had not power to deprive a citizen of his property which was denied both to a State Legislature and to Congress. This extreme power of sovereignty in the latter cases they knew could only be conferred by an amendment to the State or Federal Constitution.

The Douglas Democracy still placed their principal reliance, as they had done before the decision, on the language of the Kansas and Nebraska Act. The difference between them and the old Democracy related to the point of time intended by the act, when the people of the Territories were recognized to possess the power "to form and regulate their domestic institutions in their own way." Was this at any time they pleased after the arrival of the first settlers, or not until the people should assemble in convention to form a State government, when, in the language of the act, they were to be admitted into the Union "with or without slavery, as their constitution may prescribe at the time of their admission"? According to the construction of the Douglas Democracy, the act recognized their right to abolish slavery at any period of the Territorial existence; but according to the construction of the old Democracy, there was no recognition of this right, until the period when they should meet in convention to form a State constitution; and such was in accordance with the decision of the Supreme Court.

If the Douglas construction of the act be correct, it is morally certain that the Southern Senators and Representatives who were warm advocates of its passage, could not possibly have so understood it. If they had, they would then have voluntarily voted away the rights of their own constituents. Indeed, such a construction of the act would be more destructive to the interests of the slaveholder, than the Republican doctrine of Congressional exclusion. Better, far better for him to submit the question to Congress, where he could be deliberately heard by his representatives, than to be deprived of his slaves, after he had gone to the trouble and expense of transporting them to a Territory, by a hasty enactment of a Territorial Legislature elected annually and freed from all constitutional restraints. Such a construction of the Kansas and Nebraska Act would be in direct opposition to the policy and practice of the Government from its origin. The men who framed and built up our institutions, so far from regarding the Territories to be sovereign, treated them as mere wards of the Federal Government. Congress, as a faithful and kind guardian, watched over their infancy and promoted their growth and prosperity until they attained their majority. During the period of their pupilage the persons and property of the inhabitants were protected by the Constitution and laws of the United States. When the population had so far increased as to render this expedient, Congress gave them a Territorial Government. But in conferring upon the settlers the privilege to elect members to the popular branch of the Territorial Legislature, they took care to reserve the appointment of the Governor and the members of the Council to the President and Senate. Moreover, they expressly provided, in the language of the compromise measures of 1850, "that all the laws passed by the Legislative Assembly and Governor shall be submitted to the Congress of the United States, and if disapproved, shall be null and of no effect." This limitation on their powers was intended to restrain them from enacting laws in conflict with the Constitution, the laws, or the established policy of the United States. It produced the happiest effect. The cases are rare, indeed, in which Congress found it necessary to exercise this disapproving power. It was not then foreseen that any political party would arise in this country, claiming the right for the majority of the first settlers of a Territory, under the plea of popular sovereignty, to confiscate the property of the minority. When the population in the Territories had reached a sufficient number, Congress admitted them as States into the Union under constitutions framed by themselves, "with or without slavery," according to their own discretion.

Long experience had abundantly sanctioned the wisdom of this policy. Under its benign influence many powerful and prosperous States have been admitted into the Union. No serious difficulties had ever occurred until the attempt was made to abolish it under the construction in favor of "squatter sovereignty" given to the Kansas and Nebraska Act.

The Southern people, who had expected that after the decision of the Supreme Court their equal rights in the Territories would be respected by the Northern Democracy, were deeply mortified and disappointed to find that a large portion of this party still persevered in assailing these rights. This exasperated them, and placed in the hands of Southern disunion agitators a powerful weapon against the Union.

President Buchanan, ever since the commencement of his administration, has been persistently denounced, especially by the Douglas Democracy, for sustaining the law as pronounced by the highest judicial authority of the country. He has been charged with proving faithless to the Cincinnati platform, which he accepted and on which he was elected. To prove this would be impossible, because it is altogether silent in regard to the power of a Territorial Legislature over the question of slavery. Nay, more; whilst affirming, in general terms, the provisions of the Kansas and Nebraska Act, it specifically designates a future time when slavery may be rightfully abolished, not by the Territorial Legislature, but by the people. This is when, "acting through the legally and fairly expressed will of a majority of actual residents, and whenever the number of their inhabitants justifies it, [they assemble] to form a constitution with or without domestic slavery, and be admitted into the Union upon terms of perfect equality with the other States." Before this period the Cincinnati platform is silent on the subject. The power is claimed by its advocates as a mere inference from the general language of the Kansas and Nebraska Act. But even if the right of a Territorial Legislature to abolish slavery had been affirmed in express terms by the Cincinnati Convention, which was the President bound to obey?—a political platform, or the Constitution as expounded afterwards by the Supreme Court? the decree of a nominating convention, or the supreme law of the land? He could not hesitate in the choice under his oath faithfully and to the best of his ability "to preserve, protect, and defend the Constitution of the United States." Sad must be the condition of any country where an appeal can be taken from judicial decisions to excited popular elections! Under our free government all citizens are equal before the law. The law and the law alone is their master. When this is disregarded and defied by excited and exasperated popular majorities, anarchy and confusion must be the inevitable consequence. Public and private rights are sacrificed to the madness of the hour. The Government itself becomes helpless for their protection, and to avoid such evils history has taught us that the people will at last seek refuge in the arms of despotism. Let all free governments in future times profit by our example. Let them take warning that the late disastrous civil war, unjustifiable as it was, would most probably never have existed had not the American people disobeyed and resisted the Constitution of their country as expounded by the tribunal which they themselves had created for this express purpose.

The great Democratic party might have maintained its ascendency and saved the Union, had it not been thus hopelessly divided at this critical period. Encouraged and emboldened by its irreconcilable divisions, the Abolition or Republican party no longer confined itself to an opposition to slavery in the Territories. It soon extended its agitation to the suppression of slavery within the States. At the first it sought to save appearances, but the veil was too transparent to conceal its purposes.

CHAPTER III.

Senator Seward—The "Irrepressible Conflict"—Helper's "Impending Crisis"—The John Brown Raid—The nature of Fanaticism—The Democratic National Convention at Charleston—Its proceedings and adjournment to Baltimore—Reassembling at Baltimore and proceedings there—Its breaking up and division into the Douglas and the Breckinridge Conventions—Proceedings of each—Review of the whole and the effect on the South.

SENATOR SEWARD, of New York, was at this period the acknowledged head and leader of the Republican party. Indeed, his utterances had become its oracles. He was much more of a politician than a statesman. Without strong convictions, he understood the art of preparing in his closet, and uttering before the public, antithetical sentences well calculated both to inflame the ardor of his anti-slavery friends and to exasperate his pro-slavery opponents. If he was not the author of the "irrepressible conflict," he appropriated it to himself and converted it into a party oracle. He thus aroused passions, probably without so intending, which it was beyond his power afterwards to control. He raised a storm which, like others of whom we read in history, he wanted both the courage and the power to quell.

We quote the following extract from his famous speech at Rochester on the 25th of October, 1858:* "Free labor and slave labor, these antagonistic systems, are continually coming into close contact, and collision results. Shall I tell you what this collision means? They who think it is accidental, unnecessary, the work of interested or fanatical agitators, and therefore ephemeral, mistake the case altogether. It is an *irrepressible*

* Helper's Compendium, p. 142.

conflict between opposing and enduring forces, and it means that the United States must and will, sooner or later, become either entirely a slaveholding nation or entirely a free-labor nation. Either the cotton and rice fields of South Carolina and the sugar plantations of Louisiana will ultimately be tilled by free labor, and Charleston and New Orleans become marts for legitimate merchandise alone, or else the rye fields and wheat fields of Massachusetts and New York must again be surrendered by their farmers to slave culture and to the production of slaves, and Boston and New York become once more markets for trade in the bodies and souls of men."

However impossible that Massachusetts and New York should ever again become slaveholding States, and again engage in the African slave trade, yet such was the temper of the times that this absurd idea produced serious apprehensions in the North. It gave rise to still more serious apprehensions in the South. There they believed or affected to believe that the people of the North, in order to avoid the dreaded alternative of having slavery restored among themselves, and having their rye fields and wheat fields cultivated by slave labor, would put forth all their efforts to cut up slavery by the roots in the Southern States. These reckless fancies of Senator Seward made the deeper impression upon the public mind, both North and South, because it was then generally believed that he would be the candidate of the Republican party at the next Presidential election. In accordance with the views expressed by Senator Seward, Hinton Helper's "Impending Crisis" soon afterwards appeared, a book well calculated to alarm the southern people. This was ushered into the world by the following warm commendation from Mr. Seward himself:* "I have read the 'Impending Crisis of the South' with great attention. It seems to me a work of great merit, rich yet accurate in statistical information, and logical in analysis."

On the 9th of March, 1859, a Republican committee in New York, consisting of Horace Greeley, Thurlow Weed, and others, issued a circular warmly commending the book, and proposing to publish one hundred thousand copies of a compendium of it

* Fowler's Sectional Controversy, p. 205.

at a cheap rate for gratuitous circulation. In order to raise subscriptions for the purpose, they obtained the recommendation of this plan by sixty-eight Republican members of Congress, with Schuyler Colfax at their head. It is in the following terms: * "We the undersigned, members of the House of Representatives of the National Congress, do cordially indorse the opinion and approve the enterprise set forth in the foregoing circular."

The author of the book is by birth a North Carolinian, though of doubtful personal character, but his labors have since been recognized and rewarded by his appointment as Consul of the United States at Buenos Ayres.

Published under such auspices, the "Impending Crisis" became at once an authoritative exposition of the principles of the Republican party. The original, as well as a compendium, were circulated by hundreds of thousands, North, South, East, and West. No book could be better calculated for the purpose of intensifying the mutual hatred between the North and the South. This book, in the first place, proposes to abolish slavery in the slaveholding States by exciting a revolution among those called "the poor whites," against their rich slaveholding neighbors. To accomplish this purpose, every appeal which perverse ingenuity and passionate malignity could suggest, was employed to excite jealousy and hatred between these two classes. The cry of the poor against the rich, the resort of demagogues in all ages, was echoed and reëchoed. The plan urged upon the non-slaveholding citizens of the South was— †

1st. "Thorough organization and independent political action on the part of the non-slaveholding whites of the South."

2d. "Ineligibility of pro-slavery slaveholders. Never another vote to any one who advocates the retention and perpetuation of human slavery."

3d. "No coöperation with pro-slavery politicians—no fellowship with them in religion—no affiliation with them in society."

4th. "No patronage to pro-slavery merchants—no guestship

* Con. Globe, 1859-'60, p. 16.   † Compendium, p. 76.

in slave-waiting hotels—no fees to pro-slavery lawyers—no employment of pro-slavery physicians—no audience to pro-slavery parsons."

5th. "No more hiring of slaves by non-slaveholders."

6th. "Abrupt discontinuance of subscription to pro-slavery newspapers."

7th. "The greatest possible encouragement to free white labor."

"This, then," says Mr. Helper, "is the outline of our scheme for the abolition of slavery in the Southern States. Let it be acted upon with due promptitude, and as certain as truth is mightier than error, fifteen years will not elapse before every foot of territory, from the mouth of the Delaware to the emboguing of the Rio Grande, will glitter with the jewels of freedom. Some time during this year, next, or the year following, let there be a general convention of non-slaveholders from every slave State in the Union, to deliberate on the momentous issues now pending."* Not confining himself even within these limits, Mr. Helper proceeds to still greater extremities, and exclaims: "But, sirs, slaveholders, chevaliers, and lords of the lash, we are unwilling to allow you to cheat the negroes out of all the rights and claims to which, as human beings, they are most sacredly entitled. Not alone for ourself as an individual, but for others also, particularly for five or six millions of southern non-slaveholding whites, whom your iniquitous Statism has debarred from almost all the mental and material comforts of life, do we speak, when we say, you must sooner or later emancipate your slaves, and pay each and every one of them at least sixty dollars cash in hand. By doing this you will be restoring to them their natural rights, and remunerating them at the rate of less than twenty-six cents per annum for the long and cheerless period of their servitude from the 20th of August, 1620, when, on James River, in Virginia, they became the unhappy slaves of heartless tyrants. Moreover, by doing this you will be performing but a simple act of justice to the non-slaveholding whites, upon whom the system of slavery has

* Pages 89, 90.

weighed scarcely less heavily than upon the negroes themselves. You will, also, be applying a saving balm to your own outraged hearts and consciences, and your children—yourselves in fact—freed from the accursed stain of slavery, will become respectable, useful, and honorable members of society."

He then taunts and defies the slaveholders in this manner: "And now, sirs, we have thus laid down our ultimatum. What are you going to do about it ? Something dreadful of course! Perhaps you will dissolve the Union again. Do it, if you dare! Our motto, and we would have you to understand it, is, ' *The abolition of slavery and the perpetuation of the American Union.*' If, by any means, you do succeed in your treasonable attempts to take the South out of the Union to-day, we will bring her back to-morrow; if she goes away with you, she will return without you.

" Do not mistake the meaning of the last clause of the last sentence. We could elucidate it so thoroughly that no intelligent person could fail to comprehend it; but, for reasons which may hereafter appear, we forego the task.

" Henceforth there are other interests to be consulted in the South, aside from the interests of negroes and slaveholders. A profound sense of duty incites us to make the greatest possible efforts for the abolition of slavery; an equally profound sense of duty calls for a continuation of those efforts until the very last foe to freedom shall have been utterly vanquished. To the summons of the righteous monitor within, we shall endeavor to prove faithful; no opportunity for inflicting a mortal wound in the side of slavery shall be permitted to pass us unimproved.

" Thus, terror engenderers of the South, have we fully and frankly defined our position; we have no modifications to propose, no compromises to offer, nothing to retract. Frown, sirs, fret, foam, prepare your weapons, threat, strike, shoot, stab, bring on civil war, dissolve the Union, nay, annihilate the solar system if you will—do all this, more, less, better, worse, any thing—do what you will, sirs, you can neither foil nor intimidate us; our purpose is as firmly fixed as the eternal pillars of heaven; we have determined to abolish slavery, and so help us God, abolish it we will! Take this to bed with you to-night, sirs, and think about it, dream over it, and let us know how you feel to-morrow morning."

"Such are specimens from the book indorsed and commended by the acknowledged leader of the Republican party, after having read it "with great attention," and by sixty-eight prominent Republican members of Congress! In the midst of the excitement produced by this book, both North and South, occurred the raid of John Brown into Virginia. This was undertaken for the avowed purpose of producing a servile insurrection among the slaves, and aiding them by military force in rising against their masters.

John Brown was a man violent, lawless, and fanatical. Amid the troubles in Kansas he had distinguished himself, both by word and by deed, for boldness and cruelty. His ruling passion was to become the instrument of abolishing slavery, by the strong hand, throughout the slaveholding States. With him, this amounted almost to insanity. Notwithstanding all this, he was so secret in his purposes that he had scarcely any confidants. This appears in a striking manner from the testimony taken before the Senate Committee.* Several abolitionists had contributed money to him in aid of the anti-slavery cause generally, but he had not communicated to them for what particular purpose this was to be employed. He had long meditated an irruption into Virginia, to excite and to aid a rising of the slaves against their masters, and for this he had prepared. He had purchased two hundred Sharp's carbines, two hundred revolver pistols, and about one thousand pikes, with which to arm the slaves. These arms he had collected and deposited in the vicinity of Harper's Ferry. When the plot was ripe for execution, a little before midnight on Sunday evening, the 16th of October, 1859, he, with sixteen white and five negro confederates, rushed across the Potomac to Harper's Ferry, and there seized the armory, arsenal, and rifle factory belonging to the United States. When the inhabitants awoke in the morning they found, greatly to their terror and surprise, that these places, with the town itself, were all in possession of John Brown's force. It would be a waste of time to detail the history of this

---

* Reports of Senate Committee, 1st Session 36th Congress, No. 278, vol. ii.

raid. Suffice it to say that on Tuesday morning, 18th, the whole band, with the exception of two who had escaped, were either killed or captured. Among the latter was John Brown himself, badly wounded. In the mean time, however, his party had murdered five individuals, four of them unarmed citizens, and had wounded nine others. It is proper to observe that John Brown, after all his efforts, received no support from the slaves in the neighborhood. The news of this attack on Harper's Ferry spread rapidly over the country. All were at first ignorant of the strength of the force, and public rumor had greatly exaggerated it. The President immediately sent a detachment of marines to the spot, by which John Brown and his party were captured in the engine house, where they had fled for shelter and defence. Large numbers of volunteers from Virginia and Maryland had also hastened to the scene of action. John Brown and several of his party were afterwards tried before the appropriate judicial authorities of Virginia, and were convicted and executed.

In the already excited condition of public feeling throughout the South, this raid of John Brown made a deeper impression on the southern mind against the Union than all former events. Considered merely as the isolated act of a desperate fanatic, it would have had no lasting effect. It was the enthusiastic and permanent approbation of the object of his expedition by the abolitionists of the North, which spread alarm and apprehension throughout the South. We are told by Fowler in his "Sectional Controversy," that on the day of Brown's execution bells were tolled in many places, cannon fired, and prayers offered up for him as if he were a martyr; he was placed in the same category with Paul and Silas, for whom prayers were made by the Church, and churches were draped in mourning. Nor were these honors to his memory a mere transient burst of feeling. The Republican party have ever since honored him as a saint or a martyr in a cause which they deemed so holy. According to them, "whilst his body moulders in the dust his spirit is still marching on" in the van to accomplish his bloody purposes. Even blasphemy, which it would be improper to repeat, has been employed to consecrate his memory.

5

Fanaticism never stops to reason. Driven by honest impulse, it rushes on to its object without regard to interposing obstacles. Acting on the principle avowed in the Declaration of Independence, "that all men are created equal," and believing slavery to be sinful, it would not hesitate to pass from its own State into other States, and to emancipate their slaves by force of arms. We do not stop to inquire whether slavery is sinful. We may observe, however, that under the old and new dispensations, slaves were held both by Jews and Christians, and rules were prescribed for their humane treatment. In the present state of civilization, we are free to admit that slavery is a great political and social evil. If left to the wise ordinances of a superintending Providence, which never acts rashly, it would have been gradually extinguished in our country, peacefully and without bloodshed, as has already been done throughout nearly the whole of Christendom. It is true that other countries enjoyed facilities for emancipation which we do not possess. In them the slaves were of the same color and race with the rest of the community, and in becoming freemen they soon mingled with the general mass on equal terms with their former masters.

But even admitting slavery to be a sin, have the adherents of John Brown never reflected that the attempt by one people to pass beyond their own jurisdiction, and to extirpate by force of arms whatever they may deem sinful among another people, would involve the nations of the earth in perpetual hostilities? We Christians are thoroughly convinced that Mahomet was a false prophet; shall we, therefore, make war upon the Turkish empire to destroy Islamism? If we would preserve the peace of the world and avoid much greater evils than we desire to destroy, we must act upon the wise principles of international law, and leave each people to decide domestic questions for themselves. Their sins are not our sins. We must intrust their punishment and reformation to their own authorities, and to the Supreme Governor of nations. This spirit of interference with what we may choose to consider the domestic evils of other nations, has in former periods covered the earth with blood. Even since the advent of Christianity, until a comparatively late period, Catholics and Protestants, acting on this false principle, have, with equal sincerity, made war against each other, to put down dogmas of faith which they mutually believed to be sinful and dangerous to the soul's salvation, and this in the name of Him who descended from heaven to establish a kingdom of peace and charity on earth. Spain waged a reckless war against the poor Indians of Mexico, to root out the sin of idolatry from their midst and compel them to embrace the Christian faith; and whoever shall read the life of Cortes must admit that he acted with perfect sincerity, and was intent on their souls' salvation. Mahometans, believing Christianity to be sinful, have, in a similar spirit, made war on Christian nations to propagate their own faith.

We might fill volumes with like examples from history. These days of darkness and delusion, of doing evil that good might come, have, it is to be hoped, passed away for ever under the pure light of the Gospel. If all these acts were great wrongs in the intercourse between independent nations, if they violated the benign principles of Christianity, how much greater would the wrong have been had one portion of the sovereign States of a confederate union made war against the remainder to extirpate from them the sin of slavery! And this more especially when their common constitution, in its very terms, recognizes slavery, restores the runaway slave to his master, and even makes the institution a basis for the exercise of the elective franchise. With like reason might the State of Maine, whilst the delusion of the Maine liquor law prevailed, have made war on her sister States to enforce its observance upon their people, because drunkenness is a grievous sin in the belief of all Christians. In justification of this, she might have alleged that the intemperance tolerated among her neighbors, and not her own spirit to intermeddle with their concerns, was the cause of the war, just as it has been asserted that slavery in the Southern States was the cause of the late war. We may believe and indeed know that the people of the North, however much they may have extolled the conduct of John Brown, would never in practice have carried out his teachings and his example; but justice requires that we should make a fair allowance for the apprehensions of the Southern people, who necessarily viewed the whole scene from an opposite standpoint. Under these circumstances it is no wonder that the South should have entertained fearful apprehensions for their peace and safety, in the event that the Abolition party should succeed in obtaining the reins of the government, an event soon thereafter rendered morally certain by the breaking up of the Charleston Democratic Convention. To the history of the sad event we now proceed.

It is certain that before the meeting of the Convention, the Democratic party of the North had become seriously divided between the old and the Douglas Democracy, and that the latter at least was strongly tinctured with an anti-slavery spirit.

The Convention assembled at Charleston on the 23d of April, 1860, to nominate candidates for the offices of President and Vice-President. It was composed of delegates from all the thirty-three. States of the Union, and each State was entitled to as many votes as it had Senators and Representatives in Congress. The whole number of votes was, therefore, 303; and under the two-thirds rule which it adopted, after the example of former Conventions, 202 votes were required to make a nomination.* The Convention elected Hon. Caleb Cushing, of Massachusétts, its President.

This Convention had no sooner assembled than a radical difference of opinion was exhibited among its members in regard to the status of slavery in the Territories. The old Democratic portion, invoking the Dred Scott decision, held that slave property, under the Constitution, was entitled to the same protection therein with any other property; whilst the Douglas delegates, in opposition to this decision, maintained the power of a Territorial Legislature to impair or destroy this property in its discretion. On the day after the Convention assembled (24th April), a committee was appointed, consisting of a delegate from each State, selected by the respective State delegations, to report resolutions as a platform for the party; and on the same day it was resolved unanimously " that this Convention will not proceed to ballot for a candidate for the Presidency until the platform shall have been adopted." On the 27th of April the Committee on Resolutions made majority and minority reports.†

* Report of Proceedings, p. 11.   † 5th day, p. 45.

After a long, able, and eloquent discussion on the respective merits of the two reports, they were both, on motion of Mr. Bigler, of Pennsylvania, re-committed to the Committee on Resolutions,* with a view, if possible, to promote harmony; but this proved to be impracticable. On the sixth day of the Convention (Saturday, April 28th),† at an evening session, Mr. Avery, of North Carolina, and Mr. Samuels, of Iowa, from the majority and minority of the committee, again made opposite and conflicting reports on the question of slavery in the Territories. On this question the committee had divided from the beginning, the one portion embracing the fifteen members from the slaveholding States, with those from California and Oregon, and the other consisting of the members from all the free States east of the Rocky Mountains. On all other questions both reports substantially agreed, and therefore in regard to them no special notice is required.

The following is the report of the majority made on this subject by Mr. Avery, of North Carolina, the chairman of the committee: "*Resolved*, That the platform adopted by the Democratic party at Cincinnati be affirmed with the following explanatory resolutions: 1st. That the Government of a Territory, organized by an act of Congress, is provisional and temporary, and during its existence all citizens of the United States have an equal right to settle with their property in the Territory, without their rights, either of person or property, being destroyed or impaired by Congressional or Territorial legislation. 2d. That it is the duty of the Federal Government, in all its departments, to protect, when necessary, the rights of persons and property in the Territories, and wherever else its constitutional authority extends. 3d. That when the settlers in a Territory having an adequate population form a State Constitution, the right of sovereignty commences, and being consummated by admission into the Union, they stand on an equal footing with the people of other States, and the State thus organized ought to be admitted into the Federal Union whether its constitution prohibits or recognizes the institution of slavery." It

---

* Page 89.   † Pages 92, 93.

will be perceived that these resolutions are in exact conformity with the decision of the Supreme Court.

The following is the report of the minority, made by Mr. Samuels, of Iowa. After re-affirming the Cincinnati platform by the first resolution, it proceeds: "Inasmuch as differences of opinion exist in the Democratic party, as to the nature and extent of the powers of a Territorial Legislature, and as to the powers and duties of Congress, under the Constitution of the United States, over the institution of slavery within the Territories, *Resolved*, That the Democratic party will abide by the decisions of the Supreme Court of the United States upon questions of constitutional law."

It must strike the reader that this resolution does not meet the question, but is vague and evasive. It entirely ignores the fact that all these "questions of constitutional law" had been already decided by the Supreme Court, and that in regard to them no differences of opinion could exist among those who were willing to recognize its authority. It leaves the rights of the master over slave property in the Territories as an open question, and places them at the mercy of a majority in Territorial Legislatures, until some future decision should be made, not on this specific question, but generally "on questions of constitutional law." In fact, it treats the decision as though it had never been made. It is proper to observe that we have included the member of the committee from Massachusetts (Mr. Butler) among the sixteen votes in favor of the minority report, because, although he made a separate report of his own, this was confined to a simple recommendation of the Cincinnati platform and nothing more. The opposing reports from the Northern and the Southern members of the committee were thus distinctly placed before the Convention. It was soon manifest that should the minority report prevail, the Convention must be broken into fragments.

After some preliminary remarks, Mr. Samuels moved the adoption of the minority report as a substitute for that of the majority.* This gave rise to an earnest and excited debate. The difference between the parties was radical and irreconcila-

* Page 97.

ble. The South insisted that the Cincinnati platform, whose true construction in regard to slavery in the Territories had always been denied by a portion of the Democratic party, should be explained and settled by an express recognition of the principles decided by the Supreme Court. The North, on the other hand, refused to recognize this decision, and still maintained the power to be inherent in the people of a Territory to deal with the question of slavery according to their own discretion. The vote was then taken, and the minority report was substituted for that of the majority by a vote of one hundred and sixty-five to one hundred and thirty-eight.* The delegates from the six New England States, as well as from New York, Ohio, Indiana, Illinois, Michigan, Wisconsin, Iowa, and Minnesota, fourteen free States, cast their entire vote in favor of the minority report. New Jersey and Pennsylvania alone among the free States east of the Rocky Mountains refused to vote as States, but their delegates voted as individuals. Had all the States voted as units, without regard to the respective minorities in each; or, on the other hand, had the delegates from all the States voted as individuals, in either case the majority report would have been sustained, and the Democratic party might have been saved. It was the want of uniformity in the mode of voting that produced the disastrous result. The means employed to attain this end were skilfully devised by the minority of the Pennsylvania delegation in favor of nominating Mr. Douglas.† The entire delegation had, strangely enough, placed this power in their hands, by selecting two of their number, Messrs. Cessna and Wright, to represent the whole on the two most important committees of the Convention—that of organization and that of resolutions. These gentlemen, by adroitness and parliamentary tact, succeeded in abrogating the former practice of casting the vote of the State as a unit, and in reducing it almost to a cipher. In this manner, whilst New York indorsed with her entire thirty-five votes the peculiar views of Mr. Douglas, notwithstanding there was in her delegation a majority of only five votes in their favor on the question of Territorial sovereignty,‡ the effective strength of Pennsylvania recognizing the judgment of the Supreme

---

* Page 112. 7th day, April 30. † Page 21. ‡ Mr. Bartlett, p. 249.

Court was reduced to three votes, this being the majority of fifteen on the one side over twelve on the other.

The question next in order before the Convention was upon the adoption of the second resolution of the minority of the committee, which had been substituted for the report of the majority. On this question Georgia, Louisiana, Alabama, Arkansas, Texas, Florida, and Mississippi refused to vote.* Indeed, it soon appeared that on the question of the final adoption of this second vague and general resolution, which in fact amounted to nothing, it had scarcely any friends of either party in the Convention. The Douglas party, abandoning their own offspring, and preferring to it the Cincinnati platform, pure and simple, without explanation or addition, voted against it.† On the other hand, the old Democracy could not vote for it without admitting that the Supreme Court had not already placed the right over slave property in the Territories on the same footing with all other property, and therefore they also voted against it. In consequence the resolution was negatived by a vote of only twenty-one in its favor to two hundred and thirty-eight. ‡ Had the seven Southern States just mentioned voted, the negatives would have amounted to two hundred and eighty-two, or more than thirteen to one. Thus both the majority and the minority resolutions on the Territorial question were rejected, and nothing remained before the Convention except the Cincinnati platform.

At this stage of the proceedings § (April 30th), the States of Louisiana, Alabama, South Carolina, Mississippi, Florida, Texas, and Arkansas, having assigned their reasons for the act, withdrew in succession from the Convention.∥ After these seven States had retired, the delegation from Virginia made a noble effort to restore harmony.¶ Mr. Russell, their chairman, addressed the Convention in a solemn and impressive manner. He portrayed the alarming nature of the crisis. He expressed his fears that we were on the eve of a revolution, and if this Convention should prove a failure it would be the last National Convention of any party which would ever assemble in the

---

* Page 116. † Ibid. ‡ Ibid. § Pp. 118–125.
∥ Pp. 126, 127. ¶ 30th April, 7th day, p. 126.

United States. "Virginia," said he, "stands in the midst of her sister States, in garments red with the blood of her children slain in the first outbreak of the 'irrepressible conflict.' But, sir, not when her children fell at midnight beneath the weapon of the assassin, was her heart penetrated with so profound a grief as that which will wring it when she is obliged to choose between a separate destiny with the South, and her common destiny with the entire Republic."

Mr. Russell was not then prepared to answer, in behalf of his delegation, whether the events of the day [the defeat of the majority report, and the withdrawal of the seven States] were sufficient to justify her in taking the irrevocable step in question. In order, therefore, that they might have time to deliberate, and if they thought proper make an effort to restore harmony in the Convention, he expressed a desire that it might adjourn and afford them an opportunity for consultation.* The Convention accordingly adjourned until the next day, Tuesday, May 1st; and immediately after its reassembling the delegation from Georgia, making the eighth State, also withdrew.†

In the mean time the Virginia delegation had consulted among themselves, and had conferred with the delegations of the other Southern States which still remained in the Convention, as to the best mode of restoring harmony.‡ In consequence Mr. Howard, of Tennessee, stated to the Convention that "he had a proposition to present in behalf of the delegation from Tennessee, whenever, under parliamentary rules, it would be proper to present it." In this Tennessee was joined by Kentucky and Virginia, "the three great middle States which stand as a breakwater against fanaticism on one side and disunion on the other. He should propose the following resolution, whenever it would be in order: '*Resolved*, That the citizens of the United States have an equal right to settle with their property in the Territories of the United States; and that, under the decision of the Supreme Court of the United States, which we recognize as the correct exposition of the Constitution of the United States, neither the rights of person nor property

---

* Page 128, 8th day.   † Ibid.   ‡ Page 136.

can be destroyed or impaired by Congressional or Territorial legislation.'"*

"Mr. Russell, as chairman of the delegation from Virginia, rose to express the sentiments entertained by the delegation from that State, and the position they occupy this morning in this Convention. They came here for the double purpose of defending the rights of the South, which are involved in the great issues of the day, and of maintaining the integrity of the American Union. The events of yesterday had especially left him a delicate task to perform. Events had occurred which their constituency never contemplated when they were sent here. They desired that the Democratic party should remain complete, whatever might be done in this Convention. With these general views, the Virginia delegation had entered into consultation among themselves, and had conferred with their sister Southern States remaining in the Convention. They believed that the resolution just read by the gentleman from Tennessee [Mr. Howard] presented a reasonable basis of settlement among all parties, North and South, affirming, as it did, the doctrine of the decision of the Supreme Court, and going no further."

On a subsequent day (May 3d), Mr. Russell informed the Convention that this resolution had, " he believed, received the approbation of all the delegations from the Southern States which remained in the Convention, and also received the approbation of the delegation from New York. He was informed there was strengthe nough to pass it when in order." † Of this there could have been no doubt; with the vote of New York in its favor. Had it been adopted, what an auspicious event this would have been both for the Democratic party and the country!

Mr. Howard, however, in vain attempted to obtain a vote on his resolution. When he moved to take it up on the evening of the day it had been offered, he was met by cries of "Not in order," "Not in order." ‡ The manifest purpose was to postpone its consideration until the hour should arrive which had been fixed by a previous order of the Convention, in opposition to its first order on the same subject, for the balloting to commence

* Page 136. † Page 152. ‡ Page 138.

for a Presidential candidate, when it would be too late. This the friends of Mr. Douglas accomplished, and no vote was ever taken upon it either at Charleston or Baltimore.

Before the balloting commenced Mr. Howard succeeded, in the face of strong opposition, with the aid of the thirty-five votes from New York, in obtaining a vote of the Convention in affirmance of the two-thirds rule. On his motion they resolved, by 141 to 112 votes,* "that the President of the Convention be and he is hereby directed not to declare any person nominated for the office of President or Vice-President, unless he shall have received a number of votes equal to two-thirds of the votes of all the electoral colleges." It was well known at the time that this resolution rendered the regular nomination of Mr. Douglas impossible.

The balloting then commenced (Tuesday evening, May 1st), on the eighth day of the session.† Necessary to a nomination, under the two-thirds rule, 202 votes. On the first ballot Mr. Douglas received $145\frac{1}{2}$ votes; Mr. Hunter, of Virginia, 42; Mr. Guthrie, of Kentucky, $35\frac{1}{2}$; Mr. Johnson, of Tennessee, 12; Mr. Dickinson, of New York, 7; Mr. Lane, of Oregon, 6; Mr. Toucey, of Connecticut, $2\frac{1}{2}$; Mr. Davis, of Mississippi, $1\frac{1}{2}$, and Mr. Pearce, of Maryland, 1 vote.

The voting continued until 3d May, during which there were fifty-four additional ballotings. Mr. Douglas never rose to more than $152\frac{1}{2}$, and ended at $151\frac{1}{2}$ votes, 202 votes being necessary to a nomination. Of these votes, at least 110 were given by delegates from States which, judging from their antecedents, could not give him or any Democratic candidate a single electoral vote.

This statement proves the wisdom and foresight of those who adopted the two-thirds rule. Until 1824 nominations had been made by Congressional caucus. In these none participated except Senators from Democratic States, and Representatives from Democratic Congressional districts. The simple majority rule governed in these caucuses, because it was morally certain that, composed as they were, no candidate could be selected against the will of the Democratic States on whom his election de-

---

* Page 141. † Pages 141–152.

pended. But when a change was made to National Conventions, it was at once perceived that if a mere majority could nominate, then the delegates from Anti-Democratic States might be mainly instrumental in nominating a candidate for whom they could not give a single electoral vote. Whilst it would have been harsh and inexpedient to exclude these States from the Convention altogether, it would have been unjust to confer on them a controlling power over the nomination. To compromise this difficulty, the two-thirds rule was adopted. Under its operation it would be almost impossible that a candidate could be selected, without the votes of a simple majority of delegates from the Democratic States.

It had now become manifest that it was impossible to make a nomination at Charleston. The friends of Mr. Douglas adhered to him and would vote for him and him alone, whilst his opponents, apprehending the effect of his principles should he be elected President, were equally determined to vote against his nomination.

In the hope that some compromise might yet be effected to save the Democratic party, the Convention, on the motion of Mr. Russell, of Virginia, resolved to adjourn to meet at Baltimore on Monday, the 18th June;* and it was "respectfully recommended to the Democratic party of the several States, to make provision for supplying all vacancies in their respective delegations to this Convention when it shall assemble."

The Convention re-assembled at Baltimore on the 18th June, 1860,† according to its adjournment, and Mr. Cushing, the President, took the chair. It was greatly to be desired that the Southern delegates who had withdrawn at Charleston might resume their seats at Baltimore, and thus restore the Convention to its original integrity. In that event high hopes were still entertained that both parties might harmonize in selecting some eminent Democratic statesman, not obnoxious to either as a candidate, and thus save the Democracy of the Union from certain defeat. Every discerning citizen foresaw that without such a re-union the Democratic party would continue to be hopelessly divided, and the Republican candidates must inevitably be elected.

* Pages 152–154, 10th day, May 3d.   † Page 155.

Immediately after the reorganization of the Convention, Mr. Howard, of Tennessee, offered a resolution, " that the President of this Convention direct the sergeant-at-arms to issue tickets of admission to the delegates of the Convention, as originally constituted and organized at Charleston." Thus the vitally important question was distinctly presented. It soon, however, became manifest that no such resolution could prevail. In the absence of the delegates who had withdrawn at Charleston, the friends of Mr. Douglas constituted a controlling majority. At the threshold they resisted the admission of the original delegates, and contended that by withdrawing they had irrevocably resigned their seats. In support of this position, they relied upon the language of the resolution adjourning the Convention to Baltimore, which, as we have seen, " recommended to the Democratic party of the several States to make provision for supplying all vacancies in their respective delegations to this Convention, when it shall reassemble." On the other hand, the advocates of their readmission contended that a simple withdrawal of the delegates was not a final renunciation of their seats, but they were still entitled to reoccupy them, whenever, in their judgment, this course would be best calculated to restore the harmony and promote the success of the Democratic party; that the Convention had no right to interpose between them and the Democracy of their respective States; that being directly responsible to this Democracy, it alone could accept their resignation; that no such resignation had ever been made, and their authority therefore continued in full force, and this, too, with the approbation of their constituents.

In the mean time, after the adjournment from Charleston to Baltimore, the friends of Mr. Douglas, in several of these States, had proceeded to elect delegates to take the place of those who had withdrawn from the Convention, but not in any instance, it is believed, according to the rules and usages of the Democratic party. Indeed, it was manifest at the time, and has since been clearly proved by the event, that these delegates represented but a small minority of the party in their respective States. These new delegates, nevertheless, appeared and demanded seats.

After a long and ardent debate, the Convention adopted a resolution, offered by Mr. Church, of New York, and modified on motion of Mr. Gilmore, of Pennsylvania, as a substitute for that of Mr. Howard, to refer "the credentials of all persons claiming seats in this Convention, made vacant by the secession of delegates at Charleston, to the Committee on Credentials." They thus prejudged the question, by deciding that the seats of these delegates had been made and were still vacant. The Committee on Credentials had been originally composed of one delegate from each of the thirty-three States, but the number was now reduced to twenty-five, in consequence of the exclusion of eight of its members from the States of Georgia, Alabama, Mississippi, South Carolina, Texas, Louisiana, Arkansas, and Florida. The committee, therefore, now stood 16 to 9 in favor of the nomination of Mr. Douglas, instead of 17 to 16 against it, according to its original organization.*

The committee, through their chairman, Mr. Krum, of Missouri, made their report on the 21st June, and Governor Stevens, of Oregon, at the same time presented a minority report, signed by himself and eight other members.

It is unnecessary to give in detail these conflicting reports. It is sufficient to state that whilst the report of the majority maintained that the delegates, by withdrawing at Charleston, had resigned their seats, and these were still vacant; that of the minority, on the contrary, asserted the right of these delegates to resume their seats in the Convention, by virtue of their original appointment.

In some respects the majority report presented a strange aspect. Whilst it recommended the admission of all the new delegates from the States of Alabama and Louisiana, to the exclusion of the old, it divided Georgia equally between the conflicting parties, allowing one half to each, thus rendering the vote of the State a mere nullity. This anomaly was, however, afterwards corrected by a vote of the Convention. Indeed, the new delegates voluntarily withdrew their claim to seats.

On the next day (June 22),† the important decision was made between the conflicting reports. Mr. Stevens moved to

---

* Pages 187-191. † Page 203.

substitute the minority report for that of the majority, and his motion was rejected by a vote of 100½ to 150. Of course no vote was given from any of the excluded States, except one half vote from each of the parties in Arkansas.

The resolutions of the majority, except the ninth, relating to the Georgia delegation, were then adopted in succession. Among other motions of similar character, a motion had been made by a delegate in the majority to reconsider the vote by which the Convention had adopted the minority report, as a substitute for that of the majority, and to lay his own motion on the table. This is a common mode resorted to, according to parliamentary tactics, of defeating every hope of a reconsideration of the pending question, and rendering the first decision final.*

Mr. Cessna, always on the alert, with this view called for a vote on laying the motion to reconsider on the table. Should this be negatived, then the question of reconsideration would be open. The President stated the question to be first " on laying on the table the motion to reconsider the vote by which the Convention refused to amend the majority report of the Committee on Credentials by substituting the report of the minority." On this question New York, for the first time since the meeting at Baltimore, voted with the minority and changed it into a majority. "When New York was called," says the report of the proceedings, " and responded thirty-five votes " (in the negative), " the response was greeted with loud cheers and applause."† The result of the vote was 113½ to 138½—" so the Convention refused to lay on the table the motion to reconsider the minority report." The Convention then adjourned until the evening, on motion of Mr. Cochrane, of New York, amidst great excitement and confusion.

This vote of New York, appearing to indicate a purpose to harmonize the party by admitting the original delegates from the eight absent States, was not altogether unexpected. Although voting as a unit, it was known that her delegation were greatly divided among themselves. The exact strength of the minority was afterwards stated by Mr. Bartlett, one of its members, in

* Page 209. † Page 210.

the Breckinridge Convention.* He said: "Upon all questions and especially upon the adoption of the majority report on credentials, in which we had a long contest, the line was strictly drawn, and there were thirty on one side and forty on the other." This was equal to fifteen votes to twenty.

The position of New York casting an undivided vote of thirty-five, with Dean Richmond at their head, had been a controlling power from the commencement. Her responsibility was great in proportion. Had she cast her weight into the scale at Charleston in favor of the majority report on the resolutions and in accordance with the decision of the Supreme Court, this, as we have already seen, would have prevailed by a vote of 173 to 130. Such a result might probably have terminated the controversy between the North and the South.

After the retirement of the Southern delegations at Charleston, the delegation from New York had appeared to be willing to change their course and adopt the compromise platform proposed by Virginia, Tennessee, and Kentucky, with the approbation of the other border States still in the Convention. This was in fact nothing more than an affirmance of the decision of the Supreme Court. In advocating it, Mr. Russell, of Virginia, whose ability and spirit of conciliation had been displayed throughout, stated his belief, as we have seen, that it had "received the approbation of the delegation from New York;" and this statement was not contradicted. This would have secured its adoption. The means by which a vote upon the question was defeated at Charleston by the commencement of the balloting have already been presented. Strong expectations were, therefore, now entertained that after the New York delegation had recorded their vote against a motion which would have killed the minority report beyond hope of revival, they would now follow this up by taking the next step in advance and voting for its reconsideration and adoption.† On the evening of the very same day, however, they reversed their course and voted against its reconsideration. They were then cheered by the opposite party from that which had cheered them in the morning. Thus the action of the Convention in favor of the majority report became final and conclusive.‡

* Page 249.   † Page 211.   ‡ Page 211.

Mr. Cessna, of Pennsylvania, always eager, at once moved "that the Convention do now proceed to nominate candidates for President and Vice-President of the United States." These proceedings immediately produced the disastrous effects which must have been foreseen by all.*

Mr. Russell rose and stated, "It has become my duty now, by direction of a large majority of the delegation from Virginia, respectfully to inform you and this body, that it is not consistent with their convictions of duty to participate longer in its deliberations."†

Mr. Leader next stated "that it became his duty, as one of the delegates from North Carolina, to say that a very large majority of the delegation from that State were compelled to retire permanently from this Convention, on account, as he conceived, of the unjust course that had been pursued toward some of their fellow-citizens of the South. The South had heretofore relied upon the Northern Democracy to give them the rights which were justly due them; but the vote to-day had satisfied the majority of the North Carolina delegation that these rights were now refused them, and this being the case, they could no longer remain in the Convention."

Then followed in succession the withdrawal of the delegations from Tennessee,‡ Kentucky,§ Maryland,‖ California,¶ Oregon,** and Arkansas.†† The Convention now adjourned at half-past ten o'clock until the next morning at ten.

Soon after the assembling of the Convention ‡‡ the President, Mr. Cushing, whilst tendering his thanks to its members for their candid and honorable support in the performance of his duties, stated that notwithstanding the retirement of the delegations of several of the States at Charleston, in his solicitude to maintain the harmony and union of the Democratic party, he had continued in his post of labor. "To that end and in that sense," said he, "I had the honor to meet you, gentlemen, here at Baltimore. But circumstances have since transpired which compel me to pause. The delegations of a majority of the States have, either in whole or in part, in one form or another, ceased to par-

---

* Page 212. † Page 213. ‡ Page 213. § Page 213. ‖ Page 214.
¶ Pages 215–217. ** Page 217. †† Page 225. ‡‡ Sixth day, June 23d, page 225.

ticipate in the deliberations of the Convention. * * * In the present circumstances, I deem it a duty of self-respect, and I deem it still more a duty to this Convention, as at present organized, * * * to resign my seat as President of this Convention, in order to take my place on the floor as a member of the delegation from Massachusetts. * * * I deem this above all a duty which I owe to the members of this Convention, as to whom no longer would my action represent the will of a majority of the Convention."*

"Governor Tod, of Ohio, one of the Vice-Presidents, then took the vacant chair, and was greeted with hearty and long-continued cheers and applause from members of the Convention."

"Mr. Butler, of Massachusetts, now announced that a portion of the Massachusetts delegation desired to retire, but was interrupted by cries of 'No,' 'No,' 'Call the roll.' The indefatigable Mr. Cessna called for the original question, to wit, that the Convention now proceed to a nomination for President and Vice-President."

"The President here ordered the Secretary to call the States. Maine, New Hampshire, and Vermont were called, and they gave an unbroken vote for Stephen A. Douglas. When Massachusetts was called, Mr. Butler rose and said he had a respectful paper in his hand which he would desire the President to have read. A scene of great confusion thereupon ensued, cries of 'I object' being heard upon all sides." Mr. Butler, not to be baffled, contended for his right at this stage to make remarks pertinent to the matter, and cited in his support the practice of the Conventions at Baltimore in 1848 and 1852, and at Cincinnati in 1856. He finally prevailed, and was permitted to proceed. He then said he "would now withdraw from the Convention, upon the ground that there had been a withdrawal, in whole or in part, of a majority of the States; and further, which was a matter more personal to himself, he could not sit in a Convention where the African slave trade, which was piracy according to the laws of his country, was openly advocated."

Mr. Butler then retired, followed by General Cushing and four others of the Massachusetts delegation.

* Page 226.

The balloting now proceeded. Mr. Douglas received 173½ votes; Mr. Guthrie 9; Mr. Breckinridge 6½; Mr. Bocock and Mr. Seymour each 1; and Mr. Dickinson and Mr. Wise each half a vote. On the next and last ballot Mr. Douglas received 181½ votes, eight of those in the minority having changed their votes in his favor.

To account for this number, it is proper to state that a few delegates from five of the eight States which had withdrawn still remained in the Convention. On the last ballot Mr. Douglas received all of their votes, to wit: 3 of the 15 votes of Virginia, 1 of the 10 votes of North Carolina, 1½ of the 3 votes of Arkansas, 3 of the 12 votes of Tennessee, 3 of the 12 votes of Kentucky, and 2½ of the 8 votes of Maryland, making in the aggregate 14 votes. To this number may be added the 9 votes of the new delegates from Alabama and the 6 from Louisiana, who had been admitted to the exclusion of the original delegates. If these 29 votes from Southern States be deducted from the 181½ votes nominating Mr. Douglas, that number would be reduced to 152½.

These proceedings had now rendered it clear that Mr. Douglas could not, as he did not, receive one electoral vote from any of the sixteen Democratic States of Delaware, Maryland, Virginia, North Carolina, South Carolina, Georgia, Alabama, Louisiana, Mississippi, Texas, Florida, Tennessee, Kentucky, Arkansas, California, and Oregon. He owed his nomination almost exclusively to States which could not give him a single electoral vote. What was still more ominous of evil, the division was sectional between the free and the slaveholding States, between the North and the South. It might have been supposed that these disastrous circumstances, foreboding such dangers both to the Democratic party and the Union, would have caused his friends to pause, and at the last moment consent to some means of conciliation. But they rushed on to complete their work, regardless of consequences. The two-thirds rule interposed no obstacle in their course, although it had been expressly adopted and readopted by this Convention, and the very case had now occurred—the nomination by nearly all the Anti-Democratic States—against which its original authors, with wise foresight, intended to guard. Mr. Douglas was accordingly declared to be the regular nominee of the Democratic party of the Union,* upon the motion of Mr. Church, of New York, when, according to the report of the proceedings, " The whole body rose to its feet, hats were waved in the air, and many tossed aloft; shouts, screams, and yells, and every boisterous mode of expressing approbation and unanimity, were resorted to."

Senator Fitzpatrick, of Alabama, was then unanimously nominated as the candidate for Vice-President; and the Convention adjourned *sine die* on the 23d June, the sixth and last day of its session.† On the same day, but after the adjournment, Mr. Fitzpatrick declined the nomination, and it was immediately conferred on Mr. Herschel V. Johnson, of Georgia, by the Executive Committee. Thus ended the Douglas Convention.

But another Convention assembled at Baltimore on the same 23d June,‡ styling itself also, and with as little reason, the "National Democratic Convention." It was composed chiefly of the delegates who had just withdrawn from the Douglas Convention, and the original delegates from Alabama and Louisiana. One of their first acts was to abrogate the two-thirds rule, as had been done by the Douglas Convention. Both acted under the same necessity, because the preservation of this rule would have prevented a nomination by either. This consideration, instead of causing both to desist and appeal to the people of the States to appoint a new Convention for the salvation of the Democratic party, was totally disregarded.

Mr. Cushing was elected and took the chair as President. In his opening address he said: "Gentlemen of the Convention, we assemble here, delegates to the National Democratic Convention [applause], duly accredited thereto from more than twenty States of the Union [applause], for the purpose of nominating candidates of the Democratic party for the offices of President and Vice-President of the United States, for the purpose of announcing the principles of the party, and for the purpose of continuing and reëstablishing that party upon the firm foundations of the Constitution, the Union, and the coequal rights of the several States." §

* Pages 231-236.   † Page 239.   ‡ Page 241.   § Page 243.

Mr. Avery, of North Carolina, who had reported the majority resolutions at Charleston, now reported the same from the committee of this body, and they "were adopted unanimously, amid great applause."

The Convention then proceeded to select their candidates. Mr. Loring, on behalf of the delegates from Massachusetts, who with Mr. Butler had retired from the Douglas Convention, nominated John C. Breckinridge, of Kentucky, which Mr. Dent, representing the Pennsylvania delegation present, "most heartily seconded." Mr. Ward, from the Alabama delegation, nominated R. M. T. Hunter, of Virginia; Mr. Ewing, from that of Tennessee, nominated Mr. Dickinson, of New York; and Mr. Stevens, from Oregon, nominated General Joseph Lane. Eventually all these names were withdrawn except that of Mr. Breckinridge, and he received the nomination by a unanimous vote. The whole number of votes cast in his favor from twenty States was 103½. The vote of Mr. Douglas was considerably greater, but Mr. Breckinridge received a large majority over him from States known to be Democratic.

General Lane was unanimously nominated as the candidate for Vice-President. Thus terminated the Breckinridge Convention.

The 23d of June, 1860, was a dark and gloomy day both for the Democratic party and the Union. It foreboded nothing but evil. There could be no pretence that either candidate had been nominated according to the established rules of the party. Every individual Democrat was, therefore, left at liberty to choose between them. In many localities, especially North, their respective partisans became more violent against each other than against the common foe. No reasonable hope could remain for the election of Mr. Douglas or Mr. Breckinridge. It was morally certain that Mr. Lincoln would be the next President, and this added greatly to his strength. The result was, that of the 303 electoral votes, Mr. Douglas received but 12[*] (3 from New Jersey, and 9 from Missouri), and Mr. Breckinridge only 72 (3 from Delaware, 8 from Maryland, 10 from North Carolina, 8 from South Carolina, 10 from Georgia, 6

[*] Congressional Globe, 1860–'61, page 894.

from Louisiana, 7 from Mississippi, 9 from Alabama, 4 from Arkansas, 3 from Florida, and 4 from Texas). Virginia, North Carolina, and Tennessee cast their 39 votes for John Bell, of Tennessee, of the self-styled Constitutional Union party.

In reviewing the whole, it is clear that the original cause of the disaster was the persistent refusal of the friends of Mr. Douglas to recognize the constitutional rights of the slaveholding States in the Territories, established by the Supreme Court. These rights the Southern States could not yield after the decision, without a sense of self-degradation, and voluntary abandonment of their equality with their sister States, as members of the Union. But were they justified, for this cause, in seceding from the Convention, and pursuing a course so extreme? Far from it. Had they remained at the post of duty, like Virginia and the other border States, it would have been impossible that a candidate so obnoxious to them, on account of his principles, could have been nominated. The final result would probably then have been the nomination of some compromise candidate, which would have preserved the unity and strength of the Democratic organization. Indeed, the withdrawal of these States, under the circumstances, has afforded plausible ground for the belief of many, that this was done with a view to prepare the way for a dissolution of the Union. Although, from the votes and speeches of their delegates, there do not seem to be sufficient grounds for so harsh a judgment, yet it cannot be denied that the act was rash, unwise, and unfortunate.

An entire new generation had now come upon the stage in the South, in the midst of the anti-slavery agitation. The former generation, which had enjoyed the blessings of peace and security under the Constitution and the Union, had passed away. That now existing had grown up and been educated amid assaults upon their rights, and attacks from the North upon the domestic institution inherited from their fathers. Their post-offices had been perverted for the circulation of incendiary pictures and publications intended to excite the slaves to servile insurrection. In the North, the press, State Legislatures, anti-slavery societies, abolition lecturers, and above all the Christian pulpit, had been persistently employed in denouncing slavery as a sin, and rendering slaveholders odious. Numerous abolition petitions had been presented to Congress, from session to session, portraying slavery as a grievous sin against God and man. The Fugitive Slave Law enacted by the first Congress, as well as that of 1850, for the security of their property, had been nullified by the Personal Liberty Acts of Northern Legislatures, and by the organized assistance afforded by abolitionists for the escape of their slaves. Wilmot provisos had been interposed to defeat their constitutional rights in the common Territories, and even after these rights had been affirmed by the Supreme Court, its decision had been set at naught not only by the Republican but by the Douglas party. "The irrepressible conflict" of Senator Seward, and the Helper book, both portending the abolition of slavery in the States, had been circulated broadcast among the people. And finally the desperate fanatic, John Brown, inflamed by these teachings, had invaded Virginia, and murdered a number of her peaceful citizens, for the avowed purpose of exciting a servile insurrection; and although he had expiated his crimes on the gallows, his memory was consecrated by the abolitionists, as though he had been a saintly martyr.

In the midst of these perils the South had looked with hope to the action of the Democratic National Convention at Charleston, but in this they had been sadly disappointed. This series of events had inflamed the Southern mind with intense hostility against the North, and enabled the disunion agitators to prepare it for the final catastrophe.

It was not until after the breaking up of the Democratic party at Charleston and Baltimore, that the masses, even in the cotton States, always excepting South Carolina, could be induced to think seriously of seceding from the Union. The border States, with Virginia in the front rank, although much dissatisfied with the course of events at the North, still remained true to the Federal Government.

CHAPTER IV.

The heresy of Secession—Originated in New England—Maintained by Josiah Quincy and the Hartford Convention, by Mr. Rawle and Mr. John Quincy Adams, but opposed by the South—Southern Secession dates from South Carolina Nullification—Its character and history—The Compromise Tariff of 1833—The Nullifiers agitate for Secession—Mr. Calhoun—Mr. Cobb against it—Warnings of the Democratic party—They are treated with contempt—Secession encouraged by the Republicans—The Cotton States led to believe they would be allowed to depart in peace—President Buchanan warned them against this delusion.

THE alleged right of secession, or the right of one or more States to withdraw from the Union, is not a plant of Southern origin. On the contrary, it first sprung up in the North. At an early period after the formation of the Constitution, many influential individuals of New England became dissatisfied with the union between the Northern and Southern States, and were anxious to dissolve it. "This design," according to Mr. John Quincy Adams, "had been formed in the winter of 1803–'4, immediately after and as a consequence of the acquisition of Louisiana."* This he disclosed to Mr. Jefferson, in the year 1809. About the same time, to the confidential friends of Mr. Jefferson he "urged that a continuance of the embargo much longer would certainly be met by forcible resistance, supported by the Legislature and probably by the judiciary of the State [Massachusetts]. That to quell that resistance, if force should be resorted to by the Government, it would produce a civil war; and that, in that event, he had no doubt the leaders of the party would secure the coöperation with them of Great Britain. That their object was, and had been for several years, a dissolution of

* Letter of Dec. 30, 1828, in reply to Harrison Grey Otis and others. Appendix to Randall's Life of Jefferson, vol. iii., p. 635. Vide also vol. iii., p. 295.

the Union, and the establishment of a separate Confederation, he knew from unequivocal evidence, although not provable in a court of law ; and that in case of a civil war, the aid of Great Britain to effect that purpose would be assuredly resorted to, as it would be indispensably necessary to the design."

Afterwards, in 1828, whilst President of the United States, he reaffirmed the statement made to Mr. Jefferson, and said : " That project, I repeat, had gone to the length of fixing upon a military leader for its execution ; and although the circumstances of the times never admitted of its execution, nor even of its full development, I had yet no doubt in 1808 and 1809, and have no doubt at this time, that it is the key of all the great movements of these leaders of the Federal party in New England, from that time forward till its final catastrophe in the Hartford Convention." It is but fair to observe that these statements were denied by the parties implicated, but were still adhered to and again reaffirmed by Mr. Adams.

In this connection we may cite the speech delivered by Mr. Josiah Quincy, a leading and influential Representative from Massachusetts, on the 14th January, 1811.* In this he boldly avows and defends both the right and the duty of States to separate from the Union, should Congress pass the bill then pending before them, " to enable the people of the Territory of Orleans to form a Constitution and State Government, and for the admission of such State [Louisiana] into the Union on an equal footing with the original States."

He alleges "that the principle of this bill materially affects the liberties and rights of the whole people of the United States. To me it appears that it would justify a revolution in this country, and that in no great length of time may produce it." He then proceeds to declare as follows : " If this bill passes, it is my deliberate opinion that it is virtually a dissolution of the Union ; that it will free the States from their moral obligation, and, as it will be the right of all, so it will be the duty of some, definitely to prepare for a separation, amicably if they can, violently if they must." Upon being called to order for the utter-

---

* Gales & Seaton's Annals of Congress, 1810-'11, 3d session, p. 524.

ance of this sentiment, he repeated it and committed it to writing with his own hand.

The violation of the Constitution involved in this bill was, according to Mr. Quincy, the admission into the Union of a State composed of foreign territory, which had been outside of the limits of the United States when the Constitution was adopted. This, he contended, would result in a serious diminution of the power and influence in the Federal Government, to which Massachusetts and the other old States were justly entitled.

It is curious to observe that he justified a dissolution of the Union by the very same fallacy afterwards employed by the Southern secessionists, in applying to our Government a rule of construction applicable to mere private contracts. "Is there," said he, "a moral principle of public law better settled, or more conformable to the plainest suggestions of reason, than that the violation of a contract by one of the parties may be considered as exempting the other from its obligations?"*

Thirty-five members united with Mr. Quincy in voting against this bill, but it passed the House by a vote of 77 to 36.

We shall not refer specially to the proceedings of the Hartford Convention, which assembled in December, 1814, during the existence of our last war with Great Britain. We may observe generally, that this body manifested their purpose to dissolve the Union, should Congress refuse to redress the grievances of which they complained. The peace, however, with Great Britain, terminated their action, and consigned them to lasting and well merited reproach. During this entire period the Southern people opposed and denounced all threats and efforts to dissolve the Union as treasonable, and during the war as giving "aid and comfort" to the enemy.

The right of secession found advocates afterwards in men of distinguished abilities and unquestioned patriotism. In 1825 it was maintained by Mr. William Rawle, of Philadelphia, an eminent and universally respected lawyer, in the 23d chapter of his "View of the Constitution of the United States." In speaking of him his biographer says, that "in 1791 he was appointed District Attorney of the United States, by the Father

* Gales & Seaton's Annals of Congress, 1810–'11, 3d session, p. 577.

of his country;" and "the situation of Attorney General was more than once tendered to him by Washington, but as often declined," for domestic reasons.* But to quote a still higher authority, that of Mr. John Quincy Adams. This learned and profound statesman, in 1839, admitted the right of the people of a State to secede from the Union, whilst deprecating its exercise. We copy entire the three paragraphs relating to this subject from his "Discourse delivered before the New York Historical Society,"† on the fiftieth anniversary of General Washington's Inauguration as President of the United States:

"In the calm hours of self-possession, the right of a *State* to nullify an act of Congress, is too absurd for argument, and too odious for discussion. The right of a State to secede from the Union, is equally disowned by the principles of the Declaration of Independence. Nations acknowledge no judge between them upon earth, and their Governments, from necessity, must in their intercourse with each other decide when the failure of one party to a contract to perform its obligations, absolves the other from the reciprocal fulfilment of his own. But this last of earthly powers is not necessary to the freedom or independence of States, connected together by the immediate action of the people of whom they consist. To the people alone is there reserved, as well the dissolving, as the constituent power, and that power can be exercised by them only under the tie of conscience, binding them to the retributive justice of Heaven.

"With these qualifications, we may admit the same right as vested in the *people* of every State in the Union, with reference to the General Government, which was exercised by the people of the United Colonies, with reference to the supreme head of the British empire, of which they formed a part; and under these limitations have the people of each State in the Union a right to secede from the confederated Union itself.

"Thus stands the RIGHT. But the indissoluble link of union between the people of the several States of this confederated nation is, after all, not in the *right*, but in the *heart*. If the day should ever come (may Heaven avert it) when the affections of the people of these States shall be alienated from each other;

---

* Brown's Forum, p. 505.   † Pages 68, 69.

when the fraternal spirit shall give way to cold indifference, or collision of interest shall fester into hatred, the bands of political association will not long hold together parties no longer attracted by the magnetism of conciliated interests and kindly sympathies; and far better will it be for the people of the disunited States to part in friendship from each other, than to be held together by constraint. Then will be the time for reverting to the precedents which occurred at the formation and adoption of the Constitution, to form again a more perfect union, by dissolving that which could no longer bind, and to leave the separated parts to be reunited by the law of political gravitation to the centre."

These high authorities in the North made no impression on the Southern people. Southern secession was the bitter fruit of South Carolina nullification.

Nullification did not spring from the slavery question. It originated exclusively from hostility to a protective tariff. In the belief of the people of South Carolina, the tariff laws afforded extravagant and unconstitutional protection to domestic manufactures, greatly to their injury. They were convinced that the high import duties exacted from them enhanced unjustly the price of the articles they consumed, and at the same time depreciated the value of the cotton and other articles which they produced and exported; and that all their losses were so many forced contributions to enrich Northern manufacturers at their expense.

In this belief the people of the State were nearly unanimous; but they were almost equally divided as to whether nullification was an appropriate and constitutional remedy. Nullification assumes that each State has the rightful power to absolve itself from obedience to any particular law of Congress which it may deem oppressive, and to resist its execution by force; and yet in regard to all other laws to remain a constituent member of the Union. Thus in each State, though still under the same General Government, a different code might be in force, varying with every degree of latitude. This would produce " confusion worse confounded." Even secession can be sustained by much more plausible arguments than such a paradox.

Mr. John C. Calhoun was the acknowledged leader of the

Nullification party. As a member of the House of Representatives he had borne a conspicuous part in the declaration and prosecution of the war of 1812 against Great Britain. He had been Secretary of War during nearly the whole eight years of Mr. Monroe's Presidency, and had displayed great administrative ability in organizing and conducting his Department. He was elected in 1824, and afterwards reëlected in 1828, Vice-President of the United States, and still held this high office. He possessed eminent reasoning powers, but, in the opinion of many, was deficient in sound practical judgment. He was terse and astute in argument; but his views were not sufficiently broad and expanded to embrace at the same time all the great interests of the country, and to measure them according to their relative importance. It was his nature to concentrate all his powers on a single subject; and this, for the time being, almost to the exclusion of all others. Although not eloquent in debate, he was rapid, earnest, and persuasive. His powers of conversation were of the highest order; and it was his delight to exert them in making proselytes, especially of the young and promising. It is but just to add that his private life was a model of purity.

Under his auspices, the State Convention of South Carolina, in November, 1832, passed the well-known Nullification Ordinance. By this they declared that all the tariff acts then in force had been passed in violation of the Constitution of the United States; and that they were "null, void, and no law, nor binding upon this State, its officers or citizens." They also ordained that should the Federal Government attempt to carry these acts into effect within the limits of South Carolina, "the people of this State will thenceforth hold themselves absolved from all further obligation to maintain or preserve their political connection with the people of the other States, and will forthwith proceed to organize a separate Government, and to do all other acts and things which sovereign and independent States of right do." *

This declaration was the germ of Southern secession. It asserted the right and the duty of South Carolina to secede from the Union and establish an independent Government,

* Con. Debates, vol. ix., Part 2d, Appendix, pp. 162, 163.

whenever the Federal Government should attempt to execute the tariff laws within its limits.

At this period a large and influential minority, almost amounting to a majority of the people of South Carolina, were opposed to nullification. This party embraced the Federal judges, and the collectors and other revenue officers at the different ports. They did not believe nullification to be either a rightful or constitutional remedy for grievances, which notwithstanding they felt keenly in common with their fellow-citizens. So hostile did the parties become toward each other in the progress of the conflict, that there was imminent danger they might resort to civil war. The minority stood ready to aid the Government in enforcing the tariff laws against the nullifiers.

The Convention, in their address to the people of the United States,* proposed terms of compromise, with which should Congress comply, South Carolina would repeal the nullifying ordinance. Professing their willingness "to make a large offering to preserve the Union,"† and distinctly declaring that it was a concession on their part, they proposed to consent to a tariff imposing the same rate of duty on the protected as on the unprotected articles, "provided that no more revenue be raised than is necessary to meet the demands of the Government for constitutional purposes, and provided, also, that a duty substantially uniform be imposed upon all foreign imports." Thus their ultimatum was a uniform ad valorem horizontal tariff for revenue alone, without any discriminations whatever in favor of domestic manufactures.

At this crisis Mr. Calhoun resigned the office of Vice-President, and on the 12th December, 1832, took his seat in the Senate as one of the Senators from South Carolina, for the purpose of advocating the measures he had advised. Strange to say, South Carolina substantially succeeded in accomplishing her object by the passage of the "Compromise Act" of 2d March, 1833.‡ Under it, Congress provided for a gradual reduction of existing duties on all foreign articles competing in the home market with our domestic manufactures, until they should finally

---

* Con. Debates, vol. ix., Part 2d, Appendix, p. 168.
† Page 172.   ‡ U. S. Statutes at Large, p. 629.

sink, on the 30th June, 1842, to a uniform rate of 20 per cent. ad valorem, from and after which period this reduced duty only should be collected. Mr. Calhoun supported the bill and voted for its passage. South Carolina accepted the concession, and repealed the ordinance of nullification.

Mr. Calhoun, notwithstanding this success, was never able to indoctrinate the Southern people outside of his own State with the heresy of nullification. It soon became odious to the whole country, and has since passed into universal disrepute. But not so with its twin sister secession.

Whilst these proceedings were pending, General Jackson was ready and willing to enforce the laws against South Carolina, should they be resisted, with all the means in his power. These were, however, inadequate for the occasion. New legislation was required to enable him to act with vigor and success. For this he applied to Congress in an elaborate message of the 16th January, 1833.* This was not granted until the passage of the "Compromise Act" had rendered such legislation unnecessary. In fact, this act and "the Force Bill," as it was then called, conferring on him the necessary powers, were approved by General Jackson on the same day (2d March, 1833). Such was, at this crisis, the jealousy of executive power in Congress, that the only effective enactments of this bill were to expire, by their own limitation, at the end of the next session of Congress (June, 1834). Here it may be proper to observe, that Congress refused to revive them throughout the entire session of 1860–'61, and to confer upon President Buchanan the same powers for the collection of the revenue which they had, but only for this brief period, conferred on President Jackson.

The majority in South Carolina, encouraged by success in bringing Congress to terms on the tariff question, and smarting under the reproach of nullification, soon threw aside all reserve and rushed from this heresy into that of secession. In this they were not long after joined by the minority which had resisted nullification. The formidable aspect assumed by anti-slavery at the North consolidated the union between the nullifiers and the anti-nullifiers. Then followed the exchange of violent and vir-

* Congressional Debates, vol. ix., part 2d, Appendix, p. 145.

ulent denunciations between the slavery and anti-slavery factions, North and South, each furnishing combustibles to the other, as though they had been in alliance to destroy the Union. Although the people of South Carolina had thus become almost unanimous in their hostility to the Union, they were nevertheless divided into two parties, denominated "Disunionists" and "Coöperationists." Both were equally resolved on secession; they differed merely as to the point of time for making the movement. Whilst the former advocated immediate action by the State alone, the latter were in favor of awaiting the coöperation of one or more of the other slaveholding States.

The time-honored and Union-loving Whig and Democratic parties no longer existed in South Carolina. They had passed away amid the din of disunion. Mr. Calhoun, from the termination of nullification until the day of his death (31st March, 1850), made the wrongs and dangers of the South his almost constant theme. These he much exaggerated. In his last great speech to the Senate,* on the 4th March, 1850, a few days before his death, which, from physical weakness, was read by Mr. Mason, the Senator from Virginia, he painted these wrongs in glowing colors, and predicted that if they were not speedily redressed disunion must inevitably follow. He asked the North "to do justice, by conceding to the South an equal right in the acquired [Mexican] territory, and to do her duty by causing the stipulations in regard to fugitive slaves to be faithfully fulfilled; to cease the agitation of the slave question," and to provide for such an amendment to the Constitution as would restore to the South the means of self-protection. It is worthy of remark, that, extreme as he was, he never, on any occasion, asked for a repeal of the Missouri Compromise.

Although the earnest and impassioned appeals of Mr. Calhoun made a deep impression on the people of the Southern States, yet outside of South Carolina these failed to convince the masses that they ought to resort to extreme measures. Whilst satisfied they were suffering grievous wrongs from the Abolitionists, they were yet willing to abide by the compromise measures of 1850, and to seek redress by constitutional efforts

* Con. Globe, 1849-'50, p. 451.

within the Union. Such, it is our confident belief, continued to be the genuine sentiments of a very large majority of their people even in the cotton States for a number of years after the death of Mr. Calhoun. Still complaining, yet still hoping, they could not be persuaded to adopt rash measures, by all the zeal and eloquence of pro-slavery demagogues with which they were infested.

The friends of the Union calculated much upon the persistent opposition to South Carolina doctrines so long maintained by Georgia. Indeed Mr. Cobb, in his canvass for Governor, had made an able and powerful argument before the people of that State against the right of secession; and this was a principal reason for his selection for a seat in the Cabinet of Mr. Buchanan. Without the coöperation of this great and influential State a successful movement toward disunion would have been impracticable.

It was not until after the breaking up of the Charleston and Baltimore Conventions, as we have before observed, that the people of the cotton States, having lost all hopes of security and redress within the Union, began seriously to determine to go out of it. By this time they had become thoroughly indoctrinated with a belief in the right of secession; and they began to think earnestly of putting it into practice.

Throughout the Presidential canvass, the cotton States openly declared their purpose to secede should Mr. Lincoln be elected. In this they were now unfortunately in earnest. In ominous contrast with their former blustering, they now assumed a quiet and determined tone. No sound judging man, unless blinded by prejudice, could doubt their fixed resolution, unless the Republican party should concede their equal rights within the Territories; should cease to assail slavery in the States; should repeal the personal liberty laws of Northern Legislatures, and should fairly carry into execution the Fugitive Slave Laws. Besides, they felt confident of their power. Their territory was larger and contained a greater population than that of the thirteen original States which had established their independence against the forces of the British Empire. They, also, hoped to bring the border slaveholding States, which still remained true to the Union, into their alliance. They knew that if invaded, the Northern armies, in order to reach them, must march through these States, which they hoped would deny a right of passage to the invaders.

The Democratic party, justly appreciating the danger, everywhere throughout the canvass warned their countrymen of its approach. The Republican party, on the other hand, treated these warnings as mere electioneering expedients, and in derision ridiculed the Democrats as "Union savers." They confidently predicted that the threats of the cotton States would end in smoke, as they had ended heretofore; that they would not dare to secede; but even if they should, they could within a brief period be reduced to obedience by the overwhelming physical power of the North.

With strange inconsistency, however, immediately after Mr. Lincoln's election much was said and written by Republicans in the North calculated to delude the cotton States into the belief that they might leave the Union without serious opposition. The New York "Tribune," deservedly their leading and most influential journal, giving tone to its party everywhere, contributed much to encourage this delusion. It was doubtless actuated by hostility to a continued union with slaveholding States. Acting in the spirit of the quotation already made from the oration of John Quincy Adams before the New York Historical Society, it on the 9th of November, but three days after Mr. Lincoln's election, announced such sentiments as the following: "If the cotton States shall become satisfied that they can do better out of the Union than in it, we insist on letting them go in peace. *The right to secede may be a revolutionary one*, BUT IT EXISTS NEVERTHELESS. * * * We must ever resist the right of any State to remain in the Union and nullify or defy the laws thereof. To WITHDRAW FROM THE UNION IS QUITE ANOTHER MATTER; and whenever a considerable section of our Union shall deliberately resolve to go out, WE SHALL RESIST ALL COERCIVE MEASURES DESIGNED TO KEEP IT IN. We hope never to live in a Republic whereof one section is pinned to another by bayonets."

And again on the 17th December, three days before the

secession of South Carolina: "If it [the Declaration of Independence] justifies the secession from the British Empire of three millions of colonists in 1776, *we do not see why it would not justify the secession of five millions of Southrons from the Federal Union in* 1861. If we are mistaken on this point, why does not some one attempt to show *wherein* and why? For our own part, while we deny the right of slaveholders to hold slaves against the will of the latter, *we cannot see how twenty millions of people can rightfully hold ten, or even five, in a detested Union with them by military force.* * · * * *If seven or eight contiguous States shall present themselves authentically at Washington,* saying, 'We hate the Federal Union; we have withdrawn from it; we give you the choice between acquiescing in our secession and arranging amicably all incidental questions on the one hand and attempting to subdue us on the other,' *we could not stand up for coercion, for subjugation, for we do not think it would be just.* We hold the right of self-government *even when invoked in behalf of those who deny it to others.* So much for the question of principle."

In this course the "Tribune" persisted from the date of Mr. Lincoln's election until after his inauguration, employing such remarks as the following: "Any attempt to compel them by force to remain would be contrary to the principles enunciated in the immortal Declaration of Independence, contrary to the fundamental ideas on which human liberty is based."

Even after the cotton States had formed their confederacy, and adopted a provisional Constitution at Montgomery, on the 23d February, 1861, it gave them encouragement to proceed in the following language: "*We have repeatedly said, and we once more insist,* that the great principle embodied by Jefferson in the Declaration of American Independence, that Governments derive their just powers from the consent of the governed, is sound and just; *and that if the Slave States, the Cotton States, or the Gulf States only, choose to form an independent nation,* THEY HAVE A CLEAR MORAL RIGHT TO DO SO. *Whenever it shall be clear that the great body of Southern people have become conclusively alienated from the Union, and anxious to escape from it,* WE WILL DO OUR BEST TO FORWARD THEIR VIEWS."

In a similar spirit, leading Republicans everywhere scornfully exclaimed, "Let them go;" "We can do better without them;" "Let the Union slide," and other language of the same import.

In addition to all these considerations, the persistent refusal of Congress, from the first until the last hour of the session of 1860–'61, to take a single step in preparing for armed resistance to the execution of the laws, served to confirm the cotton States in the opinion that they might "depart in peace."

The people of the cotton States, unfortunately for themselves, were also infatuated with the belief, until the very last moment, that in case they should secede they would be sustained by a large portion if not the whole Democratic party of the North. They vainly imagined that this party, which had maintained their constitutional rights whilst they remained in the Union, would sustain them in rebellion after they had gone out of it. In this delusion they were also greatly encouraged by sympathy and support from influential and widely circulated Anti-Republican journals in the North, and especially in the city of New York.

It was in vain, therefore, that the late President warned them, as he often did, against this delusion. It was in vain he assured them that the first cannon fired against either Fort Moultrie or Fort Sumter would arouse the indignant spirit of the North—would heal all political divisions amongst the Northern people, and would unite them as one man in support of a war rendered inevitable by such an act of rebellion.

CHAPTER V.

General Scott's "Views," and the encouragement they afforded to the cotton States to secede—Their publication by him in the "National Intelligencer"—His recommendation in favor of four distinct Confederacies—His recommendation to reënforce nine of the Southern forts, and the inadequacy of the troops—The reason of this inadequacy—The whole army required on the frontiers—The refusal of Congress to increase it—Our fortifications necessarily left without sufficient garrisons for want of troops—The President's duty to refrain from any hostile act against the cotton States, and smooth the way to a compromise—The rights of those States in no danger from Mr. Lincoln's election—Their true policy was to cling to the Union.

SUCH, since the period of Mr. Lincoln's election, having been the condition of the Southern States, the "Views" of General Scott, addressed before that event to the Secretary of War, on the 29th and 30th October, 1860, were calculated to do much injury in misleading the South. From the strange inconsistencies they involve, it would be difficult to estimate whether they did most harm in encouraging or in provoking secession. So far as they recommended a military movement, this, in order to secure success, should have been kept secret until the hour had arrived for carrying it into execution. The substance of them, however, soon reached the Southern people. Neither the headquarters of the army at New York, nor afterwards in Washington, were a very secure depository for the "Views," even had it been the author's intention to regard them as confidential. That such was not the case may be well inferred from their very nature. Not confined to the recommendation of a military movement, by far the larger portion of them consists of a political disquisition on the existing dangers to the Union; on the horrors of civil war and the best means of averting so great a calamity; and also on the course which their author had resolved to pursue, as a citizen, in the approaching Presidential election. These were themes entirely foreign to a military report, and equally foreign from the official duties of the Commanding General. Furthermore, the "Views" were published to the world by the General himself, on the 18th January, 1861, in the "National Intelligencer," *and this without the consent or even previous knowledge of the President.* This was done at a critical moment in our history, when the cotton States were seceding one after the other. The reason assigned by him for this strange violation of official confidence toward the President, was the necessity for the correction of misapprehensions which had got abroad, "both in the public prints and in public speeches," in relation to the "Views."

The General commenced his "Views" by stating that, "To save time the right of secession may be conceded, and instantly balanced by the correlative right on the part of the Federal Government against an *interior* State or States to reëstablish by force, if necessary, its former continuity of territory." He subsequently explains and qualifies the meaning of this phrase by saying : ."It will be seen that the 'Views' only apply to a case of secession that makes a *gap* in the present Union. The falling off (say) of Texas, or of all the Atlantic States, from the Potomac South [the very case which has since occurred], was not within the scope of General Scott's provisional remedies." As if apprehending that by possibility it might be inferred he intended to employ force for any other purpose than to open the way through this *gap* to a State beyond, still in the Union, he disclaims any such construction, and says: " The foregoing views eschew the idea of invading a seceded State." This disclaimer is as strong as any language he could employ for the purpose.

To sustain the limited right to open the way through the *gap*, he cites, not the Constitution of the United States, but the last chapter of Paley's " Moral and Political Philosophy," which, however, contains no allusion to the subject.

The General paints the horrors of civil war in the most gloomy colors, and then proposes his alternative for avoiding them. He exclaims : " But break this glorious Union by whatever line or lines that political madness may contrive, and there would be no hope of reuniting the fragments except by the laceration and despotism of the sword. To effect such result the intestine wars of our Mexican neighbors would, in comparison with ours, sink into mere child's play.

"A smaller evil" (in the General's opinion) "would be to allow the fragments of the great Republic to form themselves into new Confederacies, probably four."

Not satisfied with this general proposition, he proceeds not only to discuss and to delineate the proper boundaries for these new Confederacies, but even to designate capitals for the three on this side of the Rocky Mountains. We quote his own language as follows :—"All the lines of demarcation between the new unions cannot be accurately drawn in advance, but many of them approximately may. Thus, looking to natural boundaries and commercial affinities, some of the following frontiers, after many waverings and conflicts, might perhaps become acknowledged and fixed:

"1. The Potomac River and the Chesapeake Bay to the Atlantic. 2. From Maryland along the crest of the Alleghany (perhaps the Blue Ridge) range of mountains to some point on the coast of Florida. 3. The line from, say the head of the Potomac to the West or Northwest, which it will be most difficult to settle. 4. The crest of the Rocky Mountains."

"The Southeast Confederacy would, in all human probability, in less than five years after the rupture, find itself bounded by the first and second lines indicated above, the Atlantic and the Gulf of Mexico, with its capital at say Columbia, South Carolina. The country between the second, third, and fourth of those lines would, beyond a doubt, in about the same time constitute another Confederacy, with its capital at probably Alton or Quincy, Illinois. The boundaries of the Pacific Union are the most definite of all, and the remaining States would constitute the Northeast Confederacy, with its capital at Albany. It, at the first thought, will be considered strange that seven slaveholding States and part of Virginia and Florida should be placed (above) in a new Confederacy with Ohio, Indiana, Illinois, etc. But when the overwhelming weight of the great Northwest is taken in connection with the laws of trade, contiguity of territory, and the comparative indifference to free soil doctrines on the part of Western Virginia, Kentucky, Tennessee, and Missouri, it is evident that but little if any coercion, beyond moral force, would be needed to embrace them; and I have omitted the temptation of the unwasted public lands which would fall entire to this Confederacy—an appanage (well husbanded) sufficient for many generations. As to Missouri, Arkansas, and Mississippi, they would not stand out a month. Louisiana would coalesce without much solicitation, and Alabama with West Florida would be conquered the first winter from the absolute need of Pensacola for a naval depot."

According to this arrangement of General Scott, all that would be left for "the Northeast Confederacy" would be the New England and Middle States; and our present proud Capitol at Washington, hallowed by so many patriotic associations, would be removed to Albany.[*]

It is easy to imagine with what power these "Views," presented so early as October, 1860, may have been employed by the disunion leaders of the cotton States to convince the people that they might depart in peace. Proceeding from the Commanding General of the army, a citizen and a soldier so eminent, and eschewing as they did the idea of invading a seceded State, as well as favoring the substitution of new Confederacies for the old Union, what danger could they apprehend in the formation of a Southern Confederacy?

This portion of the "Views," being purely political and prospective, and having no connection with military operations, was out of time and out of place in a report from the Commanding General of the Army to the Secretary of War. So, also, the expression of his personal preferences among the candidates then before the people for the office of President. "From a sense of propriety as a soldier," says the General, "I have taken no part in the pending canvass, and, as always heretofore, mean to

---

[*] It is worthy of special remark that General Scott in his autobiography recently published, vol. ii., p. 609, entirely omits to copy this part of his views on which we have been commenting; so also his supplementary views of the next day, though together they constitute but one whole. He merely copies that which relates to garrisoning the Southern forts.

stay away from the polls. My sympathies, however, are with the Bell and Everett ticket."

After all these preliminaries, we now proceed to a different side of the picture presented by the General.

In the same "Views" (the 29th October, 1860), he says that, "From a knowledge of our Southern population it is my solemn conviction that there is some danger of an early act of rashness preliminary to secession, viz., the seizure of some or all of the following posts:—Forts Jackson and St. Philip, in the Mississippi, below New Orleans, both without garrisons; Fort Morgan, below Mobile, without a garrison; Forts Pickens and M'Rea, Pensacola harbor, with an insufficient garrison for one; Fort Pulaski, below Savannah, without a garrison; Forts Moultrie and Sumter, Charleston harbor, the former with an insufficient garrison, and the latter without any; and Fort Monroe, Hampton Roads, without a sufficient garrison. In my opinion all these works should be immediately so garrisoned as to make any attempt to take any one of them by surprise or *coup de main* ridiculous."

It was his duty, as commanding general, to accompany this recommendation with a practicable plan for garrisoning these forts, stating the number of troops necessary for the purpose; the points from which they could be drawn, and the manner in which he proposed to conduct the enterprise. Finding this to be impossible, from the total inadequacy of the force within the President's power to accomplish a military operation so extensive, instead of furnishing such a plan he absolves himself from the task by simply stating in his supplemental views of the next day (30th October) that "There is one (regular) company at Boston, one here (at the Narrows), one at Pittsburg, one at Augusta, Ga., and one at Baton Rouge—in all five companies, only, within reach, to garrison or reënforce the forts mentioned in the 'Views.'"

Five companies only, four hundred men, to garrison nine fortifications scattered over six highly excited Southern States. This was all the force "within reach" so as to make any attempt to take any one of them by surprise or coup de main ridiculous.

He even disparages the strength of this small force by applying to it the diminutive adverb "*only*," or, in other words, merely, barely. It will not be pretended that the President had any power, under the laws, to add to this force by calling forth the militia, or accepting the services of volunteers to garrison these fortifications. And the small regular army were beyond reach on our remote frontiers. Indeed, the whole American army, numbering at that time not more than sixteen thousand effective men, would have been scarcely sufficient. To have attempted to distribute these five companies among the eight forts in the cotton States, and Fortress Monroe, in Virginia, would have been a confession of weakness, instead of an exhibition of imposing and overpowering strength. It could have had no effect in preventing secession, but must have done much to provoke it. It will be recollected that these views, the substance of which soon reached the Southern States, were written before Mr. Lincoln's election, and at a time when none of the cotton States had made the first movement toward secession. Even South Carolina was then performing all her relative duties, though most reluctantly, to the Government, whilst the border States, with Virginia in the first rank, were still faithful and true to the Union.

Under these circumstances, surely General Scott ought not to have informed them in advance that the reason why he had recommended this expedition was because, from his knowledge of them, he apprehended they might be guilty of an early act of rashness in seizing these forts before secession. This would necessarily provoke the passions of the Southern people. Virginia was deeply wounded at the imputation against her loyalty from a native though long estranged son.

Whilst one portion of the "Views," as we have already seen, might be employed by disunion demagogues in convincing the people of the cotton States that they might secede without serious opposition from the North, another portion of them was calculated to excite their indignation and drive them to extremities. From the impracticable nature of the "Views," and their strange and inconsistent character, the President dismissed them from his mind without further consideration.

It is proper to inform the reader why General Scott had five companies *only* within reach for the proposed service. This was because nearly the whole of our small army was on the remote frontiers, where it had been continually employed for years in protecting the inhabitants and the emigrants on their way to the far west, against the attacks of hostile Indians. At no former period had its services been more necessary than throughout the year 1860, from the great number of these Indians continually threatening or waging war on our distant settlements. To employ the language of Mr. Benjamin Stanton, of Ohio, in his report of the 18th February, 1861, from the military committee to the House of Representatives! "The regular army numbers only 18,000 men, when recruited to its maximum strength; and the whole of this force is required upon an extended frontier, for the protection of the border settlements against Indian depredations." Indeed, the whole of it had proved insufficient for this purpose. This is established by the reports of General Scott himself to the War Department. In these he urges the necessity of raising more troops, in a striking and convincing light. In that of 20th November, 1857,* after portraying the intolerable hardships and sufferings of the army engaged in this service, he says: "To mitigate these evils, and to enable us to give a reasonable security to our people on Indian frontiers, measuring thousands of miles, I respectfully suggest an augmentation of at least one regiment of horse (dragoons, cavalry, or riflemen) and at least three regiments of foot (infantry or riflemen). This augmentation would not more than furnish the reënforcements now greatly needed in Florida, Texas, New Mexico, California, Oregon, Washington Territory, Kansas, Nebraska, and Minnesota, leaving not a company for Utah."

Again, General Scott, in his report of November 13, 1858, says: † "This want of troops to give reasonable security to our citizens in distant settlements, including emigrants on the plains, can scarcely be too strongly stated; but I will only add, that as often as we have been obliged to withdraw troops from one fron-

---

* 3 Senate Documents, 1857-'58, p. 48.
† Senate Executive Documents, 1858-'59, vol. ii., part 8, p. 761.

tier in order to reënforce another, the weakened points have been instantly attacked or threatened with formidable invasion."

The President, feeling the force of such appeals, and urged by the earnest entreaties of the suffering people on the frontiers, recommended to Congress, through the War Department, to raise five additional regiments.* This, like all other recommendations to place the country in a proper state of defence, was disregarded. From what has been stated it is manifest that it was impossible to garrison the numerous forts of the United States with regular troops. . This will account for the destitute condition of the nine forts enumerated by General Scott, as well as of all the rest.

When our system of fortifications was planned and carried into execution, it was never contemplated to provide garrisons for them in time of peace. This would have required a large standing army, against which the American people have ever evinced a wise and wholesome jealousy. Every great republic, from the days of Cæsar to Cromwell, and from Cromwell to Bonaparte, has been destroyed by armies composed of free citizens, who had been converted by military discipline into veteran soldiers. Our fortifications, therefore, when completed, were generally left in the custody of a sergeant and a few soldiers. No fear was entertained that they would ever be seized by the States for whose defence against a foreign enemy they had been erected.

Under these circumstances it became the plain duty of the President, destitute as he was of military force, not only to refrain from any act which might provoke or encourage the cotton States into secession, but to smooth the way for such a Congressional compromise as had in times past happily averted danger from the Union. There was good reason to hope this might still be accomplished. The people of the slaveholding States must have known there could be no danger of an actual invasion of their constitutional rights over slave property from any hostile action of Mr. Lincoln's administration. For the protection of these, they could rely both on the judicial and the legislative branches of the Government. The Supreme Court

* Senate Documents, 1857-'58, vol. iii., p. 4.

had already decided the Territorial question in their favor, and it was also ascertained that there would be a majority in both Houses of the first Congress of Mr. Lincoln's term, sufficient to prevent any legislation to their injury. Thus protected, it would be madness for them to rush into secession.

Besides, they were often warned and must have known that by their separation from the free States, these very rights over slave property, of which they were so jealous, would be in greater jeopardy than they had ever been under the Government of the Union. Theirs would then be the only Government in Christendom which had not abolished or was not in progress to abolish slavery. There would be a strong pressure from abroad against this institution. To resist this effectually would require the power and moral influence of the Government of the whole United States. They ought, also, to have foreseen, that if their secession should end in civil war, whatever might be the event, slavery would receive a blow from which it could never recover. The true policy, even in regard to the safety of their domestic institution, was to cling to the Union.

CHAPTER VI.

Mr. Lincoln's election to the Presidency—Its danger to the Union—Warnings of the President and his trying position—His policy in the emergency, and the reasons for it—His supreme object the preservation of the Union—Meeting of Congress, and the hostility of the two parties toward each other—The wrongs of the South—How rash and causeless would be rebellion in the Cotton States—The right of secession discussed and denied in the Message—The President's position defined—Question of the power to coerce a State—Distinction between the power to wage war against a State, and the power to execute the laws against individuals—Views of Senator (now President) Johnson, of Tennessee—President Buchanan's solemn appeal in favor of the Union—His estrangement from the secession leaders—Cessation of all friendly intercourse between him and them.

On the 6th November, 1860, Abraham Lincoln was elected President of the United States, and immediately thereafter the Legislature of South Carolina passed an Act for the call of a Convention to carry the State out of the Union, calculating that by this precipitate violence she might force the other cotton States to follow in her lead.

Every discerning citizen must now have foreseen serious danger to the Union from Mr. Lincoln's election. After a struggle of many years, this had accomplished the triumph of the anti-slavery over the slaveholding States, and established two geographical parties, inflamed with malignant hatred against each other, in despite of the warning voice of Washington. It at once became manifest that the apprehensions of civil war, arising from this event, had proved as disastrous to the business of the country as if the struggle had actually commenced. Although the harvests of the year had been abundant, and commerce and manufactures had never been more prosperous, terror and alarm everywhere prevailed. In the midst of all the elements of prosperity, every material interest was at once greatly depressed. With a sound currency in abundance, the price of all public securities fell in the market. The credit of the Federal Government, which had before stood so high, was unable to resist the shock. The small necessary loans to meet the previous appropriations of Congress, could not be obtained except at ruinous rates.

Throughout more than a quarter of a century the late President, on every fitting occasion, had solemnly warned his countrymen of the approaching danger, unless the agitation in the North against slavery in the South should cease. Instead of this, it still continued to increase, year after year, with brief intervals only, until it has become at length the unhappy, though unjustifiable cause, perhaps the criminal pretext, for the secession of eleven slaveholding States from the Confederacy.

The President had less than four months to complete his term of office. The Democratic party, to which he owed his election, had been defeated, and the triumphant party had pursued his administration from the beginning with a virulence uncommon even in our history. His every act had been misrepresented and condemned, and he knew that whatever course he might pursue, he was destined to encounter their bitter hostility. No public man was ever placed in a more trying and responsible position. Indeed, it was impossible for him to act with honest independence, without giving offence both to the anti-slavery and secession parties, because both had been clearly in the wrong. In view of his position, and after mature reflection, he adopted a system of policy to which ever afterward, during the brief remnant of his term, he inflexibly adhered. This he announced and explained in the annual message to Congress of the 3d December, 1860, and in the special message thereafter of the 8th January, 1861.

The Cabinet was then composed of Lewis Cass, of Michigan, Secretary of State; Howell Cobb, of Georgia, Secretary of the Treasury; John B. Floyd, of Virginia, Secretary of War; Isaac Toucey, of Connecticut, Secretary of the Navy; Jacob Thompson, of Mississippi, Secretary of the Interior; Joseph Holt, of Kentucky, Postmaster-General, in the place of

Aaron V. Brown, of Tennessee, deceased; and Jeremiah S. Black, of Pennsylvania, Attorney-General.

The annual message throughout, before it was communicated to Congress, had been warmly approved by every member of the Cabinet, except so much of it as denied the right of secession, and maintained the duty of defending the public property and collecting the revenue in South Carolina, to which Messrs. Cobb and Thompson objected. These having now become practical questions of vital importance, both felt it would be impossible to remain in the Cabinet whilst holding opinions upon them in opposition to the known and settled convictions of the President. They accordingly resigned after the meeting of Congress, remaining in office for a brief period, to enable them to bring up and close the ordinary business of their respective departments, and thus clear the way for their successors.

At this critical moment, and but nine days after Congress had assembled, General Cass, on the 12th December, 1860, resigned the office of Secretary of State, notwithstanding the message had, but a few days before, elicited from him strong expressions of approbation. Of this resignation and the circumstances preceding and following it, we forbear to speak, not doubting it proceeded at the moment from a sense of duty. Attorney-General Black was, in consequence, appointed Secretary of State, and the vacancy thereby created was filled by the appointment of Edwin M. Stanton as Attorney-General.

Philip F. Thomas, formerly Governor of Maryland, and then Commissioner of Patents, was appointed Secretary of the Treasury, in place of Mr. Cobb, who had resigned on the 8th December, but he did not long continue in office, having also resigned on the 11th January, 1861. The reason he assigned was a difference of opinion from the President and a majority of the Cabinet in regard to the measures which had been adopted against South Carolina, and the purpose of the President to enforce the collection of the customs at the port of Charleston. Immediately thereafter, the President tendered the appointment of Secretary of the Treasury to General John A. Dix, of New York, which was, much to his satisfaction, promptly accepted.

The Interior Department remained vacant after the retirement of Mr. Thompson, but its duties were ably and faithfully performed by Moses Kelly, the chief clerk, until the close of the administration. Upon Mr. Holt's transfer, late in December, 1860, from the Post Office to the War Department, the first Assistant Postmaster-General, Horatio King, of Maine, continued for some time to perform the duties of the Department in a highly satisfactory manner, when he was appointed Postmaster-General. After these changes the Cabinet consisted of Messrs. Black, Dix, Holt, Toucey, Stanton, and King, who all remained in office until the end of Mr. Buchanan's term.

The President had earnestly desired that his Cabinet might remain together until the close of the administration. He felt sensibly the necessary withdrawal of some of its members, after all had been so long united in bonds of mutual confidence and friendship.

The President's policy was, first and above all, to propose and urge the adoption of such a fair and honorable compromise as might prove satisfactory to all the States, both North and South, on the question of slavery in the Territories, the immediate and principal source of danger to the Union; and should he fail to accomplish this object in regard to the seven cotton States, which there was too much cause to apprehend, then to employ all legitimate means to preserve and strengthen the eight remaining slave or border States in their undoubted loyalty. These States, he knew, in case of need, might prove instrumental in bringing back their erring sisters to a sense of duty.

To preserve the Union was the President's supreme object, and he considered it doubtful whether it could survive the shock of civil war. He was well aware that our wisest statesmen had often warned their countrymen, in the most solemn terms, that our institutions could not be preserved by force, and could only endure whilst concord of feeling, and a proper respect by one section for the rights of another, should be maintained. Mr. Madison in this spirit had observed, in the Federal Convention,*

* June 8, 1787. Sup. to Elliot's Debates, vol. v., p. 171.

that "Any Government for the United States, formed upon the supposed practicability of using force against the unconstitutional proceedings of the States, would prove as visionary and fallacious as the Government of [the old] Congress." And General Jackson, a high authority, especially on such a subject, had declared in his Farewell Address* (3d March, 1837), that "the Constitution cannot be maintained, nor the Union preserved, in opposition to public feeling, by the mere exertion of the coercive powers confided to the General Government. The foundations must be laid in the affections of the people; in the security it gives to life, liberty, character, and property, in every quarter of the country; and in the fraternal attachments which the citizens of the several States bear to one another, as members of one political family, mutually contributing to promote the happiness of each other. Hence [in evident reference to the slavery agitation in the North] the citizens of every State should studiously avoid every thing calculated to wound the sensibility or offend the just pride of the people of other States; and they should frown upon any proceedings within their own borders likely to disturb the tranquillity of their political brethren in other portions of the Union."

The President, whilst admitting that Mr. Madison and General Jackson may have erred in these opinions, was convinced that should a rebellion break out within the seven cotton States, this could not be overcome without a long and bloody war. From the character of our people and the history of our race, it was evident that such a war, on both sides, would be carried to desperate extremities. These seven States composed a contiguous territory of greater extent than the whole thirteen original States, and contained more than five millions of people. To vanquish them would require a very large army and an immense sacrifice of kindred blood. No person acquainted with history could be blind to the danger to which our free institutions would be exposed from such an army. History had taught us that every great Republic had fallen a victim to military power. Besides, it was morally certain that should civil war actually commence, most if not all of the border States, though

* 2 Statesman's Manual, 951.

still adhering to the Union, would eventually be drawn into the conflict. To prosecute civil war would require an expenditure of hundreds of millions of dollars. This would entail an enormous debt on ourselves and our posterity, the interest on which could only be paid by oppressive taxation. The President knew that, in the mean time, many of the great commercial, manufacturing, artisan, and laboring classes would be exposed to absolute ruin. It was therefore his supreme desire to employ all the constitutional means in his power to avert these impending calamities.

In the midst of these portentous circumstances, both present and prospective, Congress met on the first Monday of December, 1860, and the President on the next day transmitted to them his annual message. The opposing parties, instead of presenting the peaceful aspect becoming the Representatives of a great Confederacy assembled to promote the various interests of their constituents, breathed nothing but mutual defiance. There was no longer any social or friendly intercourse between the Pro-Slavery and Anti-Slavery members. South Carolina had called a Convention for the avowed purpose of adopting a secession ordinance; and the other cotton States were preparing to follow her example.

Such was the situation at the meeting of Congress, and it was most unfortunate that but few individuals in the Northern States justly appreciated the extent and magnitude of the danger. These facts stared every unprejudiced observer in the face. The danger was upon us, and how to remove it was a question for enlightened and patriotic statesmanship. The stake involved was no less than the peace and perpetuity of the Union. The evil could not be averted by any argument, however conclusive, against the right of a State peacefully to secede from the Union. This dangerous heresy had taken thorough possession of the Southern mind, and the seven cotton States were acting and preparing to act in accordance with it. There was but one mode of arresting their headlong career, and this was promptly to recognize their rights over slave property in the Territories, as they existed under the decision of the Supreme Court. If the North should refuse to do this and reject any compromise, the secession of the cotton States would be inevitable. Apart from the factitious importance with which party spirit had invested the question, it was little more in point of fact than a mere abstraction. The recognition of the decision of the Supreme Court on the part of Congress, would not have added a single slave or a single slave State to the number already existing. The natural and irreversible laws of climate would prove an insurmountable barrier against the admission of any of our Territories as a slave State into the Union.

The President, therefore, in his annual message of 3d December, 1860, appealed to Congress to institute an amendment to the Constitution recognizing the rights of the Southern States in regard to slavery in the Territories. But before we proceed to give the history and the fate of this recommendation, it is necessary to revert to previous portions of the message, in which he endeavored to hold the balance fairly between the North and the South.

And first in respect to the wrongs which the South had suffered, he says: " The long-continued and intemperate interference of the Northern people with the question of slavery in the Southern States, has at length produced its natural effects. The different sections of the Union are now arrayed against each other, and the time has arrived, so much dreaded by the Father of his Country, when hostile geographical parties have been formed.

"I have long foreseen, and often forewarned my countrymen of the now impending danger. This does not proceed solely from the claim on the part of Congress or the Territorial Legislatures to exclude slavery from the Territories, nor from the efforts of different States to defeat the execution of the fugitive slave law.

" All or any of these evils might have been endured by the South, without danger to the Union (as others have been), in the hope that time and reflection might apply the remedy. The immediate peril arises, not so much from these causes, as from the fact that the incessant and violent agitation of the slavery question throughout the North, for the last quarter of a century, has at length produced its malign influence on the slaves, and inspired them with vague notions of freedom. Hence a sense of security no longer exists around the family altar. This feeling of peace at home has given place to apprehensions of servile insurrections. Many a matron throughout the South retires at night in dread of what may befall herself and her children before the morning. Should this apprehension of domestic danger, whether real or imaginary, extend and intensify itself until it shall pervade the masses of the Southern people, then disunion will become inevitable. Self-preservation is the first law of nature, and has been implanted in the heart of man by his Creator for the wisest purpose; and no political union, however fraught with blessings and benefits in all other respects, can long continue, if the necessary consequence be to render the homes and the firesides of nearly half the parties to it habitually and hopelessly insecure. Sooner or later the bonds of such a Union must be severed. It is my conviction that this fatal period has not yet arrived; and my prayer to God is, that he would preserve the Constitution and the Union throughout all generations.

"But let us take warning in time and remove the cause of danger. It cannot be denied that for five and twenty years the agitation at the North against slavery has been incessant. In 1835, pictorial handbills and inflammatory appeals were circulated extensively throughout the South, of a character to excite the passions of the slaves, and, in the language of General Jackson, 'to stimulate them to insurrection and produce all the horrors of a servile war.'

"This agitation has ever since been continued by the public press, by the proceedings of State and County Conventions, and by abolition sermons and lectures. The time of Congress has been occupied in violent speeches on this never-ending subject; and appeals, in pamphlet and other forms, indorsed by distinguished names, have been sent forth from this central point and spread broadcast over the Union.

"How easy would it be for the American people to settle the slavery question forever, and to restore peace and harmony to this distracted country! They, and they alone, can do it. All that is necessary to accomplish the object, and all for which the slave States have ever contended, is to be let alone and permitted to manage their domestic institutions in their own way. As sovereign States, they and they alone are responsible before God and the world for the slavery existing among them. For this the people of the North are not more responsible, and have no more right to interfere, than with similar institutions in Russia or in Brazil. Upon their good sense and patriotic forbearance, I confess, I still greatly rely. Without their aid it is beyond the power of any President, no matter what may be his own political proclivities, to restore peace and harmony among the States. Wisely limited and restrained as is his power under our Constitution and laws, he alone can accomplish but little for good or for evil on such a momentous question."

The President then proceeded to show how rash and causeless would be the action of the cotton States, should they rise in revolutionary resistance against the Federal Government, at a time when their rights were in no real danger, either from the election or administration of Mr. Lincoln. He says: "And this brings me to observe, that the election of any one of our fellow-citizens to the office of President does not of itself afford just cause for dissolving the Union. This is more especially true if his election has been effected by a mere plurality and not a majority of the people, and has resulted from transient and temporary causes, which may probably never again occur. In order to justify a resort to revolutionary resistance, the Federal Government must be guilty of 'a deliberate, palpable, and dangerous exercise' of powers not granted by the Constitution. The late Presidential election, however, has been held in strict conformity with its express provisions. How, then, can the result justify a revolution to destroy this very Constitution? Reason, justice, a regard for the Constitution, all require that we shall wait for some overt and dangerous act on the part of the President elect, before resorting to such a remedy. It is said, however, that the antecedents of the President elect have been sufficient to justify the fears of the South that he will attempt to invade their constitutional rights. But are such apprehensions of contingent danger in the future sufficient to justify the immediate destruction of the noblest system of government ever devised by mortals? From the very nature of his office, and its high responsibilities, he must necessarily be conservative. The stern duty of administering the vast and complicated concerns of this Government, affords in itself a guarantee that he will not attempt any violation of a clear constitutional right.

"After all, he is no more than the chief executive officer of the Government. His province is not to make but to execute the laws, and it is a remarkable fact in our history that, notwithstanding the repeated efforts of the Anti-Slavery party, no single act has ever passed Congress, unless we may possibly except the Missouri Compromise, impairing in the slightest degree the rights of the South to their property in slaves. And it may also be observed, judging from present indications, that no probability exists of the passage of such an act by a majority of both Houses, either in the present or the next Congress. Surely, under these circumstances, we ought to be restrained from present action by the precept of Him who spake as man never spoke, that 'sufficient unto the day is the evil thereof.' The day of evil may never come unless we shall rashly bring it upon ourselves.

"It is alleged as one cause for immediate secession, that the Southern States are denied equal rights with the other States in the common Territories. But by what authority are these denied? Not by Congress, which has never passed, and I believe never will pass, any act to exclude slavery from these Territories. And certainly not by the Supreme Court, which has solemnly decided that slaves are property, and like all other property their owners have a right to take them into the common Territories and hold them there under the protection of the Constitution.

"So far, then, as Congress is concerned, the objection is not to any thing they have already done, but to what they may do hereafter. It will surely be admitted that this apprehension of future danger is no good reason for an immediate dissolution of the Union. It is true that the Territorial Legislature of Kansas, on the 23d February, 1860, passed in great haste an act over the veto of the governor, declaring that slavery 'is and shall be for ever prohibited in this Territory.' Such an act, however, plainly violating the rights of property secured by the Constitution, will surely be declared void by the judiciary, whenever it shall be presented in a legal form.

"Only three days after my inauguration the Supreme Court of the United States solemnly adjudged that this power did not exist in a Territorial Legislature. Yet such has been the factious temper of the times that the correctness of this decision has been extensively impugned before the people, and the question has given rise to angry political conflicts throughout the country. Those who have appealed from this judgment of our highest constitutional tribunal to popular assemblies, would, if they could, invest a Territorial Legislature with power to annul the sacred rights of property. This power Congress is expressly forbidden by the Federal Constitution to exercise. Every State Legislature in the Union is forbidden by its own Constitution to exercise it. It cannot be exercised in any State except by the people in their highest sovereign capacity when framing or amending their State Constitution. In like manner it can only be exercised by the people of a Territory, represented in a convention of delegates for the purpose of framing a constitution preparatory to admission as a State into the Union. Then, and not until then, are they invested with power to decide the question whether slavery shall or shall not exist within their limits. This is an act of sovereign authority and not of subordinate territorial legislation. Were it otherwise, then indeed would the equality of the States in the Territories be destroyed, and the rights of property in slaves would depend not upon the guarantees of the Constitution, but upon the shifting majorities of an irresponsible Territorial Legislature. Such a doctrine, from its intrinsic unsoundness, cannot long influence any considerable portion of our people, much less can it afford a good reason for a dissolution of the Union.

"The most palpable violations of constitutional duty which have yet been committed consist in the acts of different State Legislatures to defeat the execution of the fugitive slave law. It ought to be remembered, however, that for these acts neither Congress nor any President can justly be held responsible. Having been passed in violation of the Federal Constitution, they are therefore null and void. All the courts, both State and national, before whom the question has arisen, have, from the beginning, declared the fugitive slave law to be constitutional. The single exception is that of a State court in Wisconsin; and this has not only been reversed by the proper appellate tribunal, but has met with such universal reprobation, that there can be no danger from it as a precedent. The validity of this law has been established over and over again by the Supreme Court of the United States with perfect unanimity. It is founded upon an express provision of the Constitution, requiring that fugitive slaves who escape from service in one State to another shall be 'delivered up' to their masters. Without this provision it is a well-known historical fact that the Constitution itself could never have been adopted by the Convention. In one form or other under the acts of 1793 and 1850, both being substantially the same, the fugitive slave law has been the law of the land from the days of Washington until the present moment. Here, then, a clear case is presented, in which it will be the duty of the next President, as it has been my own, to act with vigor in executing this supreme law against the conflicting enactments of State Legislatures. Should he fail in the performance of this high duty, he will then have manifested a disregard of the Constitution and laws, to the great injury of the people of nearly one-half of the States of the Union. But are we to presume in advance that he will thus violate his duty? This would be at war with every principle of justice and of Christian charity. Let us wait for the overt act. The fugitive slave law has been carried into execution in every contested case since the commencement of the present administration; though often, it is to be regretted, with great loss and inconvenience to the master, and with considerable expense to the Government. Let us trust that the State Legislatures will repeal their unconstitutional and obnoxious enactments. Unless this shall be done without unnecessary delay, it is impossible for any human power to save the Union.

"The Southern States, standing on the basis of the Constitution, have a right to demand this act of justice from the States of the North. Should it be refused, then the Constitution, to which all the States are parties, will have been wilfully violated by one portion of them in a provision essential to the domestic security and happiness of the remainder. In that event, the injured States, after having first used all peaceful and constitutional means to obtain redress, would be justified in revolutionary resistance to the Government of the Union."

Having thus disposed of the question of revolutionary resistance, the message proceeds to discuss the right of peaceful secession from the Union claimed by the Southern States in their sovereign character. It proceeds:

"I have purposely confined my remarks to revolutionary resistance, because it has been claimed within the last few years that any State, whenever this shall be its sovereign will and pleasure, may secede from the Union in accordance with the Constitution, and without any violation of the constitutional rights of the other members of the Confederacy. That as each became parties to the Union by the vote of its own people assembled in convention, so any one of them may retire from the Union in a similar manner by the vote of such a convention.

"In order to justify secession as a constitutional remedy, it must be on the principle that the Federal Government is a mere voluntary association of States, to be dissolved at pleasure by any one of the contracting parties. If this be so, the Confederacy is a rope of sand, to be penetrated and dissolved by the first adverse wave of public opinion in any of the States. In this manner our thirty-three States may resolve themselves into as many petty, jarring, and hostile republics, each one retiring from the Union without responsibility whenever any sudden excitement might impel them to such a course. By this process a Union might be entirely broken into fragments in a few weeks, which cost our forefathers many years of toil, privation, and blood to establish.

"Such a principle is wholly inconsistent with the history as well as the character of the Federal Constitution. After it was framed with the greatest deliberation and care, it was submitted to conventions of the people of the several States for ratification. Its provisions were discussed at length in these bodies, composed of the first men of the country. Its opponents contended that it conferred powers upon the Federal Government dangerous to the rights of the States, whilst its advocates maintained that, under a fair construction of the instrument, there was no foundation for such apprehensions. In that mighty struggle between the first intellects of this or any other country, it never occurred to any individual, either among its opponents or advocates, to assert or even to intimate that their efforts were all vain labor, because the moment that any State felt herself aggrieved she might secede from the Union. What a crushing argument would this have proved against those who dreaded that the rights of the States would be endangered by the Constitution. The truth is, that it was not until some years after the origin of the Federal Government that such a proposition was first advanced. It was afterwards met and refuted by the conclusive arguments of General Jackson, who, in his message of the 16th January, 1833, transmitting the nullifying ordinance of South Carolina to Congress, employs the following language: 'The right of the people of a single State to absolve themselves at will and without the consent of the other States from their most solemn obligations, and hazard the liberty and happiness of the millions composing this Union, cannot be acknowledged. Such authority is believed to be utterly repugnant both to the principles upon which the General Government is constituted, and to the objects which it was expressly formed to attain.'

"It is not pretended that any clause in the Constitution gives countenance to such a theory. It is altogether founded upon inference, not from any language contained in the instrument itself, but from the sovereign character of the several States by which it was ratified. But is it beyond the power of a State, like an individual, to yield a portion of its sovereign rights to secure the remainder? In the language of Mr. Madison, who has been called the father of the Constitution, 'It was formed by the States—that .is, by the people in each of the States acting in their highest sovereign capacity, and formed consequently by the same authority which formed the State constitutions.' 'Nor is the Government of the United States, created by the Constitution, less a Government, in the strict sense of the term, within the sphere of its powers, than the governments created by the constitutions of the States are within their several spheres. It is, like them, organized into legislative, executive, and judiciary departments. It operates, like them, directly on persons and things; and, like them, it has at command a physical force for executing the powers committed to it.'

"It was intended to be perpetual, and not to be annulled at the pleasure of any one of the contracting parties. The old Articles of Confederation were entitled 'Articles of Confederation and Perpetual Union between the States;' and by the thirteenth article it is expressly declared that 'the articles of this confederation shall be inviolably observed by every State, and the Union shall be perpetual.' The preamble to the Constitution of the United States, having express reference to the Articles of Confederation, recites that it was established 'in order to form a more perfect union.' And yet it is contended that this 'more perfect union' does not include the essential attribute of perpetuity.

"But that the Union was designed to be perpetual, appears conclusively from the nature and extent of the powers conferred by the Constitution on the Federal Government. These powers embrace the very highest attributes of national sovereignty. They place both the sword and the purse under its control. Congress has power to make war and to make peace; to raise and support armies and navies, and to conclude treaties with foreign governments. It is invested with the power to coin money, and to regulate the value thereof, and to regulate commerce with foreign nations and among the several States. It is not necessary to enumerate the other high powers which have been conferred upon the Federal Government. In order to carry the enumerated powers into effect, Congress possesses the exclusive right to lay and collect duties on imports, and, in common with the States, to lay and collect all other taxes.

"But the Constitution has not only conferred these high powers upon Congress, but it has adopted effectual means to restrain the States from interfering with their exercise. For that purpose it has in strong prohibitory language expressly declared that 'no State shall enter into any treaty, alliance, or confederation; grant letters of marque and reprisal; coin money; emit bills of credit; make any thing but gold and silver coin a tender in payment of debts; pass any bill of attainder, *ex post facto* law, or law impairing the obligation of contracts.' Moreover, 'without the consent of Congress no State shall lay any imposts or duties on any imports or exports, except what may be absolutely necessary for executing its inspection laws,' and if they exceed this amount, the excess shall belong to the United States. And 'no State shall, without the consent of Congress, lay any duty of tonnage, keep troops or ships of war in time of peace, enter into any agreement or compact with another State, or with a foreign power, or engage in war, unless actually invaded or in such imminent danger as will not admit of delay.'.

"In order still further to secure the uninterrupted exercise of these high powers against State interposition, it is provided 'that this Constitution and the laws of the United States which shall be made in pursuance thereof, and all treaties made or which shall be made under the authority of the United States, shall be the supreme law of the land; and the judges in every State shall be bound thereby, any thing in the Constitution or laws of any State to the contrary notwithstanding.'

"The solemn sanction of religion has been superadded to the obligations of official duty, and all Senators and Representatives of the United States, all members of State Legislatures, and all executive and judicial officers, 'both of the United States and of the several States, shall be bound by oath or affirmation to support this Constitution.'

"In order to carry into effect these powers, the Constitution has established a perfect Government in all its forms, legislative, executive, and judicial; and this Government to the extent of its powers acts directly upon the individual citizens of every State, and executes its own decrees by the agency of its own officers. In this respect it differs entirely from the Government under the old confederation, which was confined to making requisitions on the States in their sovereign character. This left it in the discretion of each whether to obey or to refuse, and they often declined to comply with such requisitions. It thus became necessary, for the purpose of removing this barrier, and 'in order to form a more perfect union,' to establish a Government which could act directly upon the people and execute its own laws without the intermediate agency of the States. This has been accomplished by the Constitution of the United States. In short, the Government created by the Constitution, and deriving its authority from the sovereign people of each of the several States, has precisely the same right to exercise its power over the people of all these States in the enumerated cases, that each one of them possesses over subjects not delegated to the United States, but 'reserved to the States respectively or to the people.'

"To the extent of the delegated powers the Constitution of the United States is as much a part of the constitution of each State, and is as binding upon its people, as though it had been textually inserted therein.

"This Government, therefore, is a great and powerful Government, invested with all the attributes of sovereignty over the special subjects to which its authority extends. Its framers never intended to implant in its bosom the seeds of its own destruction, nor were they at its creation guilty of the absurdity of providing for its own dissolution. It was not intended by its framers to be the baseless fabric of a vision, which, at the touch of the enchanter, would vanish into thin air, but a substantial and mighty fabric, capable of resisting the slow decay of time, and of defying the storms of ages. Indeed, well may the jealous patriots of that day have indulged fears that a Government of such high powers might violate the reserved rights of the States, and wisely did they adopt the rule of a strict construction of these powers to prevent the danger. But they did not fear, nor had they any reason to imagine that the Constitution would ever be so interpreted as to enable any State by her own act, and without the consent of her sister States, to discharge her people from all or any of their federal obligations.

"It may be asked, then, are the people of the States without redress against the tyranny and oppression of the Federal Government? By no means. The right of resistance on the part of the governed against the oppression of their governments cannot be denied. It exists independently of all constitutions, and has been exercised at all periods of the world's history. Under it, old governments have been destroyed and new ones have taken their place. It is embodied in strong and express language in our own Declaration of Independence. But the distinction must ever be observed that this is revolution against an established Government, and not a voluntary secession from it by virtue of an inherent constitutional right. In short, let us look the danger fairly in the face; secession is neither more nor less than revolution. It may or it may not be a justifiable revolution; but still it is revolution."

The President having thus attempted to demonstrate that the Constitution affords no warrant for secession, but that this was inconsistent both with its letter and spirit, then defines his own position. He says:

"What, in the mean time, is the responsibility and true position of the Executive? He is bound by solemn oath, before God and the country, 'to take care that the laws be faithfully executed,' and from this obligation he cannot be absolved by any human power. But what if the performance of this duty, in whole or in part, has been rendered impracticable by events over which he could have exercised no control? Such, at the present moment, is the case throughout the State of South Carolina, so far as the laws of the United States to secure the administration of justice by means of the Federal judiciary are concerned. All the Federal officers within its limits, through whose agency alone these laws can be carried into execution, have already resigned. We no longer have a district judge, a district attorney, or a marshal in South Carolina. In fact, the whole machinery of the Federal Government necessary for the distribution of remedial justice among the people has been demolished, and it would be difficult, if not impossible, to replace it.

"The only acts of Congress on the statute book bearing upon this subject are those of the 28th February, 1795, and 3d March, 1807. These authorize the President, after he shall have ascertained that the marshal, with his *posse comitatus*, is unable to execute civil or criminal process in any particular case, to call forth the militia and employ the army and navy to aid him in performing this service, having first by proclamation commanded the insurgents 'to disperse and retire peaceably to their respective abodes within a limited time.' This duty cannot by possibility be performed in a State where no judicial authority exists to issue process, and where there is no marshal to execute it, and where, even if there were such an officer, the entire population would constitute one solid combination to resist him.

"The bare enumeration of these provisions proves how inadequate they are without further legislation to overcome a united opposition in a single State, not to speak of other States who may place themselves in a similar attitude. Congress alone has power to decide whether the present laws can or cannot be amended so as to carry out more effectually the objects of the Constitution.

"The same insuperable obstacles do not lie in the way of executing the laws for the collection of the customs. The revenue still continues to be collected, as heretofore, at the custom-house in Charleston, and should the collector unfortunately resign, a successor may be appointed to perform this duty.

"Then, in regard to the property of the United States in South Carolina. This has been purchased for a fair equivalent, 'by the consent of the Legislature of the State,' 'for the erection of forts, magazines, arsenals,' &c., and over these the authority 'to exercise exclusive legislation' has been expressly granted by the Constitution to Congress. It is not believed that any attempt will be made to expel the United States from this property by force; but if in this I should prove to be mistaken, the officer in command of the forts has received orders to act strictly on the defensive. In such a contingency the responsibility for consequences would rightfully rest upon the heads of the assailants.

"Apart from the execution of the laws, so far as this may be practicable, the Executive has no authority to decide what shall be the relations between the Federal Government and South Carolina. He has been invested with no such discretion. He possesses no power to change the relations heretofore existing between them, much less to acknowledge the independence of that State. This would be to invest a mere executive officer with the power of recognizing the dissolution of the Confederacy among our thirty-three sovereign States. It bears no resemblance to the recognition of a foreign *de facto* Government, involving no such responsibility. Any attempt to do this would, on his part, be a naked act of usurpation. It is, therefore, my duty to submit to Congress the whole question in all its bearings."

Then follows the opinion expressed in the message, that the Constitution has conferred no power on the Federal Government to coerce a *State* to remain in the Union. The following is the language: "The question fairly stated is, 'Has the Constitution delegated to Congress the power to coerce a State into submission which is attempting to withdraw, or has actually withdrawn from the Confederacy?' If answered in the affirmative, it must be on the principle that the power has been conferred upon Congress to make war against a State.

"After much serious reflection, I have arrived at the conclusion that no such power has been delegated to Congress or to any other department of the Federal Government. It is manifest, upon an inspection of the Constitution, that this is not among the specific and enumerated powers granted to Congress; and it is equally apparent that its exercise is not 'necessary and proper for carrying into execution' any one of these powers. So far from this power having been delegated to Congress, it was expressly refused by the Convention which framed the Constitution.

"It appears from the proceedings of that body that on the 31st May, 1787, the clause '*authorizing an exertion of the force of the whole against a delinquent State*' came up for consideration. Mr. Madison opposed it in a brief but powerful speech, from which I shall extract but a single sentence. He observed: 'The use of force against a State would look more like a declaration of war than an infliction of punishment, and would probably be considered by the party attacked as a dissolution of all previous compacts by which it might be bound.' Upon his motion the clause was unanimously postponed, and was never, I believe, again presented. Soon afterwards, on the 8th June, 1787, when incidentally adverting to the subject, he said : 'Any government for the United States, formed on the supposed practicability of using force against the unconstitutional proceedings of the States, would prove as visionary and fallacious as the government of Congress,' evidently meaning the then existing Congress of the old confederation."

The Republican party have severely but unjustly criticized this portion of the message, simply because they have not chosen to take the distinction between the power to make war against a State in its sovereign character, and the undoubted power to enforce the laws of Congress directly against individual citizens thereof within its limits. It was chiefly to establish this very distinction that the Federal Constitution was framed. The Government of the old Confederation could act only by requisitions on the different States, and these, as we have seen, obeyed or disobeyed according to their own discretion. In case of disobedience, there was no resort but to actual force against them, which would at once have destroyed the Confederacy. To remove the necessity for such a dangerous alternative, the present Constitution, passing over the Governments of the States, conferred upon the Government of the United States the power to execute its own laws directly against their people. Thus all danger of collision between the Federal and State authorities was removed, and the indissoluble nature of the Federal Union established. The Republican party have, notwithstanding, construed the message to mean a denial by the President of the power to enforce the laws against the citizens of a State after secession, and even after actual rebellion. The whole tenor, not only of this message, but of the special message of the 8th January, 1861, contradicts and disproves this construction. Indeed, in the clause of the first, immediately preceding that relied upon, and whilst South Carolina was rapidly rushing to secession, he expressed his determination to execute the revenue laws whenever these should be resisted, and to defend the public property against all assaults. And in the special message, after South Carolina and other States had seceded, he reiterated this declaration, maintaining both his right and his duty to employ military force for this purpose. Having proved secession to be a mere nullity, he considered the States which had seceded to be still within the Union, and their people equally bound as they had been before to obey the laws.

The Disunionists, unlike the Republicans, placed the correct construction upon both messages, and therefore denounced them in severe terms.

The President was gratified to observe that Senator Johnson, of Tennessee, a few days after the date of the first message, placed this subject in its true light, and thereby exposed himself to similar denunciations. In his speech of 18th December, 1860 ("Congressional Globe," p. 119), he says: "I do not believe the Federal Government has the power to coerce a State, for by the eleventh amendment of the Constitution of the United States it is expressly provided that you cannot even put one of the States of this Confederacy before one of the courts of the country as a party. As a State, the Federal Government has no power to coerce it; but it is a member of the compact to which it agreed in common with the other States, and this Government has the right to pass laws, and to enforce those laws upon individuals within the limits of each State. While the one proposition is clear, the other is equally so. This Government can, by the Constitution of the country, and by the laws enacted in conformity with the Constitution, operate upon individuals, and has the right and the power, not to coerce a State, but to enforce and execute the law upon individuals within the limits of a State."

Sound doctrine, and in conformity with that of the framers of the Constitution! Any other might, according to Mr. Madison, have been construed by the States in rebellion as a dissolution of their connection with the other States, and recognized them as independent belligerents on equal terms with the United States. Happily our civil war was undertaken and prosecuted in self-defence, not to coerce a State, but to enforce the execution of the laws within the States against individuals, and to suppress an unjust rebellion raised by a conspiracy among them against the Government of the United States.

After an impartial review of all the circumstances, and a careful consideration of the danger of the crisis, the President determined to recommend to Congress to initiate such amendments to the Constitution as would recognize and place beyond dispute the rights of the Southern people, as these had been expounded by the Supreme Court. Whilst acknowledging that the cotton States were without justifiable cause for their threatened attempts to break up the Union, either by peaceful secession, as they claimed the right to do, or by forcible rebellion, he could not deny that they had suffered serious wrongs through many years from the Northern abolition party. To deny them such a security would be at war with the noblest feelings of patriotism, and inconsistent with the friendly sentiments which ought ever to be cherished between the people of sister States. We ought first to do our duty toward the cotton States; and if thereafter they should persist in attempting to dissolve the Union, they would expose themselves to universal condemnation. We should first "cast the beam out of our own eye," and then we might see clearly how to deal with our brothers' faults. Besides, such a course would have confirmed the loyalty of the border slaveholding States. And above all, we were bound to make this concession, the strong to the weak, when the object was to restore the fraternal feelings which had presided at the formation of the Constitution, to reëstablish the ancient harmony between the States, and to prevent civil war. Neither the Chicago platform, nor any other political platform, ought to have stood in the way of such a healing measure. The President, therefore, appealed to Congress to propose and recommend " to the legislatures of the several States the remedy for existing evils which the Constitution has itself provided for its own preservation. This has been tried at different critical periods of our history, and always with eminent success. It is to be found in the fifth article providing for its own amendment. Under this article amendments have been proposed by two-thirds of both houses of Congress, and have been 'ratified by the legislatures of three-fourths of the several States,' and have consequently become parts of the Constitution. To this process the country is indebted for the clause prohibiting Congress from passing any law respecting an establishment of religion, or abridging the freedom of speech or of the press, or of the right of petition. To this we are, also, indebted for the Bill of Rights, which secures the people against any abuse of power by the Federal Government. Such were the apprehensions justly entertained by the friends of State rights at that period as to have rendered it extremely doubtful whether the Constitution could have long survived without those amendments.

"Again, the Constitution was amended by the same process, after the election of President Jefferson by the House of Representatives, in February, 1803. This amendment was rendered necessary to prevent a recurrence of the dangers which had seriously threatened the existence of the Government during the pendency of that election. The article for its own amendment was intended to secure the amicable adjustment of conflicting constitutional questions like the present, which might arise between the Governments of the States and that of the United States. This appears from contemporaneous history." * * *

"The explanatory amendment might be confined to the final settlement of the true construction of the Constitution on three special points:

"1. An express recognition of the right of property in slaves in the States where it now exists or may hereafter exist.

"2. The duty of protecting this right in all the common Territories throughout their Territorial existence, and until they shall be admitted as States into the Union, with or without slavery, as their constitutions may prescribe.

"3. A like recognition of the right of the master to have his slave, who has escaped from one State to another, restored and 'delivered up' to him, and of the validity of the fugitive slave law enacted for this purpose, together with a declaration that all State laws impairing or defeating this right are violations of the Constitution, and are consequently null and void. It may be objected that this construction of the Constitution has already been settled by the Supreme Court of the United States, and what more ought to be required? The answer is, that a very large proportion of the people of the United States still contest the correctness of this decision, and never will cease from agitation and admit its binding force until clearly established by the people of the several States in their sovereign character. Such an explanatory amendment would, it is believed, forever terminate the existing dissensions, and restore peace and harmony among the States.

"It ought not to be doubted that such an appeal to the arbitrament established by the Constitution itself, would be received with favor by all the States of the Confederacy. In any event, it ought to be tried in a spirit of conciliation before any of these States shall separate themselves from the Union."

The President accompanied his recommendations by a solemn appeal in favor of the Union. He says:

"But may I be permitted solemnly to invoke my countrymen to pause and deliberate, before they determine to destroy this, the grandest temple which has ever been dedicated to human freedom since the world began. It has been consecrated by the blood of our fathers, by the glories of the past, and by the hopes of the future. The Union has already made us the most prosperous, and ere long will, if preserved, render us the most powerful nation on the face of the earth. In every foreign region of the globe the title of American citizen is held in the highest respect, and when pronounced in a foreign land it causes the hearts of our countrymen to swell with honest pride. Surely when we reach the brink of the yawning abyss, we shall recoil with horror from the last fatal plunge.

"By such a dread catastrophe, the hopes of the friends of freedom throughout the world would be destroyed, and a long night of leaden despotism would enshroud the nations. Our example for more than eighty years would not only be lost, but it would be quoted as a conclusive proof that man is unfit for self-government.

"It is not every wrong—nay, it is not every grievous wrong—which can justify a resort to such a fearful alternative. This ought to be the last desperate remedy of a despairing people, after every constitutional means of conciliation had been exhausted. We should reflect that, under this free Government, there is an incessant ebb and flow in public opinion. The slavery question, like every thing human, will have its day. I firmly believe that it has reached and passed the culminating point. But if, in the midst of the existing excitement, the Union shall perish, the evil may then become irreparable."

This message proved unsatisfactory both to the Republican party and to the Pro-Slavery party in the cotton States. The leaders of this latter party in Congress, and especially Mr. Jefferson Davis, objected to it because of its earnest argument against secession, and the determination expressed to collect the revenue in the ports of South Carolina, by means of a naval force, and to defend the public property. From this moment they alienated themselves from the President. Soon thereafter, when he refused to withdraw Major Anderson from Fort Sumter, on the demand of the self-styled South Carolina Commissioners, the separation became complete. For more than two months before the close of the session all friendly intercourse between them and the President, whether of a political or social character, had ceased.

CHAPTER VII.

Refusal of Congress to act either with a view to conciliation or defence—The Senate Committee of Thirteen and its proceedings—Mr. Crittenden submits his Compromise to the Committee—Its nature—The Committee unable to agree—Testimony of Messrs. Douglas and Toombs that the Crittenden Compromise would have arrested secession in the Cotton States—Mr. Crittenden proposes to refer his amendment to the people of the several States by an act of ordinary legislation—His remarks in its favor—Proceedings thereon—Expression of public opinion in its favor—President Buchanan recommends it—Recommendation disregarded and proposition defeated by the Clark amendment—Observations thereon—Peace Convention proposed by Virginia—Its meeting and proceedings—Amendment to the Constitution reported by Mr. Guthrie, chairman of the committee—Its modification on motion of Mr. Franklin, and final adoption by the Convention—Virginia and North Carolina vote with Connecticut, Maine, Massachusetts, New Hampshire, and Vermont against it—Its rejection by the United States Senate—The House of Representatives refuse even to receive it—Every Republican member in both branches of Congress opposed to it.

IN this perilous condition of the country it would scarcely be believed, were it not demonstrated by the record, that Congress deliberately refused, throughout the entire session, to pass any act or resolution either to preserve the Union by peaceful measures, or to furnish the President or his successor with a military force to repel any attack which might be made by the cotton States. It neither did the one thing nor the other. It neither presented the olive branch nor the sword. All history proves that inaction in such an emergency is the worst possible policy, and can never stay the tide of revolution. On the contrary, it affords the strongest encouragement to rebellion. The sequel will prove the correctness of these opinions.

Then, first, as to the action of Congress on the President's recommendation to adopt amendments to the Constitution. Soon after its meeting, on the motion of Senator Powell, of Kentucky, "so much of the President's Message as relates to the present agitated and distracted condition of the country, and the grievances between the slaveholding and the non-slaveholding States," * was referred to a special committee, consist

* Senate's Report of Committees, 2d session, 36th Congress, 1860-61, No. 288

ing of thirteen members. This committee was composed of the most distinguished and influential Senators. They were true representatives of the political parties to which they respectively belonged. It consisted of five Republicans: Messrs. Seward, Collamer, Wade, Doolittle, and Grimes; five from slaveholding States: Messrs. Powell, Hunter, Crittenden, Toombs, and Davis; and three Northern Democrats: Messrs. Douglas, Bigler, and Bright. The latter three were intended to act as mediators between the extreme parties on the committee.

No legislative body, in the history of nations, had ever created a committee upon whose action more important consequences depended. Beyond question, they had it in their power justly and honorably to preserve the peace of the country and the integrity of the Union.

The committee first met on the 21st December, 1860, and, preliminary to any other proceeding, they "resolved that no proposition shall be reported as adopted, unless sustained by a majority of each of the classes of the committee; Senators of the Republican party to constitute one class, and Senators of the other parties to constitute the other class." This resolution was passed, because any report they might make to the Senate would be in vain unless sanctioned by at least a majority of the five Republican Senators. On the next day (the 22d), Mr. Crittenden submitted to the committee " A Joint Resolution " (the same which he had two days before presented to the Senate), "proposing certain amendments to the Constitution of the United States," now known as the Crittenden Compromise. This was truly a compromise of conflicting claims, because it proposed that the South should surrender their adjudged right to take slaves into all our Territories, provided the North would recognize this right in the Territories south of the old Missouri Compromise line. This amendment offered terms to the North far less favorable to the South than their existing rights under the decision of the Supreme Court.

The Constitution, as expounded by this decision, opens all the Territories, both North and South, as the common property of the States, to the introduction and protection of slave property. Mr. Crittenden's amendment proposed to restrict this general right and confine it to the Territories south of the latitude of 36° 30′. It prohibited slavery forever from all Territories, "now held or hereafter acquired," north of this line, whilst south of it slavery was "recognized as existing, and shall not be interfered with by Congress, but shall be protected as property by all the departments of the Territorial Government during its continuance; and when any Territory north or south of said line, within such boundaries as Congress may prescribe, shall contain' the population requisite for a member of Congress, it shall be admitted into the Union with or without slavery, as the Constitution of such new State may provide." *

This amendment yielded every thing to the North, except a mere abstraction. It gave, in point of fact, all the vast territories of the United States to perpetual freedom, with the single exception of New Mexico. And in regard to this, it is scarcely necessary to state to any person in the least degree acquainted with geography, that New Mexico could never practically become a slaveholding State. As to the Indian Territory south of 36° 30′, it belongs not to the United States, but is secured to the Indians by solemn treaties, founded upon full and indeed ample equivalents.

At the first it was confidently expected that this amendment would be yielded by the North as a peace offering to the South. It was in substance and in fact neither more nor less than an offer to restore the Missouri Compromise, against the repeal of which the Republican party in Congress, in 1854, had so justly struggled. It was hailed by the people throughout the country as the rainbow upon the cloud, promising peace and perpetuity to the Union. Indeed, who could fail to believe that when the alternative was presented to the Senators and Representatives of the Northern States, either to yield to their brethren in the South the barren abstraction of carrying their slaves into New Mexico, or to expose the country to the imminent peril of civil war, they would choose the side of peace and union? The period for action was still propitious. It will be recollected that Mr. Crittenden's amendment was submitted before any of our forts had been seized, before any of the cotton States, except

* Senate Report of the Proceedings of the Committee, Dec. 31, 1860.

South Carolina, had seceded, and before any of the Conventions which had been called in the remaining six of these States had assembled. Under such circumstances it would have been true wisdom to seize the propitious moment before it fled forever, and even yield, if need be, a trifling concession to patriotic policy, if not to abstract justice, rather than expose the country to a great impending calamity. And how small the concession required even from a sincere anti-slavery Republican! In the language of Mr. Crittenden: "The sacrifice to be made for its preservation [that of the Union] is comparatively worthless. Peace and harmony and union in a great nation were never purchased at so cheap a rate as we now have it in our power to do. It is a scruple only, a scruple of as little value as a barleycorn, that stands between us and peace and reconciliation and union; and we stand here pausing and hesitating about that little atom which is to be sacrificed."*

Notwithstanding these powerful arguments in favor of the Crittenden Compromise, it was rejected by the Committee of Thirteen, every one of its five Republican members, together with Messrs. Davis and Toombs, from the cotton States, having voted against it. Indeed, not one of all the Republicans in the Senate, at any period or in any form, voted in its favor, doubtless for the reason that it tolerated slavery within New Mexico, in opposition to the Chicago platform. This they held paramount to every other consideration.

The committee, having failed to arrive at a satisfactory conclusion, reported their disagreement to the Senate on the 31st December, 1860, in a resolution declaring that they had "not been able to agree upon any general plan of adjustment."† Thus on the last day of the year 1860 vanished the reasonable prospect that any of the seven cotton States would voluntarily remain in the Union. Soon thereafter the Conventions of Florida on the 7th January, Mississippi the 9th, Alabama the 11th, Georgia the 19th, Louisiana the 25th, and Texas the 5th February, adopted ordinances of secession by overwhelming majorities. Several of these States, after the evil example of South Carolina,

---

* Con. Globe, 3d Jan., 1861, p. 237.
† Senate Report of Committee, 1860–'61, No. 288.

proceeded to seize the public property within their limits; and the authorities of Louisiana, even before her ordinance of secession, more outrageous than the rest, robbed the Branch Mint and Sub-Treasury at New Orleans of a large amount of money.

But was Mr. Crittenden correct in believing, notwithstanding the adverse vote of Messrs. Davis and Toombs in the committee, that the adoption of his amendment would have arrested secession in the cotton States? There is good reason to believe that he was, with the exception of South Carolina; and she could not long have remained in a state of isolation. On this question we have the published testimony of two members of the Committee of Thirteen, which has never since been contradicted. Mr. Douglas, in his speech of the 3d January, 1861, but three days after the report of the committee and within the hearing of all its members, said: "If you of the Republican side are not willing to accept this [a proposition for adjustment made by himself] nor the proposition of the Senator from Kentucky (Mr. Crittenden), pray tell us what you are willing to do. I address the inquiry to the Republicans alone, for the reason that in the Committee of Thirteen, a few days ago, every member from the South, including those from the cotton States (Messrs. Toombs and Davis), expressed their readiness to accept the proposition of my venerable friend from Kentucky (Mr. Crittenden), as a final settlement of the controversy, if tendered and sustained by the Republican members. Hence the sole responsibility of our disagreement, and the only difficulty in the way of an amicable adjustment, is with the Republican party."*

And Mr. Douglas, afterwards, on the 2d of March, 1861, reaffirmed his former statement. In replying to Senator Pugh (of Ohio), he said: "The Senator has said that if the Crittenden proposition could have been passed early in the session, it would have saved all the States except South Carolina. I firmly believe it would. While the Crittenden proposition was not in accordance with my cherished views, I avowed my readiness and eagerness to accept it, in order to save the Union, if we could unite upon it. No man has labored harder than I have to get it passed. I can confirm the Senator's declaration that Sen-

* Appendix to Con. Globe, 1860–'61, p. 41.

ator Davis himself, when on the Committee of Thirteen, was ready, at all times, to compromise on the Crittenden proposition. I will go further and say that Mr. Toombs was also ready to do so." *

Besides, on the 7th January, 1861, Mr. Toombs, only twelve days before his State seceded, said: "But although I insist upon this perfect equality in the Territories, when it was proposed, as I understand the Senator from Kentucky now proposes, that the line of 36° 30' shall be extended, acknowledging and protecting our property on the south side of that line, for the sake of peace, permanent peace, I said to the Committee of Thirteen, and I say here, that with other satisfactory provisions, I would accept it," etc., etc.†

Mr. Crittenden did not despair of ultimate success, notwithstanding his defeat before the Committee of Thirteen. After this, indeed, he could no longer expect to carry his compromise as an amendment to the Constitution by the necessary two-thirds vote of Congress. It was, therefore, postponed by the Senate on his own motion.‡ As a substitute for it he submitted to the Senate, on the 3d January, 1861, a joint resolution (S. No. 54), which might be passed by a bare majority of both Houses. This was to refer his rejected amendment, by an ordinary Act of Congress, to a direct vote of the people of the several States. This he prefaced by some striking remarks. He said: "The times on which we have fallen, sir, are of a very extraordinary character; full of danger to the peace of the country, and even to the union of the country. Its extraordinary character seems to require of us all efforts, ordinary and extraordinary, for the purpose of averting the danger which now so threateningly hangs over us. The measure which I am about to propose, sir, is of that extraordinary character; and I shall be at a loss for a justification and excuse for it, if it cannot be found in the perilous condition of public affairs, and in that great law, the safety of the people."

He then proceeded to offer his resolution in the following language: "Whereas the Union is in danger, and, owing to the

* Con. Globe, 1860-'61, p. 1391.   † Ibid., p. 270.
‡ Ibid., p. 237.

unhappy divisions existing in Congress, it would be difficult, if not impossible, for that body to concur in both its branches by the requisite majority, so as to enable it either to adopt such measures of legislation, or to recommend to the States such amendments to the Constitution, as are deemed necessary and proper to avert that danger; and whereas in so great an emergency the opinion and judgment of the people ought to be heard, and would be the best and surest guide to their Representatives: Therefore, *Resolved*, That provision ought to be made by law without delay for taking the sense of the people and submitting to their vote the following resolution [the same as in his former amendment], as the basis for the final and permanent settlement of those disputes that now disturb the peace of the country and threaten the existence of the Union."

It was supposed that this resolution would conciliate the support of some at least, if not all, of the Republican Senators. By referring the questions in dispute to the legitimate fountain of all political power, it would relieve them from previous committals to the Chicago platform. Besides, it was believed that they would not assume the responsibility of denying to the people of their own States the opportunity of expressing an opinion at the ballot-box on questions involving no less a stake than the peace and safety of the Union. Nevertheless, it will appear from the sequel, that not a single Republican Senator ever voted for the resolution. Had Congress thought proper to refer the Crittenden Compromise to the people of the several States, no person who observed the current of public opinion at the time, can fail to believe that outside of South Carolina it would have received their approbation. Memorials in its favor poured into Congress from all portions of the North, even from New England.* One of these presented to the Senate was from "the Mayor and members of the Board of Aldermen and the Common Council of the city of Boston, and over 22,000 citizens of the State of Massachusetts, praying the adoption of the compromise measures proposed by Mr. Crittenden." † It may be proper here to observe that the resolution of Mr. Crit-

---

* Index to Senate Journal, pp. 494, 495, and 496.
† Senate Journal, 1860–'61, p. 218.

tenden did not provide in detail for holding elections by which "the sense of the people" could be ascertained. To supply this omission, Senator Bigler, of Pennsylvania, the able, indefatigable, and devoted friend of the measure, on the 14th January, 1861, brought in "A bill to provide for taking the sense of the people of the United States on certain proposed amendments to the Constitution of the United States;" but never was he able, notwithstanding his persevering efforts, to induce the Senate even to consider this bill.

President Buchanan, in the mean time, and from the beginning, exerted all his constitutional influence in favor of these measures. In his special message to Congress of the 8th January, 1861, after depicting the deplorable consequences which had already resulted to the country from the bare apprehension of civil war and the dissolution of the Union, he says: "Let the question be transferred from political assemblies to the ballot-box, and the people themselves would speedily redress the serious grievances which the South have suffered. But, in Heaven's name, let the trial be made before we plunge into armed conflict upon the mere assumption that there is no other alternative. Time is a great conservative power. Let us pause at this momentous point, and afford the people, both North and South, an opportunity for reflection. Would that South Carolina had been convinced of this truth before her precipitate action! I, therefore, appeal through you to the people of the country, to declare in their might that the Union must and shall be preserved by all constitutional means. I most earnestly recommend that you devote yourselves exclusively to the question how this can be accomplished in peace. All other questions, when compared with this, sink into insignificance. The present is no time for palliatives; action, prompt action is required. A delay in Congress to prescribe or to recommend a distinct and practical proposition for conciliation, may drive us to a point from which it will be almost impossible to recede.

"A common ground on which conciliation and harmony can be produced is surely not unattainable. The proposition to compromise by letting the North have exclusive control of the territory above a certain line, and to give Southern institutions protection below that line, ought to receive universal approbation. In itself, indeed, it may not be entirely satisfactory, but when the alternative is between a reasonable concession on both sides and a dissolution of the Union, it is an imputation on the patriotism of Congress to assert that its members will hesitate for a moment."

This earnest recommendation was totally disregarded. It would be a useless labor to recapitulate all the proceedings in the Senate upon the proposition of Mr. Crittenden to refer his amendment to a vote of the people. On the 14th January, 1861, he made an unsuccessful attempt to have it considered, but it was postponed until the day following.* On this day it was again postponed by the vote of every Republican Senator present, in order to make way for the Pacific Railroad bill.† On the third attempt (January 16), he succeeded, but by a majority of a single vote, in bringing his resolution before the body. Every Republican Senator present voted against its consideration. A direct vote upon the resolution, so earnestly desired by the country, now seemed inevitable. The parliamentary tactics of the Republican party, however, defeated this object. Mr. Clark, a Republican Senator from New Hampshire, moved to strike out the entire preamble and resolution of Mr. Crittenden, and in lieu thereof insert as a substitute a preamble and resolution of a directly opposite character, and in accordance with the Chicago platform. This motion prevailed by a vote of 25 to 23, every Republican Senator present having voted in its favor.‡ Thus Mr. Crittenden's proposition to refer the question to the people was buried under the Clark amendment. This continued to be its position for more than six weeks, until the day before the final adjournment of Congress, 2d March, when it was far too late for final action even had there been a majority in its favor. This superincumbent weight was then removed, and the proposition itself was defeated by a vote of 19 in the affirmative against 20 in the negative.§ Thus the Republican party accomplished their object, and thus terminated every rea-

* Con. Globe, 1860–'61, . 361–363. † Ibid., p. 381.
‡ Ibid., p. 409. § Ibid., p. 1405.

sonable hope of any compromise between the North and the South.

It is proper for future reference that the names of those Senators who constituted the majority on this momentous question, should be placed upon record. Every vote given from the six New England States was in opposition to Mr. Crittenden's resolution. These consisted of Mr. Clark, of New Hampshire; Messrs. Sumner and Wilson, of Massachusetts; Mr. Anthony, of Rhode Island; Messrs. Dixon and Foster, of Connecticut; Mr. Foot, of Vermont; and Mr. Fessenden, of Maine. The remaining twelve votes, in order to make up the 20, were given by Messrs. Bingham and Wade, of Ohio; Mr. Trumbull, of Illinois; Messrs. Bingham and Chandler, of Michigan; Messrs. Grimes and Harlan, of Iowa; Messrs. Doolittle and Durkee, of Wisconsin; Mr. Wilkinson, of Minnesota; Mr. King, of New York; and Mr. Ten Eyck, of New Jersey. It is also worthy of observation, that neither Mr. Hale, of New Hampshire, Mr. Simmons, of Rhode Island, Mr. Collamer, of Vermont, Mr. Seward, of New York, nor Mr. Cameron, of Pennsylvania, voted on the question, although it appears from the journal that all these gentlemen were present in the Senate on the day of the vote. It would be vain to conjecture the reasons why these five Senators refrained from voting on an occasion so important.

It will be recollected that a direct vote of the Senate on the Crittenden resolution was defeated by the adoption of the Clark amendment, at so early a period of the session as the 16th January, when there was still time for action. This amendment prevailed only in consequence of the refusal of six secession Senators to vote against it. They thus played into the hands of the Republican Senators, and rendered them a most acceptable service. These were Messrs. Benjamin and Slidell, of Louisiana; Mr. Iverson, of Georgia; Messrs. Hemphill and Wigfall, of Texas; and Mr. Johnson, of Arkansas. Had these gentlemen voted with their brethren from the border slaveholding States and the other Democratic Senators, the Clark amendment would have been defeated, and the Senate would then have been brought to a direct vote on the Crittenden resolution.

Had this been effected and the Crittenden resolution adopted by the Senate, as it might have been by the votes of the recusant Senators, this would have awakened the people of the country to their true condition, and might have aroused them into action in sufficient time before the close of the session to avert the impending danger. As it was, they remained in a state of suspense, and still continued to hope until the very day before the termination of Congress, when all hope was finally extinguished. Such conduct on the part of these six Senators cannot be too severely censured. They thus deserted the Democratic Senators from the border slaveholding and other States, at the hour of their utmost need. It is but a poor excuse for their defection to say, as they did, that the Republican Senators, whose votes were necessary to any effectual compromise, had steadily repudiated the Crittenden propositions in every form, and for this reason they were already on the eve of abandoning their seats in the Senate.

Whilst the lovers of peace were almost despairing for the fate of the Crittenden amendment, their hope of its final triumph was revived by the interposition of Virginia.* The General Assembly of that Commonwealth, on the 19th January, 1861, adopted resolutions expressing " the deliberate opinion " " that unless the unhappy controversy which now divides the States of the Confederacy shall be satisfactorily adjusted, a permanent dissolution of the Union is inevitable." For the purpose of averting " so dire a calamity," they extended an invitation "to all such States, whether slaveholding or non-slaveholding, as are willing to unite with Virginia in an earnest effort to adjust the present unhappy controversies, in the spirit in which the Constitution was originally framed," to appoint Commissioners for this purpose, to meet on the 4th February, 1861, at the City of Washington. The resolutions expressed a favorable opinion of the Crittenden Compromise, with some modifications, and the belief that " it would be accepted as a satisfactory adjustment by the people of this Commonwealth." Such was the origin of the Peace Convention. The best hopes of the country were now fixed on the border slave States, in-

* Con. Globe, 1860–'61, p. 601.

cluding North Carolina and Tennessee. These great and powerful commonwealths still remained faithful to the Union. They had hitherto stood aloof from secession, and had manifested an earnest desire not only to remain in the Union themselves, but to exert their powerful influence to bring back the seceding sisters. Virginia had ever ranked as chief among the Southern States, and had exercised great influence over their counsels. She had now taken the lead in the grand design to save the Union, and it became the duty of the President to render her all the aid in his power in a cause so holy. Every reflecting man foresaw that if the present movement of Virginia should fail to impress upon Congress and the country the necessity for adopting a peaceful compromise, like that proposed by Mr. Crittenden, there was imminent danger that all the border slave States would follow the cotton States, which had already adopted ordinances of secession, and unite with them in an attempt to break up the Union. Indeed, as has been already seen, the Virginia Legislature had declared that, in case of failure, such a dissolution was "inevitable."

The Peace Convention met on the 4th February.* It was composed of one hundred and thirty-three commissioners, representing twenty-one States. A bare inspection of the list will convince all inquirers of the great respectability and just influence of its members. Among them there were many venerable and distinguished citizens from the border States, earnestly intent upon restoring and saving the Union. Their great object was to prevail upon their associates from the North to unite with them in such recommendations to Congress as would prevent their own States from seceding, and enable them to bring back the cotton States which had already seceded. It will be recollected that on the 4th February, when the Peace Convention assembled, six of the cotton States, South Carolina, Alabama, Mississippi, Georgia, Louisiana, and Florida, had already adopted ordinances of secession; and that but four days thereafter (8th February) deputies from these States had adopted and published at Montgomery, Alabama, a Provisional Constitution for the so-called Confederate States. The Union was then crumbling to

* Con. Globe, 1860-'61, p. 125.

pieces. One month only of the session of Congress remained. Within this brief period it was necessary that the Convention should recommend amendments to the Constitution in sufficient time to enable both Houses to act upon them before their final adjournment. It was also essential to success that these amendments should be sustained by a decided majority of the commissioners both from the Northern and the border States. It was, however, soon discovered that the same malign influence which had caused every Republican member of Congress to oppose the Crittenden Compromise, would probably defeat the patriotic purpose for which the Convention had assembled.

On Wednesday, the 6th February, a resolution was adopted,* on motion of Mr. Guthrie, of Kentucky, to refer the resolutions of the General Assembly of Virginia, and all other kindred subjects, to a committee to consist of one commissioner from each State, to be selected by the respective State delegations; and to prevent delay they were instructed to report on or before the Friday following (the 8th), "what they may deem right, necessary, and proper to restore harmony and preserve the Union."

This committee, instead of reporting on the day appointed, did not report until Friday, the 15th February,† and thus a precious week was lost. The reason for this delay shall be expressed in the language of Mr. Reverdy Johnson, a member of the committee and a commissioner from Maryland. In his letter of 13th May, 1863, to the editors of the "Journal of Commerce," in answer to allegations made by Mr. David D. Field, who had also been a member of the committee from New York, he says: "In the committee to whom the whole subject was referred, and at whose head was placed Mr. Guthrie, of Kentucky, and of which Mr. Field was a member, efforts to this end [reasonable guarantees to the South on the subject of slavery] were made again and again, but in vain. And what was finally agreed upon and reported, met with the sanction of but a bare majority of the committee, Mr. Field not being of that majority. The discussions in every meeting of the committee were earnest, and a part of the Southern members (I was of the number) im-

---
* Official Journal of the Convention, pp. 9 and 10. † Ibid., p. 21.

plored their Northern brethren to agree to something that there was any reason to believe would be satisfactory to the South. I saw then that unanimity could alone render the propositions of the committee effective. I also saw, and as the result has proved, that no satisfactory adjustment attained, an attempt at least would be made to sever the Union." (The cotton States had already attempted to sever it so far as this was in their power.)

The amendments reported by a majority of the committee, through Mr. Guthrie, their chairman, were substantially the same with the Crittenden Compromise; but on motion of Mr. Johnson, of Maryland, the general terms of the first and by far the most important section were restricted to the *present* Territories of the United States.* On motion of Mr. Franklin, of Pennsylvania, this section was further amended, but not materially changed, by the adoption of the substitute offered by him. Nearly in this form it was afterwards adopted by the Convention.† The following is a copy: "In all the present territory of the United States north of the parallel of thirty-six degrees and thirty minutes of north latitude, involuntary servitude, except in punishment of crime, is prohibited. In all the present territory south of that line, the status of persons held to involuntary service or labor, as it now exists, shall not be changed; nor shall any law be passed by Congress or the Territorial Legislature to hinder or prevent the taking of such persons from any of the States of this Union to said territory, nor to impair the rights arising from said relation; but the same shall be subject to judicial cognizance in the Federal courts, according to the course of the common law. When any Territory north or south of said line, within such boundary as Congress may prescribe, shall contain a population equal to that required for a member of Congress, it shall, if its form of government be republican, be admitted into the Union on an equal footing with the original States, with or without involuntary servitude, as the Constitution of such State may provide."

Mr. Baldwin, of Connecticut, and Mr. Seddon, of Virginia, on opposite extremes, made minority reports, which they pro-

* Official Journal, p. 42.   † Ibid., p. 70.

posed to substitute for that of the majority. Mr. Baldwin's report was a recommendation "to the several States to unite with Kentucky in her application to Congress to call a Convention for proposing amendments to the Constitution of the United States, to be submitted to the Legislatures of the several States, or to Conventions therein, for ratification, as the one or the other mode of ratification may be proposed by Congress, in accordance with the provisions in the fifth article of the Constitution." *

Of the two modes prescribed by the Constitution for its own amendment, this was the least eligible at the existing crisis, because by far the most dilatory. Instead of calling upon Congress, then in session and which could act immediately, to propose specific amendments to the Legislatures of the several States, it adopted the circuitous mode of requesting these Legislatures, in the first instance, to apply to Congress to call a Convention. Even should two-thirds of them respond in the affirmative to this request, the process would necessarily occasion a delay of years in attaining the object, when days were all-important. This would entirely defeat the patriotic purpose of the Peace Convention. It was called to obtain, if possible, a direct vote of two-thirds of both Houses before the end of the session in favor of such amendments as it might recommend. Could such a vote be obtained, it was confidently expected by the friends of the Union that its moral influence would, for the present, satisfy the border States; would arrest the tide beginning to rise among their people in favor of secession, and might enable them to exercise an effective influence in reclaiming the States which had already seceded. Affairs were then so urgent that long before the State Legislatures could possibly ask Congress to call a Convention as required by Mr. Baldwin's proposition, the cause of the Union might be hopeless. It was, therefore, rejected.

This proposition of Mr. Baldwin, evasive and dilatory as it was, nevertheless received the votes of eight of the twenty-one States.† These consisted of the whole of the New England States, except Rhode Island, and of Illinois, Iowa, and New York, all being free States. This was an evil omen.

* Official Journal pp. 24 and 25.   † Ibid., p. 63.

The first amendment reported by Mr. Seddon differed from that of the majority inasmuch as it embraced not only the present but all future Territories.* This was rejected.† His second amendment, which, however, was never voted upon by the Convention, went so far as distinctly to recognize the right of secession.

It cannot be denied that there was in the Convention an extreme Southern rights element, headed by Mr. Seddon. This manifested itself throughout its proceedings. These show how naturally extremes meet. On more than one important occasion, we find the vote of Virginia and North Carolina, though given in each case by a bare majority of their commissioners, side by side with the vote of Massachusetts and Vermont. It would be too tedious to trace the proceedings of the Convention from the report of the committee made by Mr. Guthrie until its final adjournment. It is sufficient to say that more than ten days were consumed in discussion and in voting upon various propositions offered by individual commissioners. The final vote was not reached until Tuesday, the 26th February, when it was taken on the first and vitally important section, as amended.‡

This section, on which all the rest depended, was negatived by a vote of eight States to eleven. Those which voted in its favor were Delaware, Kentucky, Maryland, New Jersey, Ohio, Pennsylvania, Rhode Island, and Tennessee. And those in the negative were Connecticut, Illinois, Iowa, Maine, Massachusetts, Missouri, New York, North Carolina, New Hampshire, Vermont, and Virginia. It is but justice to say that Messrs. Ruffin and Morehead, of North Carolina, and Messrs. Rives and Summers, of Virginia, two of the five commissioners from each of these States, declared their dissent from the vote of their respective States. So, also, did Messrs. Bronson, Corning, Dodge, Wool, and Granger, five of the eleven New York commissioners, dissent from the vote of their State. On the other hand, Messrs. Meredith and Wilmot, two of the seven commissioners from Pennsylvania, dissented from the majority in voting in favor of the section. Thus would the Convention have ter-

* Off. Journal, pp: 26, 27, and 28. † Ibid., p. 28. ‡ Ibid., p. 70.

minated but for the interposition of Illinois. Immediately after the section had been negatived, the commissioners from that State made a motion to reconsider the vote, and this prevailed. The Convention afterwards adjourned until the next morning. When they reassembled (February 27), the first section was adopted, but only by a majority of nine to eight States, nine being less than a majority of the States represented. This change was effected by a change of the vote of Illinois from the negative to the affirmative; by Missouri withholding her vote, and by a tie in the New York commissioners, on account of the absence of one of their number, rendering it impossible for the State to vote. Still Virginia and North Carolina, in the one extreme, and Connecticut, Maine, Massachusetts, New Hampshire, and Vermont, in the other, persisted in voting in the negative. From the nature of this vote, it was manifestly impossible that two-thirds of both Houses of Congress should act favorably on the amendment, even if the delay had not already rendered such action impracticable before the close of the session.

It would be useless to refer to the voting on the remaining sections of the amendment, which were carried by small majorities.* The Convention, on the same day, through Mr. Tyler, their President, communicated to the Senate and House of Representatives the amendment they had adopted, embracing all the sections, with a request that it might be submitted by Congress, under the Constitution, to the several State Legislatures. In the Senate this was immediately referred to a select committee, on motion of Mr. Crittenden. The committee, on the next day (28th Feb.), † reported a joint resolution (No. 70) proposing it as an amendment to the Constitution, but he was never able to bring the Senate to a direct vote upon it.‡ Failing in this, he made a motion to substitute the amendment of the Peace Convention for his own.§ This he prefaced by declaring that he looked upon the result of the deliberations of that body "as affording the best opportunity for a general concurrence among the States, and among the people." He, therefore, "had determined to take it in preference to his own proposi-

---

* Senate Journal, pp. 332, 333.   † Ibid., p. 337.   ‡ Ibid., p. 384.
§ Con. Globe, 1860–'61, p. 1404.

tion, and had so stated to many of the members of the Convention." He further said that he had "examined the propositions offered by that Convention; they contain, in my judgment, every material provision that is contained in the resolution called the Crittenden Resolution." He also had adopted this course " out of deference to that great body of men selected on the resolution of Virginia, and invited by Virginia herself. The body having met, and being composed of such men, and a majority of that Convention concurring in these resolutions, I think they come to us with a sanction entitling them to consideration." Mr. Crittenden's reasons failed to convince the Senate, and his motion was rejected by a large majority (28 to 7).* Then next in succession came the memorable vote on Mr. Crittenden's own resolution, and it was in its turn defeated, as we have already stated, by a majority of 20 against 19.

We cannot take leave of this venerable patriot, who so wisely appreciated the existing danger, without paying a just tribute to the vigor and perseverance of his repeated efforts to ward off from his country the direful calamity of disunion and civil war. Well did he merit the almost unanimous vote of the Virginia Convention, on the 11th March, tendering him the thanks of the people of Virginia for "his recent able, zealous, and patriotic efforts in the Senate of the United States, to bring about a just and honorable adjustment of our national difficulties." † This vote, we may remark, was far from being complimentary to the conduct of a majority of their own commissioners (Messrs. Tyler, Brockenbrough, and Seddon) in the Peace Convention.

In the House of Representatives, the amendment proposed by the Convention was treated with still less respect than it had been by the Senate.‡ The Speaker was refused leave even to present it.§ Every effort made for this purpose was successfully resisted by leading Republican members. The consequence is that a copy of it does not even appear in the Journal.

Although the amendment was somewhat less favorable to the South, and ought, therefore, to have been more acceptable to the North than the Crittenden amendment, yet like this it

* Senate Journal, p. 386. † National Intelligencer, March 14, 1861.
‡ Con. Globe, pp. 1331, 1332, 1333. § House Journal, pp. 446, 448, 449.

encountered the opposition of every Republican member in both Houses of Congress. Nevertheless, it presented a basis of compromise which, had it been conceded by the North, might and probably would have been accepted by the people of the border States, in preference to the fearful alternative of their secession from the Union.

CHAPTER VIII.

Congress passes no measures to enable the President to execute the laws or defend the Government—They decline to revive the authority of the Federal Judiciary in South Carolina, suspended by the resignation of all the judicial officers—They refuse authority to call forth the militia or accept volunteers, to suppress insurrections against the United States, and it was never proposed to grant an appropriation for this purpose—The Senate declines throughout the entire session to act upon the nomination of a Collector of the Port of Charleston—Congress refuses to grant to the President the authority long since expired, which had been granted to General Jackson for the collection of the revenue—The 36th Congress expires, leaving the law just as they found it—General observations.

WE have already seen that Congress, throughout the entire session, refused to adopt any measures of compromise to prevent civil war, or to retain first the cotton or afterwards the border States within the Union. Failing to do this, and whilst witnessing the secession of one after another of the cotton States, the withdrawal of their Senators and Representatives, and the formation of their Confederacy, it was the imperative duty of Congress to furnish the President or his successor the means of repelling force by force, should this become necessary to preserve the Union. They, nevertheless, refused to perform this duty with as much pertinacity as they had manifested in repudiating all measures of compromise.

1. At the meeting of Congress a Federal Judiciary had ceased to exist in South Carolina. The District Judge, the District Attorney, and the United States Marshal had resigned their offices. These ministers of justice had all deserted their posts before the act of secession, and the laws of the United States could no longer be enforced through their agency. We have already seen that the President, in his message, called the

attention of Congress to this subject, but no attempt was made in either House to provide a remedy for the evil.

2. Congress positively refused to pass a law conferring on the President authority to call forth the militia, or accept the services of volunteers, to suppress insurrections which might occur in any State against the Government of the United States. It may appear strange that this power had not long since been vested in the Executive. The Act of February 28, 1795,* the only law applicable to the subject, provides alone for calling forth the militia to suppress insurrections against State Governments, without making any similar provision for suppressing insurrections against the Government of the United States. If any thing were required beyond a mere inspection of the act to render this clear, it may be found in the opinion of Attorney-General Black, of the 20th November, 1860. Indeed it is a plain *casus omissus.* This palpable omission, which ought to have been instantly supplied, was suffered to continue until after the end of Mr. Buchanan's administration, when on the 29th July, 1861, Congress conferred this necessary power on the President.† The framers of the Act of 1795 either did not anticipate an insurrection within any State against the Federal Government, or if they did, they purposely abstained from providing for it. Even in regard to insurrections against a State Government, so jealous were they of any interference on the part of the Federal Government with the rights of the States, that they withheld from Congress the power to protect any State " against domestic violence," except " on the application of the Legislature, or of the Executive (when the Legislature cannot be convened)." Under the Act of 1795, therefore, the President is precluded from acting even upon his own personal and absolute knowledge of the existence of such an insurrection. Before he can call forth the militia for its suppression, he must first be applied to for this purpose by the appropriate State authorities, in the manner prescribed by the Constitution. It was the duty of Congress, immediately after their meeting, to supply this defect in our laws, and to confer an absolute authority on the President to call forth the militia, and accept the services of volun-

---

* 1 Stat. at Large, p. 424. † 12 U. S. Stat. at Large, p. 281.

teers, to suppress insurrections against the United States, whenever or wherever they might occur. This was a precautionary measure which, independently of existing dangers, ought long since to have formed a part of our permanent legislation. But no attempt was ever made in Congress to adopt it until after the President's special message of the 8th January, 1861, and then the attempt entirely failed. Meanwhile the aspect of public affairs had become more and more threatening. Mr. Crittenden's amendment had been defeated before the Committee of Thirteen, on the last day of December; and it was also highly probable that his proposition before the Senate to refer it to a vote of the people of the States, would share the same fate. South Carolina and Florida had already seceded, and the other cotton States had called Conventions for the purpose of seceding. Nay, more, several of them had already seized the forts, magazines, and arsenals within their limits. Still all this failed to produce any effect upon Congress. It was at this crisis the President sent his special message to Congress (8th January, 1861), by which he endeavored to impress them with the necessity for immediate action. He concealed nothing from them. Whilst still clinging to the fading hope that they might yet provide for a peaceful adjustment of our difficulties, and strongly recommending this course, he says: "Even now the danger is upon us. In several of the States which have not yet seceded, the forts, arsenals, and magazines of the United States have been seized. This is by far the most serious step which has been taken since the commencement of the troubles. * * * The seizure of this property, from all appearances, has been purely aggressive, and not in resistance to any attempt to coerce a State or States to remain in the Union." He also stated the well-known fact that our small army was on the remote frontiers, and was scarcely sufficient to guard the inhabitants against Indian incursions, and consequently our forts were without sufficient garrisons.

Under these circumstances he appeals to Congress in the following language: "But the dangerous and hostile attitude of the States toward each other has already far transcended and cast in the shade the ordinary executive duties already provided for by law, and has assumed such vast and alarming proportions as to place the subject entirely above and beyond executive control. The fact cannot be disguised that we are in the midst of a great revolution. In all its various bearings, therefore, I commend the question to Congress, as the only human tribunal, under Providence, possessing the power to meet the existing emergency. To them exclusively belongs the power to declare war, or to authorize the employment of military force in all cases contemplated by the Constitution; and they alone possess the power to remove grievances which might lead to war, and to secure peace and union to this distracted country. On them, and on them alone, rests the responsibility."

Congress might, had they thought proper, have regarded the forcible seizure of these forts and other property, including that of the Branch Mint at New Orleans with all the treasure it contained, as the commencement of an aggressive war. Beyond question the cotton States had now committed acts of open hostility against the Federal Government. They had always contended that secession was a peaceful constitutional remedy, and that Congress had no power to make war against a sovereign State for the purpose of coercing her to remain in the Union. They could no longer shelter themselves under this plea. They had by their violent action entirely changed the position they had assumed; and instead of peacefully awaiting the decision of Congress on the question of coercion, they had themselves become the coercionists and assailants. This question had, therefore, passed away. No person has ever doubted the right or the duty of Congress to pass laws enabling the President to defend the Union against armed rebellion. Congress, however, still shrunk from the responsibility of passing any such laws. This might have been commendable had it proceeded from a sincere desire not to interpose obstacles to a compromise intended to prevent the effusion of fraternal blood and restore the Union. Still in any event the time had arrived when it was their duty to make at the least contingent provisions for the prosecution of the war, should this be rendered inevitable. This had become the more necessary as Congress would soon expire, and the new Congress could not be convened for a considerable period after the old one had ceased to exist, because a large portion of the Representatives had not then been elected. These reasons, however, produced no effect.

The President's special message * was referred, two days after its date (10th January), by the House of Representatives to a special committee, of which Mr. Howard, of Michigan, was chairman. Nothing was heard from this committee for the space of twenty days. They then, on the 30th January, through Mr. John H. Reynolds, of New York, one of its members, reported a bill † enabling the President to call forth the militia or to accept the services of volunteers for the purpose of protecting the forts, magazines, arsenals, and other property of the United States; and to "recover possession" of such of these as "has been or may hereafter be unlawfully seized or taken possession of by any combination of persons whatever." Had this bill become a law, it would have been the duty of the President at once to raise a volunteer or militia force to recapture the forts which had been already seized. But Congress was not then prepared to assume such a responsibility. Mr. Reynolds accordingly withdrew his bill from the consideration of the House on the very day it was reported. On his own motion it was recommitted, and thus killed as soon as it saw the light. It was never heard of more.

Then, after another pause of nineteen days, and only a fortnight before the close of the session, the Committee on Military Affairs, through Mr. Stanton, of Ohio, their chairman, on the 18th February reported another bill § on the subject, but of a more limited character than that which had been withdrawn. It is remarkable that it contains no provision touching the recovery of the forts and other property which had been already seized by the delinquent States. It did no more than provide that the powers already possessed by the President, under the Act of 1795, to employ the militia in suppressing insurrections against a State Government, should be "extended to the case of insurrections against the authority of the United States," with the additional authority to "accept the services of such volunteers

---

* Con. Globe, p. 816.   † Ibid., p. 645, bills of H. R., No. 698.
§ Ibid., p. 1001, bill 1003, H. R.

as may offer their services for the purpose mentioned." Thus all hostile action for the recovery of the forts already seized was excluded from the bill. It is difficult to conceive what reasonable objection could be made to this bill, except that it did not go far enough and embrace the forts already seized; and more especially as when it was reported we may recollect that the Confederate Congress had already been ten days in session at Montgomery, Alabama, and had adopted a Provisional Constitution. Notwithstanding all this, the House refused to act upon it. The bill was discussed on several occasions until Tuesday, 26th February. On that day a motion was made by Mr. Corwin, of Ohio, to postpone its consideration until Thursday, the 28th February.* Mr. Stanton, the reporter of the bill, resisted this motion, stating that such a postponement would be fatal to it. "It will," said he, "be impossible after that to have it passed by the Senate" (before the 4th March). He, therefore, demanded the ayes and noes; and notwithstanding his warning, Mr. Corwin's motion prevailed by a vote of 100 to 74, and thus the bill was defeated.

It may be proper to observe that Mr. Corwin, whose motion killed the bill, was a confidential friend of the President elect, then present in Washington, and was soon thereafter appointed minister to Mexico.

But even had Congress passed this bill, it would have proved wholly inefficient for want of an appropriation to carry it into effect. The Treasury was empty; but had it been full, the President could not have drawn from it any, even the most trifling sum, without a previous appropriation by law. The union of the purse with the sword, in the hands of the Executive, is wholly inconsistent with the idea of a free government. The power of the legislative branch to withhold money from the Executive, and thus restrain him from dangerous projects of his own, is a necessary safeguard of liberty. This exists in every government pretending to be free. Hence our Constitution has declared that "no money shall be drawn from the Treasury but in consequence of appropriations made by law." It is, therefore, apparent that even if this bill had become a

* Con. Globe, 1232.

law, it could not have been carried into effect by the President without a direct violation of the Constitution. Notwithstanding these insuperable obstacles, no member of either House, throughout the entire session, ever even proposed to raise or appropriate a single dollar for the defence of the Government against armed rebellion. Congress not only refused to grant the President the authority and force necessary to suppress insurrections against the United States; but the Senate, by refusing to confirm his nomination of a collector of the customs for the port of Charleston, effectually tied his hands and rendered it impossible for him to collect the revenue within that port. In his annual message he had expressed the opinion that "the same insuperable obstacles do not lie in the way of executing the [existing] laws for the collection of customs on the seaboard of South Carolina as had been interposed to prevent the administration of justice under the Federal authority within the interior of that State." At all events he had determined to make the effort with the naval force under his command. He trusted that this might be accomplished without collision; but if resisted, then the force necessary to attain the object must be applied. Accordingly, whilst informing Congress "that the revenue still continues to be collected as heretofore at the custom house in Charleston," he says that "should the collector unfortunately resign, a successor may be appointed to perform this duty." The collector (William F. Colcock) continued faithfully to perform his duties until some days after the State had seceded, when at the end of December he resigned. The President, immediately afterwards, on the 2d January, nominated to the Senate, as his successor, Mr. Peter McIntire, of Pennsylvania, a gentleman well qualified for the office. The selection could not have been made from South Carolina, because no citizen of that State would have accepted the appointment. The Senate, throughout their entire session, never acted upon the nomination of Mr. McIntire; and without a collector of customs duly appointed, it was rendered impossible for the President, under any law in existence, to collect the revenue.

But even if the Senate had confirmed Mr. McIntire's nomination, it is extremely doubtful whether the President could lawfully have collected the revenue against the forcible resistance of the State, unless Congress had conferred additional powers upon him. For this purpose Mr. Bingham, of Ohio, on the 3d January, 1861,* the day after Mr. McIntire's nomination to the Senate, reported a bill from the Judiciary Committee, further to provide for the collection of duties on imports. This bill embraced substantially the same provisions, long since expired, contained in the Act of 2d March, 1833, commonly called "the Force Bill," to enable General Jackson to collect the revenue outside of Charleston, "either upon land or on board any vessel." Mr. Bingham's bill was permitted to slumber on the files of the House until the 2d March, the last day but one before Congress expired,† when he moved for a suspension of the rules, to enable the House to take it up and consider it, but his motion proved unsuccessful. Indeed, the motion was not made until so late an hour of the session that even if it had prevailed, the bill could not have passed both Houses before the final adjournment. Thus the President was left both without a collector of customs, and most probably without any law which a collector could have carried into effect, had such an officer existed. Mr. Bingham's bill shared the fate of all other legislative measures, of whatever character, intended either to prevent or to confront the existing danger. From the persistent refusal to pass any act enabling either the outgoing or the incoming administration to meet the contingency of civil war, it may fairly be inferred that the friends of Mr. Lincoln, in and out of Congress, believed he would be able to settle the existing difficulties with the cotton States in a peaceful manner, and that he might be embarrassed by any legislation contemplating the necessity of a resort to hostile measures.

The 36th Congress expired on the 3d March, 1861, leaving the law just as they had found it. They made no provision whatever for the suppression of threatened rebellion, but deliberately refused to grant either men or money for this purpose. It was this violation of duty which compelled President Lincoln to issue a proclamation convening the new Congress, in special session, immediately after the attack on Fort Sumter.

* Con. Globe, p. 236, bills H. R., No. 910.   † H. Journal, p. 465

Urgent and dangerous emergencies may have arisen, or may hereafter arise in the history of our country, rendering delay disastrous, such as the bombardment of Fort Sumter by the Confederate Government, which would for the moment justify the President in violating the Constitution, by raising a military force without the authority of law, but this only during a recess of Congress. Such extreme cases are a law unto themselves. They must rest upon the principle that it is a lesser evil to usurp, until Congress can be assembled, a power withheld from the Executive, than to suffer the Union to be endangered, either by traitors at home or enemies from abroad. In all such cases, however, it is the President's duty to present to Congress, immediately after their next meeting, the causes which impelled him thus to act, and ask for their approbation; just as, on a like occasion, a British minister would ask Parliament for a bill of indemnity. It would be difficult, however, to conceive of an emergency so extreme as to justify or even excuse a President for thus transcending his constitutional powers whilst Congress, to whom he could make an immediate appeal, was in session. Certainly no such case existed during the administration of the late President. On the contrary, not only was Congress actually in session, but bills were long pending before it for extending his authority in calling forth the militia, for enabling him to accept the services of volunteers, and for the employment of the navy, if necessary, outside of ports of entry for the collection of the revenue, all of which were eventually rejected. Under these circumstances, had the President attempted, of his own mere will, to exercise these high powers, whilst Congress were at the very time deliberating whether to grant them to him or not, he would have made himself justly liable to impeachment. This would have been for the Executive to set at defiance both the Constitution and the legislative branch of the Government.

CHAPTER IX.

The forts in Charleston harbor—Conduct toward them and the reasons for it—To guard against surprise reënforcements ready—Instructions to Major Anderson—Interview with South Carolina members—General Scott again recommends the garrisoning of all the forts—Reasons against it—The compromise measures still depending—Want of troops—Observations on General Scott's report to President Lincoln—His letter to Secretary Seward, and the manner in which it, with the report, was brought to light and published—Mr. Buchanan's reply to the report—General Scott's statement of the interview with President Buchanan on 15th December, and observations thereupon—The example of General Jackson in 1833, and why it was inapplicable.

It is now necessary to recur to the condition of the forts and other public property of the United States within South Carolina, at the date of the President's annual message, on the 3d December, 1860. In regard to that property the message says: "This has been purchased for a fair equivalent, by the consent of the Legislature of the State, for the 'erection of forts, magazines, arsenals,' and over these the authority 'to exercise exclusive legislation' has been expressly granted by the Constitution to Congress. It is not believed that any attempt will be made to expel the United States from this property by force, but if in this I should prove to be mistaken, the officer in command of the forts has received orders to act strictly on the defensive. In such a contingency the responsibility for consequences would rightfully rest upon the heads of the assailants." Thus if war must come, the President had determined to fix the whole responsibility for its commencement on South Carolina. In order to estimate correctly the wisdom of this defensive policy, it is necessary to revert to the condition of the country on the 3d December, 1860, when it was announced. At this period we may divide the Southern States into three classes, holding opinions variant from each other.

1. There was South Carolina, which had been the avowed and persistent advocate of disunion for more than a quarter of a century. She had already called a Convention for the purpose of seceding from the Union. Her leading secessionists were ever on the alert to seize upon any action of the Federal Government which they might wrest to the purpose of alienating the 'other slaveholding States from their attachment to the Union, and enlisting them in her cause.

2. The second class was composed of the six other cotton States. The people of these, although highly excited against the abolitionists, were still unwilling to leave the Union. They would have been content, notwithstanding the efforts of secession demagogues, with a simple recognition of their adjudged rights to take slaves into the Territories, and hold them there like other property, until a territorial convention, assembled to frame a State constitution, should decide the question. To this decision, whatever it might be, they professed their willingness to submit. Indeed, as has already been seen from the statements of Messrs. Douglas and Toombs in the Senate, they would have consented to abandon their rights in all the Territories north of 36° 30', leaving what should remain to them little more than a name.

3. The third class consisted of the border slaveholding States, with Virginia at the head. A large majority of their people, although believing in the right of peaceful secession, had resisted all the efforts of the extreme men in their midst, and were still devoted to the Union. Of this there could be no better proof than the result of the election held in Virginia, February 4, 1861, for the choice of delegates to her State Convention, even after the cotton States had all seceded.* This showed that a very large majority of the delegates elected were in favor of remaining in the Union.

Under these circumstances, it is easy to imagine what would have been the effect on the other Southern States of sending a feeble force of United States troops to Fort Moultrie at this criti-

---

* Appleton's Annual Cyclopœdia for 1861, p. 730.

cal conjuncture. Had collision been the consequence, and blood been shed immediately before the meeting of Congress, the other cotton States, from their well-known affinities, would have rushed to the support of South Carolina. She would thus have accomplished her long-sought object. Indeed, it was the current report of the day that her leading disunionists had declared the spilling of a little blood would be necessary to secure the coöperation of other Southern States. Besides, in the President's opinion, there was no necessity, at the time, for any reënforcement to secure the forts in the harbor of Charleston. He was convinced that while the other slaveholding States were ready and willing to compromise with the North, South Carolina would not dare to attack Fort Moultrie. This conviction did not spring from any confidence in her spirit of forbearance; it arose from a certain knowledge that such an outrage would be condemned not only by the border but by the cotton States. It would estrange and separate them from her, at the very moment she was most solicitous to conciliate them. Whoever was in Washington at the time cannot fail to recollect the denunciations in advance of leading Southern men against such an unprovoked attack. The public property stood within her limits—three forts, a custom house, an arsenal, and a post office, covered by the flag of the country. From these she knew she had nothing to fear unless she should first make the attack. Such an outrage as the seizure of a fort of the United States by any State had never before been imagined. There must be a fearful suspense between the conception and the commission of such an act. It was the supreme object of the President to promote, by all the means in his power, such a fair and honorable adjustment between the North and the South as would save the country from the scourge of civil war. It was, therefore, his evident policy to isolate South Carolina, as far as possible, from the other Southern States; and for this purpose to refrain from any act which might enable her to enlist them in her cause. If, after all, she should attack Fort Moultrie, this act would have met their universal condemnation. Besides, nothing short of such an attack could have united the people of the North in suppressing her revolt. They were then far from being prepared for civil war.

On the contrary, they were intent on a peaceful solution of our difficulties, and would have censured any act of the administration which might have defeated this purpose and precipitated them into hostilities. The true policy was that expressed by President Lincoln to the seceded cotton States in his inaugural months afterward, in which he informs them, " You can have no conflict without being yourselves the aggressors." Although the President believed (and this with good cause, as the event has shown), that under the existing circumstances, South Carolina would not attack any of the forts in the harbor of Charleston whilst he suffered their *status quo* to remain ; yet in this it was possible he might be mistaken. To guard against surprise after the secession of the State, which was then imminent, he had prepared an expedition as powerful as his limited means would afford, to send reënforcements to Major Anderson, at the first moment of danger. For this purpose the Secretary of the Navy had stationed the Brooklyn, a powerful war steamer, then completely ready for sea, in Hampton Roads, to take on board for Charleston three hundred disciplined troops, with provisions and munitions of war, from the neighboring garrison of Fortress Monroe.

Having thus provided for the reënforcement of the forts, in case of need, the Secretary of War despatched Assistant Adjutant-General Buell to Major Anderson, at Fort Moultrie, with instructions how he should act in his present position. These were communicated to him on the 11th December, 1860. Whilst they instructed the Major to avoid every act of aggression, they directed him, in case of an attack upon, or an attempt to take possession of, any of the three forts under his command, to defend them to the last extremity. Furthermore, he was authorized, as a precautionary measure, should he believe his force insufficient for the defence of all three, to remove it at his discretion from Fort Moultrie to Fort Sumter, whenever he should have tangible evidence of a design, on the part of South Carolina, to proceed to a hostile act. We say to Fort Sumter, because the third fort, Castle Pinckney, was wholly indefensible. From the important bearing of these instructions upon subsequent events, they are entitled to textual insertion. They are as follows:* "You are aware of the great anxiety of the Secretary of War, that a collision of the troops with the people of the State shall be avoided, and of his studied determination to pursue a course with reference to the military force and forts in this harbor, which shall guard against such a collision. He has, therefore, carefully abstained from increasing the force at this point, or taking any measures which might add to the present excited state of the public mind, or which would throw any doubt on the confidence he feels that South Carolina will not attempt by violence to obtain possession of the public works or interfere with their occupancy. But as the counsel and acts of rash and impulsive persons may possibly disappoint these expectations of the Government, he deems it proper that you shall be prepared with instructions to meet so unhappy a contingency. He has, therefore, directed me verbally to give you such instructions. You are carefully to avoid every act which would needlessly tend to provoke aggression, and for that reason you are not, without evident and imminent necessity, to take up any position which could be construed into the assumption of a hostile attitude, but you are to hold possession of the forts in this harbor, and if attacked you are to defend yourself to the last extremity. The smallness of your force will not permit you, perhaps, to occupy more than one of the three forts, but an attack on or attempt to take possession of either one of them will be regarded as an act of hostility, and you may then put your command into either of them which you may deem most proper to increase its power of resistance. You are also authorized to take similar defensive steps whenever you have tangible evidence of a design to proceed to a hostile act." *

The President having observed that Major Buell, in reducing to writing at Fort Moultrie the instructions he had verbally received, required Major Anderson, in case of attack, *to defend himself to the last extremity*, immediately caused the Secretary of War to modify this instruction. This extreme was not required by any principle of military honor or by any rule of war. It was sufficient for him to defend himself until no reasonable hope should remain of saving the fort. The instructions

* Ex. Doc., H. R., vol. vi., No. 26, p. 10.

were accordingly so modified, with the approbation of General Scott.

The President having determined not to disturb the *status quo* at Charleston, as long as our troops should continue to be hospitably treated by the inhabitants, and remain in unmolested possession of the forts, was gratified to learn, a short time thereafter, that South Carolina was equally intent on preserving the peace. On the 8th December, 1860, four of the Representatives in Congress from that State sought an interview, and held a conversation with him concerning the best means of avoiding a hostile collision between the parties. In order to guard against any misapprehension on either side, he suggested that they had best reduce their verbal communication to writing, and bring it to him in that form. Accordingly, on the 10th December, they delivered to him a note, dated on the previous day, and signed by five members, in which they say: "In compliance with our statement to you yesterday, we now express to you our strong convictions that neither the constituted authorities, nor any body of the people of the State of South Carolina, will either attack or molest the United States forts in the harbor of Charleston, previously to the action of the Convention; and we hope and believe not until an offer has been made, through an accredited representative, to negotiate for an amicable arrangement of all matters between the State and the Federal Government, provided that no reënforcements be sent into these forts, and their relative military status shall remain as at present." * Both in this and in their previous conversation, they declared that in making this statement, they were acting solely on their own responsibility, and expressly disclaimed any authority to bind their State. They, nevertheless, expressed the confident belief that they would be sustained both by the State authorities and by the Convention, after it should assemble. Although the President considered this declaration as nothing more than the act of five highly respectable members of the House from South Carolina, yet he welcomed it as a happy omen, that by means of their influence collision might be prevented, and time afforded to all parties for reflection and for a peaceable adjust-

---

* Ex. Doc., H. R., vol. vi., No. 96, p. 9, &c.

ment. From abundant caution, however, he objected to the word "provided" in their statement, lest, if he should accept it without remark, this might possibly be construed into an agreement on his part not to reënforce the forts. Such an agreement, he informed them, he would never make. It would be impossible for him, from the nature of his official responsibility, thus to tie his own hands and restrain his own freedom of action. Still, they might have observed from his message, that he had no present design, under existing circumstances, to change the condition of the forts at Charleston. He must, notwithstanding, be left entirely free to exercise his own discretion, according to exigencies as they might arise. They replied that nothing was further from their intention than such a construction of this word; they did not so understand it, and he should not so consider it.

It was at this moment, on the 15th December, 1860, after the President's policy had been fixed and announced in his annual message; after the "Brooklyn" had been made ready to go to the relief of Major Anderson in case of need; after he had received instructions in accordance with this policy; after the President's pacific interview with the South Carolina members, and before any action had yet been taken on the first Crittenden Compromise, that General Scott deemed it proper to renew his former recommendation to garrison the nine Southern fortifications. This appears from his report to President Lincoln, of the 30th March, 1861, entitled "Southern Forts; a Summary," &c., of which we shall often hereafter have occasion to speak. It is scarcely a lack of charity to infer that General Scott knew at the time when he made this recommendation (on the 15th December) that it must be rejected. The President could not have complied with it, the position of affairs still remaining unchanged, without at once reversing his entire policy, and without a degree of inconsistency amounting almost to self-stultification. The Senators from the cotton States and from Virginia, where these forts are situated, were still occupied with their brother Senators in devising measures of peace and conciliation. For this patriotic purpose the Committee of Thirteen were about to be appointed, and they remained in session until the last day of the month. Meanwhile all the Southern Senators in Congress professed their willingness to adopt the Crittenden Compromise, so much and so justly lauded afterwards by General Scott himself. If at this moment, whilst they were engaged in peaceful consultation with Senators from the North, the President had despatched military expeditions to these nine forts, it was easy to foresee what would be the disastrous effect, not only in the cotton, but in all the border States. Its first effect would have been to dissolve the existing conferences for a peaceable adjustment.

This, the General's second recommendation, was wholly unexpected. He had remained silent for more than six weeks from the date of his supplemental "Views," convinced, as the President inferred, that he had abandoned the idea of garrisoning all these forts with "the five companies only" within his reach. Had the President never so earnestly desired to reënforce the nine forts in question, at this time, it would have been little short of madness to undertake the task, with the small force at his command. Without authority to call forth the militia or accept the services of volunteers for the purpose, this whole force now consisted of six hundred recruits, obtained by the General since the date of his "Views," in addition to the five regular companies. Our army was still out of reach on the remote frontiers, and could not be withdrawn, during midwinter, in time for this military operation. Indeed, the General had never suggested such a withdrawal. He knew that had this been possible, the inhabitants on our distant frontiers would have been immediately exposed to the tomahawk and scalping knife of the Indians. Our weak condition in regard to troops within reach is demonstrated by the insignificant number of these he was able to collect in Washington on the 4th March following. This was to resist an attempt which he apprehended would be made by an armed force to prevent the inauguration of President Lincoln and to seize the public property. The General was so firmly convinced of the reality of this plot, that nothing could shake his faith. It was in vain that a committee of the House of Representatives, after hearing the General himself, and after full investigation, had reported that his apprehensions were unfounded.* Besides, the

* February 14, 1861. House Reports of Committees, vól. ii., No. 79.

President, relying on his own sources of information, had never entertained any similar apprehensions. The stake, notwithstanding, was so vast and the General so urgent, that he granted him permission to bring to Washington all the troops he could muster to resist an imaginary but dreaded enemy. The whole number of these, including even the sappers and miners whom he had withdrawn from West Point, amounted to no more than six hundred and fifty-three, rank and file. These troops, with a portion of the district militia, the General had posted in different parts of the city, and had stationed sentinels on the tops of the highest houses and other eminences, so that all was ready to attack the enemy at the first moment of their appearance; but never did an inauguration pass more peacefully and quietly. It is due to President Lincoln to state, that throughout his long progress in the same carriage with the late President, both on the way to the Capitol and the return from it, he was far from evincing the slightest apprehension of danger.

Had the President attempted to distribute the General's thousand men, as he proposed, among the numerous forts in the cotton States, as well as Fortress Monroe, their absurd inadequacy to the object would have exhibited weakness instead of strength. It would have provoked instead of preventing collision. It would have precipitated a civil war with the cotton States without the slightest preparation on the part of Congress, and would at once have destroyed the then prevailing hopes of compromise. Worse than all, it would have exasperated Virginia and the other border States, then so intent on remaining in the Union, and might have driven them at once into hostile action.

And now it becomes our painful duty to examine the report of General Scott to President Lincoln of 30th March, 1861. This was first published at the General's instance, eighteen months after its date, in the "National Intelligencer" of the 21st October, 1862. It cannot be denied that the report throughout is an indiscriminate censure of President Buchanan's conduct in dealing with the Southern forts. It evidently proceeded from a defective memory prejudiced by a strong bias. It rests mainly on vague and confused recollections of private conversations alleged to have been held with the President several months before its date. These having occurred between the commander-in-chief and the commanding General of the army, on important military questions, pertaining to their respective official duties, were, in their nature, strictly confidential. Were this otherwise, it would destroy that freedom and unreserve which ought to characterize such consultations, and instead thereof, the parties would be ever on their guard in the interchange of opinions, often greatly to the prejudice of the public interest. Had the General resolved to violate a confidence as sacred as that between the President and a member of his Cabinet, such is the treachery of the best human memory, he ought, at the least, to have submitted his statements to Mr. Buchanan before he had embodied them in his report. Had he done this, we venture to say from the sequel that most of them would have never seen the light.

When President Buchanan retired from office, he had reason to believe he had parted from the General on terms mutually amicable. Although in former years their friendly intercourse had been for a season interrupted, yet he believed all this had been forgotten. A suspicion never entered his mind that the General held in reserve a quiver of arrows to assail his public character upon his retirement from office.

This report does not allege that it had been made in consequence of a call from President Lincoln. From its face it appears to have been a pure volunteer offering on the part of the General. It deals with the past and not with the future. It is remarkable that it does not contain a word of advice to President Lincoln, such as might have been expected from the commanding General, as to the manner of recovering the forts which before its date had been already seized by the Confederates. On the contrary, it reveals the strange fact that the General, so late as the 12th March, and after the so-called Confederate Government of the cotton States was in full operation at Montgomery, had advised President Lincoln to evacuate Fort Sumter, and this in direct opposition to what had been the well-known and oft-expressed determination of Mr. Buchanan. We need scarcely remark that President Lincoln acted wisely in disregarding this counsel. It was founded on an alleged military necessity. Had the fort been actually invested by a hostile force so superior as to render resistance hopeless, this would have justified a capitulation in order to save a useless sacrifice of life. Its voluntary abandonment, however, to the Confederacy, would have gone far toward a recognition of their independence.

The General, in this report, would have President Lincoln believe, on the authority of a Richmond newspaper, that "had Scott been able to have got these forts in the condition he desired them to be, the Southern Confederacy would not now exist." Strange hallucination! In plain English, that South Carolina, which throughout an entire generation had determined on disunion, and had actually passed an ordinance of secession to carry this purpose. into effect, and the remaining six powerful cotton States ready to follow her evil example, unless their adjudged rights should be recognized by Congress, and which together have since sent into the field such numerous and powerful armies, would at once have been terrified into submission by the distribution of four hundred troops in October, or one thousand in December, among their numerous fortifications!

Very different must have been his opinion on the 3d March following, when he penned his famous letter to Secretary Seward. In this he exclaims: "Conquer the seceded [cotton] States by invading armies. No doubt this might be done in two or three years by a young and able general—a Wolfe, a Dessaix, a Hoche, with three hundred thousand disciplined men, estimating a third for garrisons, and the loss of a yet greater number by skirmishes, sieges, battles and Southern fevers. The destruction of life and property on the other side would be frightful, however perfect the moral discipline of the invaders. The conquest completed, at that enormous waste of human life to the North and the Northwest, with at least $250,000,000 added thereto, and *cui bono?* Fifteen devastated provinces! not to be brought into harmony with their conquerors, but to be held for generations by heavy garrisons, at an expense quadruple the net duties or taxes it would be possible to extort from them, followed by a protector or an emperor." In view of these fearful forebodings, we are not surprised that he should have despaired of the Union, and been willing to say to the cotton States, "Wayward sisters, depart in peace." Nor that he should have fallen back on his opinion expressed in the "Views" (29th October, 1860), that "a smaller evil [than such a civil war] would be to allow the fragments of the great Republic to form themselves into new Confederacies."

The General, however, in the same letter to Secretary Seward, presents his alternative for all these evils. He advises Mr. Lincoln's administration " to throw off the old and assume a new designation—the Union party; adopt the conciliatory measures proposed by Mr. Crittenden, or the Peace Convention, and my life upon it, we shall have no new case of secession, but, on the contrary, an early return of many if not all of the States which have already broken off from the Union. Without some equally benign measure, the remaining slaveholding States will probably join the Montgomery Confederacy in less than sixty days, when this city, being included in a foreign country, would require a permanent garrison of at least thirty-five thousand troops." His advice to adopt the Crittenden Compromise would have been excellent had it been given to his Republican friends in Congress in the previous December, before any State had seceded, and before any fort had been seized, instead of then recommending to President Buchanan to despatch small bands of United States soldiers to each of the forts. This recommendation, had it been followed at the time, would at once have defeated this very Crittenden Compromise, so much desired, and served only to provoke the cotton States into secession. It would have been the stone of Cadmus cast among the armed men sprung from the dragon's teeth, and the signal for immediate fratricidal war and mutual destruction. The advice to President Lincoln was out of season, after both the Crittenden Compromise and the measures proposed by the Peace Convention had been finally rejected by Congress, and whilst the Confederacy of the cotton States was in active existence.

Before we proceed to analyze in further detail the General's report, it is curious to note the reason for its publication. This was a consequence of the publication of his letter to Secretary Seward, which was in its very nature confidential. At this period, in October, 1862, when the rebellion had assumed a formidable aspect, and when his sinister predictions appeared to be in the course of fulfilment, he read the original draft, in his own handwriting, to a friend. This gentleman, whilst extolling the far-seeing sagacity and the prophetic spirit it displayed, begged for the draft as an invaluable keepsake. This appeal to the General proved irresistible. The manuscript was delivered to the friend, who soon thereafter read it, amid great applause, at a public meeting in the city of New York, and whilst a highly excited political canvass was depending for the office of Governor. The letter thus published, implying a direct censure on President Lincoln for not having followed the advice it had given, created no little astonishment, because of the prevalent belief at the time, that the General was under many obligations to the administration for liberal and indulgent treatment in the face of discomfiture and defeat. The letter having thus been first published by his friend, it was soon thereafter republished in the "National Intelligencer," of the 21st October, 1862, under the General's own authority, and in addition, a copy of his report to President Lincoln. Why he thus connected these two documents, so distinct and even opposite in character, it would be difficult to decide. It has been conjectured he may have thought that the censure of Mr. Buchanan in the report might prove an antidote to that against Mr. Lincoln in the Seward letter. Whatever may have caused the publication of this report, Mr. Buchanan has cause to rejoice that it was brought to light during his lifetime. It might, otherwise, have slumbered on the secret files of the Executive Department until after his death, and then been revealed to posterity as authentic history. And here it is proper to mention, that a few days after the publication of the report, Mr. Buchanan replied to it in a letter published in the "National Intelligencer," of the 1st November, 1862. This gave rise to a correspondence between himself and General Scott, which, on both sides, was formally addressed to the editors of that journal, and was published by them in successive numbers. This continued throughout the autumn. It might at first be supposed that the errors in the report had been sufficiently exposed in the course of this correspondence; but in the present historical sketch of President Buchanan's conduct, it is impossible to pass over the strictures made upon it by General Scott. The two are inseparably joined together.

The General, in his report, prefaces the statement of his conversation with President Buchanan, by saying, that on the 13th December he had "personally urged upon the Secretary of War the same 'views' [those of the previous October], viz., strong garrisons in the Southern forts; those of Charleston and Pensacola harbors at once; those on Mobile Bay and the Mississippi below New Orleans, next, &c., &c. I again pointed out the organized companies, and the [600] recruits at the principal depots available for the purpose. The Secretary did not concur in my views." This, indeed, he could not have done so early as the 13th December, without placing himself in direct opposition to the well-defined policy of the President. An interview was, therefore, appointed for the 15th December, between the President and the General. "By appointment," says the General, "the Secretary accompanied me to the President, December 15th, when the same topics, secessionism, &c., were again pretty fully discussed." He does not furnish the President's answer to the proposition to send strong garrisons to the Southern forts. This must unquestionably have referred to the topics of which his mind was then full, viz., the promising aspect of compromise at the moment; the certain effect of such a measure in defeating it; the inadequacy of the force at command for so extended an operation; and the policy which had been laid down in his annual message. Not a word of all this. But the General's memory seems to have improved with the lapse of years and the progress of the rebellion. In his report to President Lincoln, he speaks of but one conversation with President Buchanan, that of the 15th December, whilst in his letter of the 8th November, 1862, to the "National Intelligencer," a portion of the correspondence to which we have referred, he alleges he had, on the 28th and 30th of the same December, repeated the recommendation to garrison all the Southern forts. In this statement, if material, it would be easy to prove he was mistaken. Indeed, President Buchanan has in his possession a note from the General himself, dated on Sunday, 30th December, stating that by indisposition he was confined to the house on that day, and could not therefore call upon him. Of this hereafter.

According to the report, he merely mentions in general terms the recruits he had obtained for the expedition, without allotting them among the several forts. According to the letter, he informed President Buchanan that the number of recruits at New York and Carlisle barracks was about six hundred, "besides the five companies of regulars near at hand, making about one thousand men." And he also stated how he would distribute them among the several forts. In this distribution he left only "about two hundred men for the twin forts of Moultrie and Sumter, Charleston harbor." He also declared in this letter, that "he considered the force quite adequate to the occasion." But, as if rendered conscious of its inadequacy by the logic of events, he alleges that President Buchanan "might have called forth volunteers to garrison these forts, without any special legislation," and this, too, "with the full approbation of every loyal man in the Union." That is, that on the 15th December, 1860, before any State had seceded, he might without law have usurped this authority, when the law-making power was actually in session and had made no movement to grant it, and when all were intent, not on war, but on measures of compromise. In this letter he charges the Secretary of War, "with or without the President's approbation," with "having nearly denuded our whole eastern seaboard of troops." In doing this, he must surely have forgotten that he himself had eloquently urged that all the force on the frontiers was not sufficient for the protection of our distant fellow-citizens, and had therefore advocated the raising of an additional force by Congress for this very purpose.

It would seem from the report that the President confined his observations at their interview exclusively to the reënforcement of the forts in Charleston harbor, for which General Scott, according to his own statement, in the letter to the "National Intelligencer," could spare but two hundred men, the remaining eight hundred being required for the other fortifications. The President having expressed the opinion, according to the report, "that there was at the moment no danger of an early secession beyond South Carolina," he proceeded to state, " in reply to my [General Scott's] arguments for immediately reënforcing Fort Moultrie, and sending a garrison to Fort Sumter," that " the time has not arrived for doing so ; that he should wait the action of the Convention of South Carolina, in the expectation that a commission would be appointed and sent to negotiate with him and Congress, respecting the secession of the State and the property of the United States held within its limits ; and that if Congress sh'ould decide against the secession, then he would send a reënforcement, and telegraph the commanding officer (Major Anderson) of Fort Moultrie to hold the forts (Moultrie and Sumter) against attack."

Now it is probable that in the course of this conversation, the President may have referred to the rumor then current, that the South Carolina Convention intended to send commissioners to Washington to treat with the Government, but it is quite impossible he could have stated that the reënforcement of the forts should await the result of their mission. Why ? Because the *Brooklyn* had been for some time ready to proceed to Fort Moultrie, dependent on no other contingency than that of its attack or danger of attack. Least of all was it possible the President could have said that if Congress should decide against secession, he would then telegraph to Major Anderson " to hold the forts (Moultrie and Sumter) against attack," when instructions of a similar but stronger character had already been sent and delivered to him, and were of record in the War Department. It is strange that the President should, according to the General, have made any future action in regard to these forts dependent upon his own decision, or that of Congress, on the question of secession, when he had in his annual message, but a few days before, condemned the doctrine as unconstitutional, and he well knew it would be equally condemned by Congress.

It is curious to note a trait of the fault-finding temper of the General in this conversation. In it he makes the Secretary of War observe, " with animation," " We have a vessel of war (the *Brooklyn*) held.in readiness at Norfolk, and he would then send three hundred men in her from Fort Monroe to Charleston ; " but the General objected to this arrangement, saying in answer, "that so many men could not be withdrawn from that garrison, but could be taken from New York," &c., &c. In this report to President Lincoln the General exultingly declares, "that if the Secretary's three hundred men had then (on the 15th December), or some time later, been sent to Forts Moultrie and Sumter, both would now have been in the possession of the United States," &c. And again, "It would have been easy to reenforce this fort (Sumter) down to about the 12th February." In making these declarations, he must surely have forgotten not only his own objection to sending these very "three hundred men" from Fortress Monroe, but also the fate of the *Star of the West*, in the early part of January, with his recruits from New York, which had been substituted under his advice and direction for the *Brooklyn*.

The reader must have observed that we speak argumentatively and doubtingly of the General's statement of this conversation. We do this simply because President Buchanan, although a party to it, has no recollection whatever of its particulars. The reason doubtless is, that, believing General Scott to have been aware before the interview that the President would not violate his announced policy by sending one thousand men to all the Southern forts, or two hundred to those in Charleston harbor, he must have considered this renewed recommendation rather a matter of form, springing from a motive which he will not attempt to conjecture, than any thing more serious. But whatever may have been the cause of his want of memory, the fact is certainly true. He sincerely wishes it were otherwise.

We may observe generally in regard to this report, that the attempt, at the end of more than three months, filled with the most important and stirring events, to write out charges against President Buchanan, must almost necessarily do him injustice. Fairly to accomplish such a task, the writer ought to have tested his own recollection by a reference to dates and official documents within his reach. Not having done this, the report is confused throughout, sometimes blending in the same sentence occurrences of distinct date and opposite nature. When these come to be unravelled, it will appear in the sequel that they are often contradicted by official and other unimpeachable testimony.

And here it is due to General Scott to mention, that on the evening of their interview (15th December), he addressed a note to President Buchanan, reminding him that General Jackson, during the period of South Carolina nullification, had sent reënforcements to Fort Moultrie to prevent its seizure by the nullifiers and to enforce the collection of the revenue. This example was doubtless suggested for imitation. But the times had greatly changed during more than a quarter of a century which had since elapsed. In 1833 South Carolina stood alone. She had then the sympathy of no other Southern State. Her nullification was condemned by them all. Even her own people were almost equally divided on the question. But instead of this, in December, 1860, they were unanimous, and the other cotton States were preparing to follow her into secession, should their rights in the Territories be denied by Congress. Besides, the President had already declared his purpose to collect the revenue by the employment of vessels of war stationed outside of the port of Charleston, whenever its collection at the custom house should be resisted. He hoped thereby to avoid actual collision; but, whether or not, he had resolved at every hazard to collect the revenue. Such was the state of affairs on the 15th December, 1860. Meanwhile the forts and all other public property were unmolested, and Major Anderson and his troops continued to be supplied and treated in the kindest manner.

CHAPTER X.

South Carolina adopts an ordinance of secession, and appoints Commissioners to treat with the General Government—Their arrival in Washington—Major Anderson's removal from Fort Moultrie to Fort Sumter—The President's interview with the Commissioners, who demand a surrender of all the forts—His answer to this demand—Their insolent reply, and its return to them—Its presentation to the Senate by Mr. Davis—Secretary Floyd requested to resign—He resigns and becomes a secessionist—Fort Sumter threatened—The *Brooklyn* ordered to carry reënforcements to the fort—The *Star of the West* substituted at General Scott's instance—She is fired upon—Major Anderson demands of Governor Pickens a disavowal of the act—The Governor demands the surrender of the fort—The Major proposes to refer the question to Washington—The Governor accepts—Colonel Hayne and Lieutenant Hall arrive in Washington on the 13th January—The truce—Letter from Governor Pickens not delivered to the President until the 31st January—The answer to it—Colonel Hayne's insulting reply—It is returned to him—Virginia sends Mr. Tyler to the President with a view to avoid hostilities—His arrival in Washington and his proposals—Message of the President.

ON the 20th December, 1860, the South Carolina Convention adopted an ordinance of secession, and on the 22d appointed three of their most distinguished citizens to proceed forthwith to Washington to treat with the Government of the United States concerning the relations between the parties. These were Robert W. Barnwell, James H. Adams, and James L. Orr. They arrived in Washington on Wednesday, the 26th December. On the next morning they received intelligence by telegraph that Major Anderson had, on Christmas night, secretly dismantled Fort Moultrie; had spiked his cannon, had burnt his gun-carriages, and had removed with his troops to Fort Sumter, as if from an impending attack. This information they sent to the President. He received it with astonishment and regret. With astonishment, because he had believed Major Anderson to be in security at Fort Moultrie; and this more especially whilst the commissioners appointed but three days before were on their way to Washington. With regret, because this movement would probably impel the other cotton and border States into active sympathy with South Carolina, and thereby defeat the measures of compromise still before the Committee of Thirteen of the Senate, from which he had hoped to confine secession to that State alone. The President never doubted for a moment that Major Anderson believed before the movement that he had "the tangible evidence" of an impending attack required by his instructions. Still it was difficult to imagine that South Carolina would be guilty of the base perfidy of attacking any of these forts during the pendency of her mission to Washington, for the avowed purpose of preserving the peace and preventing collision. Such treacherous conduct would have been considered infamous among all her sister States. She has always strenuously denied that such was her intention. .

In this state of suspense the President determined to await official information from Major Anderson himself. After its receipt, should he be convinced upon full examination that the Major, on a false alarm, had violated his instructions, he might then think seriously of restoring for the present the former *status quo* of the forts. This, however, was soon after known to be impossible, in consequence of the violent conduct of South Carolina in seizing all the other forts and public property in the harbor and city of Charleston.

It was under these circumstances that the President, on Friday, the 28th December, held his first and only interview with the commissioners from South Carolina. He determined to listen with patience to what they had to communicate, taking as little part himself in the conversation as civility would permit. On their introduction he stated that he could recognize them only as private gentlemen and not as commissioners from a sovereign State; that it was to Congress, and to Congress alone, they must appeal. He, nevertheless, expressed his willingness to communicate to that body, as the only competent tribunal, any propositions they might have to offer. They then proceeded, evidently under much excitement, to state their grievances arising out of the removal of Major Anderson to Fort Sumter, and declared that for these they must obtain redress preliminary to entering upon the negotiation with which they had been intrusted; that it was impossible for them to make any proposition until this removal should be satisfactorily explained; and they even insisted upon the immediate withdrawal of the Major and his troops, not only from Fort Sumter, but from the harbor of Charleston, as a *sine qua non* to any negotiation.

In their letter to the President of the next day, they repeat this demand, saying: * " And, in conclusion, we would urge upon you the immediate withdrawal of the troops from the harbor of Charleston. Under present circumstances they are a standing menace which renders negotiation impossible, and, as our recent experience shows, threatens to bring to a bloody issue questions which ought to be settled with temperance and judgment." This demand, accompanied by an unmistakable threat of attacking Major Anderson if not yielded, was of the most extravagant character. To comply with it, the commissioners must have known, would be impossible. Had they simply requested that Major Anderson might be restored to his former position at Fort Moultrie, upon a guarantee from the State that neither it nor the other forts or public property should be molested; this, at the moment, might have been worthy of serious consideration. But to abandon all these forts to South Carolina, on the demand of commissioners claiming to represent her as an independent State, would have been a recognition, on the part of the Executive, of her right to secede from the Union. This was not to be thought of for a moment.

The President replied to the letter of the commissioners on Monday, 31st December. In the mean time information had reached him that the State authorities, without waiting to hear from Washington, had, on the day after Major Anderson's removal, seized Fort Moultrie, Castle Pinckney, the custom house, and post office, and over them all had raised the Palmetto flag; and moreover, that every officer of the customs, collector, naval officer, surveyor, appraisers, together with the postmaster, had resigned their appointments; and that on Sunday, the 30th December, they had captured from Major Hum-

* Ex. Doc., H. R., vol. vi., No. 26, p. 6.

phreys, the officer in charge, the arsenal of the United States, containing public property estimated to be worth half a million of dollars. The Government was thus expelled from all its property except Fort Sumter, and no Federal officers, whether civil or military, remained in the city or harbor of Charleston. The secession leaders in Congress attempted to justify these violent proceedings of South Carolina as acts of self-defence, on the assumption that Major Anderson had already commenced hostilities. It is certain that their tone instantly changed after his removal; and they urged its secrecy, the hour of the night when it was made, the destruction of his gun-carriages, and other attendant incidents, to inflame the passions of their followers. It was under these circumstances that the President was called upon to reply to the letter of the South Carolina commissioners, demanding the immediate withdrawal of the troops of the United States from the harbor of Charleston. In this reply he peremptorily rejected the demand in firm but courteous terms, and declared his purpose to defend Fort Sumter by all the means in his power against hostile attacks, from whatever quarter they might proceed. (*Vide* his letter of the 31st December, 1860, Ex. Doc. No. 26, H. R., 36th Congress, 2d Session, accompanying President's message of 8th January, 1861.) To this the commissioners sent their answer, dated on the 2d January, 1861. This was so violent, unfounded, and disrespectful, and so regardless of what is due to any individual whom the people have honored with the office of President, that the reading of it in the Cabinet excited indignation among all the members. With their unanimous approbation it was immediately, on the day of its date, returned to the commissioners with the following indorsement: "This paper, just presented to the President, is of such a character that he declines to receive it." Surely no negotiation was ever conducted in such a manner, unless, indeed, it had been the predetermined purpose of the negotiators to produce an open and immediate rupture.

It may be asked, why did the President, at his interview with the South Carolina commissioners, on the 28th December, offer to lay the propositions they had to make before Congress, when he must have been morally certain they would not meet a favorable response? This was to gain time for passion to subside, and for reason to resume her sway; to bring the whole subject before the representatives of the people in such a manner as to cause them to express an authoritative opinion on secession, and the other dangerous questions then before the country, and adopt such measures for their peaceable adjustment as might possibly reclaim even South Carolina herself; but whether or not, might prevent the other cotton States from following her evil and rash example.

The insulting letter of the commissioners, which had been returned to them, was notwithstanding presented to the Senate by Mr. Jefferson Davis, immediately after the reading of the President's special message of the 8th January; and such was the temper of that body at the time, that it was received and read, and entered upon their journal. Mr. Davis, not content with this success, followed it up by a severe and unjust attack against the President, and his example was followed by several of his adherents. From this time forward, as has been already stated, all social and political intercourse ceased between the disunion Senators and the President.

It is worth notice, that whilst this letter of the commissioners was published at length in the "Congressional Globe," among the proceedings of the Senate, their previous letter to the President of the 28th December, and his answer thereto of the 31st, were never published in this so-called official register, although copies of both had accompanied his special message. By this means the offensive letter was scattered broadcast over the country, whilst the letter of the President, to which this professed to be an answer, was buried in one of the numerous and long after published volumes of executive documents.

It is proper to advert to the allegation of the commissioners, in their letter of the 28th December, that the removal of Major Anderson to Fort Sumter was made in violation of pledges given by the President. They also say that "since our arrival an officer of the United States, acting, as we are assured, not only without but against your orders, has dismantled one fort and occupied another, thus altering to a most important extent the condition of affairs under which we came." As to the alleged pledge, we have already shown that no such thing existed. It has never been pretended that it rests upon any pretext except the note of the 9th December, delivered to the President by the South Carolina members of Congress, and what occurred on that occasion. All this has been already stated. But if additional evidence were wanting to refute the assertion of a pledge, this might be found in the statement published afterwards in Charleston by two of their number (Messrs. Miles and Keitt),[*] who, in giving an account of this interview, do not pretend or even intimate that any thing passed even in their opinion on either side in the nature of a pledge. By what officer, then, was the assurance given to the commissioners since their arrival in Washington, that Major Anderson had acted not only without but against the President's order? It was none other than the Secretary of War himself, notwithstanding it was in obedience to his own instructions but a few days before that the removal was made from Fort Moultrie to Fort Sumter. This appears from the letter of Major Anderson to the War Department of the 27th December, the day after his removal, which unfortunately did not arrive in Washington until some days after its date. In this he says: "I will add that many things convinced me that the authorities of the State designed to proceed to a hostile act" (against Fort Moultrie), the very contingency on which the Secretary had not only authorized but directed the Major to remove his troops to Fort Sumter, should he deem this a position of greater security. These instructions were in a certain sense peculiarly his own. They were prepared and transmitted to Major Anderson by himself. Throughout they do not mention the name of the President, though in the main they expressed his views.

We can refer to a probable cause for this strange conduct on the part of the Secretary. This was, that three days before the South Carolina commissioners reached Washington, the President had communicated to him (23d December), through a distinguished friend and kinsman of his own, a request that he should resign his office, with a statement of the reason why this

[*] Appleton's "American Annual Cyclopædia" for 1861, p. 703.

was made. When he heard this request he displayed much feeling, but said he would comply with the President's wishes. It is proper to state the reason for this request. On the night before it was made (22d December), the fact was first made known to the President that 870 State bonds for $1,000 each, held in trust by the Government for different Indian tribes, had been purloined from the Interior Department by Godard Bailey, the clerk in charge of them, and had been delivered to William H. Russell, a member of the firm of "Russell, Majors & Waddell." Upon examination, it was discovered that this clerk, in lieu of the bonds abstracted, had from time to time received bills of corresponding amount from Russell, drawn by the firm on John B. Floyd, Secretary of War, and by him accepted and indorsed, and this without any lawful authority. In consequence there was found in the safe where the Indian bonds had been kept, a number of these accepted bills, exactly equal in amount to $870,000. These acceptances were thirteen in number, commencing on the 13th September, 1860, and had been received by Mr. Bailey, according to his own statement, "as collateral security for the return of the bonds," and as such had been placed by him in the safe. It is remarkable that the last of them, dated on the 13th December, 1860, for $135,000, had been drawn for the precise sum necessary to make the aggregate amount of the whole number of bills exactly equal to that of the abstracted bonds.

And here it is due to Secretary Thompson to state, though a digression, that on Monday morning, the 24th December, at his own instance, the House of Representatives appointed a committee "to investigate and report upon the subject," of which Hon. Mr. Morris, of Illinois, a rancorous opponent of the administration, was the chairman. After a full investigation, the committee made their report on the 12th February, 1861.[*] In this they state: "They deem it but justice to add that they have discovered nothing to involve the late Secretary, Hon. Jacob Thompson, in the slightest degree in the fraud, and nothing to indicate that he had any complicity in the transaction, or that he had any knowledge of it until the time of the disclosure by

---

[*] Report of Committee, H. R., 1860–'61, vol. ii., No. 78, p. 3.

Godard Bailey." It is to be regretted, for the sake of public justice, that all the circumstances connected with the abstraction of these bonds had not been subjected to a judicial investigation. This was rendered impossible by the action of the committee itself, in examining John B. Floyd and William H. Russell as witnesses. For this reason they were relieved from all criminal responsibility by the Act of Congress of the 24th January, 1857,[*] of the existence of which the committee seem to have been ignorant. This act provides that no person examined as a witness before a committee of either House of Congress, "shall be held to answer criminally in any court of justice for any fact or act" "touching which he shall have testified." In this manner both Mr. Floyd and Mr. Russell escaped without trial.

To return from our digression. Secretary Floyd's apparent complicity with this fraudulent transaction covered him with suspicion, and, whether this were well or ill founded, rendered it impossible, in the opinion of the President, that he should remain in the Cabinet; and hence the request that he should resign. What effect this request may have produced in suddenly converting him from having been until then an avowed and consistent opponent of secession to one of its most strenuous supporters, may be readily inferred. Certain it is, that immediately after the arrival of the South Carolina commissioners, he became the intimate associate of leading secession Senators, who had just before been in the habit of openly condemning his official conduct.

On the evening of the day after the arrival of these commissioners he boldly assumed his new position, and became the only witness to a pledge which his own instructions of a few days before prove could never have existed. On that evening, in the face of all these facts, he read to the President, in Cabinet council, in a discourteous and excited tone, hitherto unknown, a paper declaring that "it is evident now, from the action of the commander at Fort Moultrie, that the solemn pledges of this Government have been violated by Major Anderson," and that "one

---

[*] 11 Laws U. S., p. 155.

remedy only is left, and that is to withdraw the garrison from the harbor of Charleston altogether." This evidently foreshadowed the demand made by the commissioners on the following day (28th December), of which we have already treated. This proposition the President heard with astonishment. As he had stated in his reply to them of the 31st December: "Such an idea was never thought of by me. No allusion had ever been made to it in any communication between myself and any human being."

The Secretary, on the 29th December, sent to the President the resignation of his office. By this he offered to discharge its duties until his successor should be appointed. It was instantly accepted without reference to this offer, and Postmaster General Holt was transferred to the War Department.

The President had not made the personal acquaintance of Mr. Floyd before his appointment. Though never in Congress, he had been, like his father, Governor of Virginia. Mr. Buchanan had been favorably impressed by the fact that he had refused to accept a recommendation from the Electoral College of Virginia for a seat in the Cabinet, assigning as a reason that the President, in making selections for this high and confidential office, ought to be left free and untrammelled to the exercise of his own judgment.

The removal of Major Anderson to Fort Sumter, and the seizure by South Carolina of all the remaining public property at Charleston, altogether changed the aspect of affairs from what it had been at the date of the interview between General Scott and the President. Fort Sumter was now threatened with an immediate attack. The time had arrived for despatching the *Brooklyn* on her destined expedition for its relief. At this crisis General Scott, being too unwell to call in person, addressed a note to the President, on Sunday, the 30th December, asking his permission to send, without reference to the War Department, and otherwise as secretly as possible, two hundred and fifty recruits from New York harbor to reënforce Fort Sumter, together with some extra muskets or rifles, ammunition and subsistence stores, expressing the hope " that a sloop-of-war and cutter may be ordered for the same purpose as early as to-morrow" (31st December).

The President immediately decided to order reënforcements; but he preferred to send them by the *Brooklyn*, which had remained in readiness for this service. He thought that a powerful war steamer with disciplined troops on board would prove more effective than a sloop-of-war and cutter with raw recruits. Accordingly on the next morning (Monday) he instructed the Secretaries of War and the Navy to despatch the *Brooklyn* to Fort Sumter. On the evening of this day the General called to congratulate him on the fact that the Secretaries had already issued appropriate orders to the respective army and navy officers, and stated that these were then in his own pocket.

In contradiction to this prompt action, it is difficult to imagine how the General could have asserted, in his report to President Lincoln, that "the South Carolina commissioners had already been many days in Washington, and no movement of defence [on the part of the United States] had been permitted." In regard to the "*many days*" delay:—These commissioners arrived in Washington on the 26th December; the General sent his request to the President on Sunday, the 30th; and on Monday morning he himself received the necessary orders for the departure of the expedition. General Scott, notwithstanding this prompt response to his request, proceeds still further, and charges the President with having "refused to allow any attempt to be made" to reënforce Fort Sumter, "because he was holding negotiations with the South Carolina commissioners," although this alleged refusal occurred at the very time (31st December) when he himself had in his own hands the order for the *Brooklyn* to proceed immediately to Fort Sumter. Nay, more: "Afterwards," says the General, "Secretary Holt and myself endeavored, in vain, to obtain a ship-of-war for the purpose, and were finally obliged to employ the passenger steamer *Star of the West.*" After this statement, will it be credited that the *Star of the West* was employed in place of the *Brooklyn* at the pressing instance of General Scott himself? And yet such is the fact. The President yielded to this unfortunate change with great reluctance, and solely in deference to the opinion of the commanding General on a question of military strategy. What a failure and confusion of memory the report to President Lincoln exhibits!

At the interview with President Buchanan on the evening of the 31st December, the General seemed cordially to approve the matured plan of sending reënforcements by the *Brooklyn*. Why, then, the change in his opinion? At this interview the President informed him he had sent a letter but a few hours before to the South Carolina commissioners, in answer to a communication from them, and this letter would doubtless speedily terminate their mission;—that although he had refused to recognize them in an official character, yet it might be considered improper to transmit the orders then in his possession to the *Brooklyn* until they had an opportunity of making a reply, and that the delay for this purpose could not, in his opinion, exceed forty-eight hours. In this suggestion the General promptly concurred, observing that it was gentlemanly and proper. He, therefore, retained the orders to await the reply. On the morning of the 2d January the President received and returned the insolent communication of the South Carolina commissioners without an answer, and thus every obstacle was removed from the immediate transmission of the orders. In the mean time, however, the General had unluckily become convinced, after advising with an individual believed to possess much knowledge and practical experience in naval affairs, that the better plan to secure both secrecy and success would be to send to Fort Sumter a fast side-wheel mercantile steamer from New York with the two hundred and fifty recruits.

Such was the cause of the change, according to the undoubted information communicated to the President at the time by the Secretaries of War and the Navy. For this reason alone was the *Star of the West* substituted for the service instead of the *Brooklyn*. The change of programme caused a brief delay; but the *Star of the West*, with recruits on board, left New York for Charleston on the afternoon of the 5th January. On the evening of the same day, however, on which this ill-fated steamer went to sea, General Scott despatched a telegram to his son-in-law, Colonel Scott, of the United States army, then at New York, to countermand her departure; but this did not reach him until after she had left the harbor.

The cause of this countermand proves how much wiser it would have been to employ the *Brooklyn* in the first instance on this important service. This shall be stated in the language of Secretary Holt in his letter of the 5th March, 1861, in reply to certain allegations which had been made and published * by Mr. Thompson, the late Secretary of the Interior. In this he says: "The countermand spoken of (by Mr. Thompson) was not more cordially sanctioned by the President than it was by General Scott and myself; not because of any dissent from the order on the part of the President, but because of a letter received that day from Major Anderson, stating, in effect, that he regarded himself secure in his position; and yet more from intelligence which late on Saturday evening (5th January, 1861) reached the Department, that a heavy battery had been erected among the sand hills, at the entrance to Charleston harbor, which would probably destroy any unarmed vessel (and such was the *Star of the West*) which might attempt to make its way to Fort Sumter. This important information satisfied the Government that there was no present necessity for sending reënforcements, and that when sent they should go not in a vessel of commerce, but of war. Hence the countermand was despatched by telegraph to New York; but the vessel had sailed a short time before it reached the officer (Colonel Scott) to whom it was addressed."

General Scott, as well as the Secretaries of War and the Navy, convinced of the blunder which had been committed in substituting the *Star of the West* for the *Brooklyn*, proceeded to provide, as far as might be possible, against anticipated disaster. For this purpose the Secretary of the Navy, on the 7th January, despatched an order to the commander of the *Brooklyn* (Farragut), and General Scott simultaneously forwarded to him a despatch to be delivered to the U. S. officer in command of the recruits on the *Star of the West*. By this the commander of the recruits was informed that Captain Farragut had been in-

* "National Intelligencer," 5th March, 1861

structed to afford him "aid and succor in case your [his] ship be shattered or injured; *second*, to convey this order of recall, in case you cannot land at Fort Sumter, to Fort Monroe, Hampton Roads, there to await further orders." In a postscript he was further directed "to land his troops at Fort Monroe and discharge the ship." The sequel will show that these precautions were useless.

The *Star of the West*, under the command of Captain McGowan, proceeded on her ill-starred voyage, amid anxious apprehensions for the fate of the recruits and mariners on board. She arrived in Charleston harbor on the 9th of January, the flag of the United States flying at her mast-head; and whilst endeavoring to approach Fort Sumter, was fired upon by order of Governor Pickens. She then immediately changed her course and returned to New York. Fortunately no lives were lost, nor was the vessel materially injured. This statement of facts proves incontestably that the President, so far from refusing, was not only willing but anxious, within the briefest period, to reënforce Fort Sumter.

On the very day and immediately after this outrage on the *Star of the West*, Major Anderson sent a flag to Governor Pickens, informing him of the reason why he had not opened fire from Fort Sumter on the batteries which had attacked the *Star of the West*. This was because he presumed the act had been unauthorized. He demanded its disavowal, and if this were not sent in a reasonable time he would consider it war, and fire on any vessel that attempted to leave the harbor. Had he adhered to his purpose, the civil war would then have commenced. This demand of Major Anderson, so worthy of an American officer, was totally disregarded by the Governor. Instead of disavowing the act or apologizing for it, he had the audacity, but two days after the outrage, to send the Hon. A. G. Magrath and General D. F. Jamison, whom he styled as "both members of the Executive Council and of the highest position in the State," to Major Anderson, for the purpose of persuading him to surrender the fort. In the letter which they bore from the Governor, dated on the 11th January, they were instructed to present to

Major Anderson "considerations of the gravest public character, and of the deepest interest to all who deprecate the improper waste of life, to induce the delivery of Fort Sumter to the constituted authorities of the State of South Carolina, with a pledge on its part to account for such public property as may be in your charge."

This Major Anderson appears to have regarded, not merely as an effort to persuade him voluntarily to surrender the fort, but as an absolute demand for its surrender. In either case, however, his instructions, already quoted, prescribed his line of duty. Under these he ought to have peremptorily informed the emissaries of the Governor that he would not surrender, but would defend the fort against attack by all the means in his power. In this course he would not only have obeyed his instructions, but have acted in accordance with the explicit determination of the President, announced but eleven days before (31st December) to the South Carolina commissioners. But Major Anderson, notwithstanding these considerations, as well as his own declared purpose but two days before to consider the attack on the *Star of the West* as war, and to act accordingly, unless it should be explained and disavowed, now proposed to Governor Pickens to refer the question of surrender to Washington. In his answer of the same date to the Governor's menacing request, whilst stating that he could not comply with it, and deeply regretting that the Governor should have made a demand of him with which he could not comply, he presents the following alternative: "Should your Excellency deem fit, prior to a resort to arms, to refer this matter to Washington, it would afford me the sincerest pleasure to depute one of my officers to accompany any messenger you may deem proper to be the bearer of your demand." This proposition was promptly accepted by the Governor, and in pursuance thereof he sent on his part Hon. I. W. Hayne, Attorney-General of South Carolina, to Washington; whilst Major Anderson sent as his deputy Lieutenant J. Norman Hall, of the first artillery, then under his command in the fort. These gentlemen immediately set out for Washington, and arrived together on the evening of the 13th January, 1861.

Thus, greatly to the surprise of the President, had a truce or suspension of arms been concluded between Major Anderson and Governor Pickens, to continue, from its very nature, until he should again decide against the surrender of Fort Sumter. This was what the writers on public law denominate " a partial truce under which hostilities are suspended only in certain places, as between a town and the army besieging it." * Until this decision should be made by the President, Major Anderson had thus placed it out of his own power to ask for reënforcements, and equally out of the power of the Government to send them without a violation of the public faith pledged by him as the commandant of the fort. In the face of these facts, the President saw with astonishment that General Scott, in his report to President Lincoln, had stated that the expedition under Captain Ward, of three or four small steamers, "had been kept back," not in consequence of this truce between Major Anderson and Governor Pickens, "but by something like a truce or armistice concluded here [in Washington], embracing Charleston and Pensacola harbors, agreed upon between the late President and certain principal seceders of South Carolina, Florida, Louisiana, &c., and this truce lasted to the end of the administration." From the confused and inaccurate memory of the General, events altogether distinct in their nature are so blended in his report to President Lincoln, that it is difficult to disentangle them. Such is eminently the case in mixing up the facts relative to Charleston and Pensacola in the same sentences. In order to render each clear, we shall first treat of Charleston and afterwards of Pensacola.

The expedition of the *Star of the West* had scarcely returned to New York, when the news of the truce between Major Anderson and Governor Pickens reached Washington (13th January). Between the two events it was physically impossible to prepare and send a second expedition, and this could not be done afterwards until the truce should expire, without a violation of public faith. It did not last, as the General asserts, "to the end of the administration," but expired by its own lim-

* Vattel's Law of Nations, p. 404.

itation on the 5th February, the day when Secretary Holt finally and peremptorily announced to the South Carolina commissioner that the President would not under any circumstances surrender Fort Sumter. It is possible that, under the laws of war, the President might have annulled this truce after due notice to Governor Pickens. This, however, would have cast a serious reflection on Major Anderson for having concluded it, who, beyond question, had acted from the purest and most patriotic motives. Neither General Scott nor any other person, so far as is known, ever proposed to violate it. Indeed, from his peculiar temper of mind and military training, he would have been the last man to make such a proposition; and yet, in his report to President Lincoln, he does not make the most distant allusion to the fact, well known to him, that such a truce had ever been concluded. Had he done this, he would at once have afforded conclusive evidence against sending reënforcements until it should expire. On the contrary, instead of the actual truce, "something like a truce," according to his statement, was made, not in Charleston, but in Washington, and not between the actual parties to it, but "between the late President and certain principal seceders of South Carolina." Nothing more unfounded and unjust could have been attributed to President Buchanan.

Major Anderson may probably have committed an error in not promptly rejecting the demand, as he understood it, of Governor Pickens for the surrender of Fort Sumter, instead of referring it to Washington. If the fort were to be attacked, which was then extremely doubtful, this was the propitious moment for a successful resistance. The Governor, though never so willing, was not in a condition to make the assault. He required time for preparation. On the other hand, Major Anderson was then confident in his power to repel it. This is shown by his letters to the War Department of the 31st December and 6th January. From these it appears that he not only felt safe in his position, but confident that he could command the harbor of Charleston, and hold the fort in opposition to any force which might be brought against him. Such was, also, the oft-expressed conviction at Washington of Lieutenant Hall, whom he had selected as his deputy, as well as that of Lieutenant Theodore Talbot, likewise of the 1st artillery, who had left Fort Sumter on the 9th January, 1861, as a bearer of despatches. Still, had Governor Pickens attacked the fort, this would have been the commencement of civil war between the United States and South Carolina. This every patriot desired to avoid as long as a reasonable hope should remain of preserving peace. And then such a hope did extensively prevail, founded upon the expectation that the Crittenden Compromise, or some equally healing measure, might be eventually adopted by Congress. How far this consideration may account for Major Anderson's forbearance when the *Star of the West* was fired upon, and for his proposal two days thereafter to refer the question of the surrender of the fort to Washington, we can only conjecture. If this were the cause, his motive deserves high commendation.

Colonel Hayne, the commissioner from South Carolina, as already stated, arrived in Washington on the 13th January. He bore with him a letter from Governor Pickens addressed to the President. On the next morning he called upon the President and stated that he would deliver this letter in person on the day following. The President, however, admonished by his recent experience with the former commissioners, declined to hold any conversation with him on the subject of his mission, and requested that all communications between them might be in writing. To this he assented. Although the President had no actual knowledge of the contents of the Governor's letter, he could not doubt it contained a demand for the surrender of the fort. Such a demand he was at all times prepared peremptorily to reject. This Colonel Hayne must have known, because the President had but a fortnight before informed his predecessors this was impossible, and had never been thought of by him in any possible contingency. The President confidently expected that the letter would be transmitted to him on the day after the interview, when his refusal to surrender the fort would at once terminate the truce, and leave both parties free to act upon their own responsibility. Colonel Hayne, however, did not transmit this letter to the President on the 15th January, according to his promise, but withheld it until the 31st of that month. The reason for this vexatious delay will constitute a curious portion of our narrative, and deserves to be mentioned in some detail. (*Vide* the President's message of 8th February, 1861, with the accompanying documents, Ex. Doc., H. R., vol. ix., No. 61.)

The Senators from the cotton States yet in Congress appeared, strangely enough, to suppose that through their influence the President might agree not to send reënforcements to Fort Sumter, provided Governor Pickens would stipulate not to attack it. By such an agreement they proposed to preserve the peace. But first of all it was necessary for them to prevail upon Colonel Hayne not to transmit the letter to the President on the day appointed, because they well knew that the demand which it contained would meet his prompt and decided refusal. This would render the conclusion of such an agreement impossible.

In furtherance of their plan, nine of these Senators, with Jefferson Davis at their head, addressed a note to Colonel Hayne, on the 15th January, requesting him to defer the delivery of the letter. They proposed that he should withhold it until they could ascertain from the President whether he would agree not to send reënforcements, provided Governor Pickens would engage not to attack the fort. They informed the Colonel that should the President prove willing in the first place to enter into such an arrangement, they would then strongly recommend that he should not deliver the letter he had in charge for the present, but send to South Carolina for authority from Governor Pickens to become a party thereto. Colonel Hayne, in his answer to these Senators of the 17th January, informed them that he had not been clothed with power to make the arrangement suggested, but provided they could get assurances with which they were entirely satisfied that no reënforcements would be sent to Fort Sumter, he would withhold the letter with which he had been charged, refer their communication to the authorities of South Carolina, and await further instructions.

On the 19th January this correspondence between the Senators and Colonel Hayne was submitted to the President, accompanied by a note from three of their number, requesting him to take the subject into consideration. His answer to this note was delayed no longer than was necessary to prepare it in proper form. On the 22d January it was communicated to these Senators in a letter from the Secretary of War. This contained an express refusal to enter into the proposed agreement. Mr. Holt says: "I am happy to observe that, in your letter to Colonel Hayne, you express the opinion that it is 'especially due from South Carolina to our States, to say nothing of other slaveholding States, that she should, so far as she can consistently with her honor, avoid initiating hostilities between her and the United States or any other power.' To initiate such hostilities against Fort Sumter would, beyond question, be an act of war against the United States. In regard to the proposition of Colonel Hayne, 'that no reënforcements will be sent to Fort Sumter in the interval, and that public peace will not be disturbed by any act of hostility toward South Carolina,' it is impossible for me to give you any such assurances. The President has no authority to enter into such an agreement or understanding. As an executive officer, he is simply bound to protect the public property so far as this may be practicable; and it would be a manifest violation of his duty to place himself under engagements that he would not perform this duty, either for an indefinite or limited period. At the present moment it is not deemed necessary to reënforce Major Anderson, because he makes no such request and feels quite secure in his position. Should his safety, however, require reënforcements, every effort will be made to supply them."

It was believed by the President that this peremptory refusal to enter into the proposed agreement, would have caused Colonel Hayne immediately to present the letter he had in charge and thus terminate his mission, thereby releasing both parties from the obligations of the truce. In this expectation the President was disappointed. The secession Senators again interposed, and advised Colonel Hayne still longer to withhold the letter from the President, and await further instructions from

Charleston. In his answer of 24th January to their note containing this advice, he informs them that although the letter from the Secretary of War " was far from being satisfactory," yet in compliance with their request he " would withhold the communication with which he was at present charged, and refer the whole matter to the authorities of South Carolina, and would await their reply." On the 30th this reply was received, and on the next day Colonel Hayne transmitted to the President the letter of Governor Pickens demanding the surrender of the fort, with a long communication from himself. This letter is dated " Headquarters, Charleston, January 12, 1861," and is as follows:

"SIR: At the time of the separation of the State of South Carolina from the United States, Fort Sumter was, and still is, in the possession of troops of the United States, under the command of Major Anderson. I regard that possession as not consistent with the dignity or safety of the State of South Carolina, and have this day [it was the day previous] addressed to Major Anderson a communication to obtain from him the possession of that fort by the authorities of this State. The reply of Major Anderson informs me that he has no authority to do what I required, but he desires a reference of the demand to the President of the United States. Under the circumstances now existing, and which need no comment by me, I have determined to send to you Hon. I. W. Hayne, the Attorney-General of the State of South Carolina, and have instructed him to demand the delivery of Fort Sumter, in the harbor of Charleston, to the constituted authorities of the State of South Carolina. The demand I have made of Major Anderson, and which I now make of you, is suggested by my earnest desire to avoid the bloodshed which a persistence in your attempt to retain possession of that fort will cause, and which will be unavailing to secure to you that possession, but induce a calamity most deeply to be deplored. If consequences so unhappy shall ensue, I will secure for this State, in the demand which I now make, the satisfaction of having exhausted every attempt to avoid it.

"In relation to the public property of the United States

within Fort Sumter, the Hon. I. W. Hayne, who will hand you this communication, is authorized to give you the pledge of the State that the valuation of such property will be accounted for by this State, upon the adjustment of its relations with the United States, of which it was a part."

On the 6th February, the Secretary of War, on behalf of the President, replied to this demand, as well as to the letter of Colonel Hayne accompanying it. Our narrative would be incomplete without this admirable and conclusive reply. It is as follows:

"WAR DEPARTMENT, *February* 6, 1861.*

"SIR: The President of the United States has received your letter of the 31st ultimo, and has charged me with the duty of replying thereto.

"In the communication addressed to the President by Governor Pickens, under date of the 12th January, and which accompanies yours now before me, his Excellency says: 'I have determined to send to you the Hon. I. W. Hayne, the Attorney-General of the State of South Carolina, and have instructed him to demand the surrender of Fort Sumter, in the harbor of Charleston, to the constituted authorities of the State of South Carolina. The demand I have made of Major Anderson, and which I now make of you, is suggested because of my earnest desire to avoid the bloodshed which a persistence in your attempt to retain the possession of that fort will cause, and which will be unavailing to secure to you that possession, but induce a calamity most deeply to be deplored.' The character of the demand thus authorized to be made appears (under the influence, I presume, of the correspondence with the Senators to which you refer) to have been modified by subsequent instructions of his Excellency, dated the 26th, and received by yourself on the 30th January, in which he says: 'If it be so that Fort Sumter is held as property, then, as property, the rights, whatever they may be, of the United States, can be ascertained, and for the satisfaction of these rights the pledge of the State of South Carolina you are authorized to give.' The full scope and precise purport of your instructions, as thus modi-

---

* H. R. Ex. Doc., 1860-'61, vol. ix., Doc., No 61.

fied, you have expressed in the following words: 'I do not come as a military man to demand the surrender of a fortress, but as the legal officer of the State—its attorney-general—to claim for the State the exercise of its undoubted right of eminent domain, and to pledge the State to make good all injury to the rights of property which arise from the exercise of the claim.' And lest this explicit language should not sufficiently define your position, you add: 'The proposition now is that her [South Carolina's] law officer should, under authority of the Governor and his council, distinctly pledge the faith of South Carolina to make such compensation, in regard to Fort Sumter and its appurtenances and contents, to the full extent of the money value of the property of the United States, delivered over to the authorities of South Carolina by your command.' You then adopt his Excellency's train of thought upon the subject, so far as to suggest that the possession of Fort Sumter by the United States, 'if continued long enough, must lead to collision,' and that 'an attack upon it would scarcely improve it as property, whatever the result; and if captured, it would no longer be the subject of account.'

"The proposal, then, now presented to the President, is simply an offer on the part of South Carolina to buy Fort Sumter and contents as property of the United States, sustained by a declaration, in effect, that if she is not permitted to make the purchase she will seize the fort by force of arms. As the initiation of a negotiation for the transfer of property between friendly governments, this proposal impresses the President as having assumed a most unusual form. He has, however, investigated the claim on which it professes to be based, apart from the declaration that accompanies it. And it may be here remarked, that much stress has been laid upon the employment of the words 'property' and 'public property' by the President in his several messages. These are the most comprehensive terms which can be used in such a connection, and surely, when referring to a fort or any other public establishment, they embrace the entire and undivided interest of the Government therein.

"The title of the United States to Fort Sumter is complete and incontestable. Were its interest in this property purely proprietary, in the ordinary acceptation of the term, it might probably be subjected to the exercise of the right of eminent domain; but it has also political relations to it of a much higher and more imposing character than those of mere proprietorship. It has absolute jurisdiction over the fort and the soil on which it stands. This jurisdiction consists in the authority to 'exercise exclusive legislation' over the property referred to, and is therefore clearly incompatible with the claim of eminent domain now insisted upon by South Carolina. This authority was not derived from any questionable revolutionary source, but from the peaceful cession of South Carolina herself, acting through her legislature, under a provision of the Constitution of the United States. South Carolina can no more assert the right of eminent domain over Fort Sumter than Maryland can assert it over the District of Columbia. The political and proprietary rights of the United States in either case rest upon precisely the same ground.

"The President, however, is relieved from the necessity of further pursuing this inquiry by the fact that, whatever may be the claim of South Carolina to this fort, he has no constitutional power to cede or surrender it. The property of the United States has been acquired by force of public law, and can only be disposed of under the same solemn sanctions. The President, as the head of the executive branch of the government only, can no more sell and transfer Fort Sumter to South Carolina than he can sell and convey the Capitol of the United States to Maryland or to any other State or individual seeking to possess it. His Excellency the Governor is too familiar with the Constitution of the United States, and with the limitations upon the powers of the Chief Magistrate of the government it has established, not to appreciate at once the soundness of this legal proposition. The question of reënforcing Fort Sumter is so fully disposed of in my letter to Senator Slidell and others, under date of the 22d of January, a copy of which accompanies this, that its discussion will not now be renewed. I then said: 'At the present moment it is not deemed necessary to reënforce Major Anderson, because he makes no such request. Should his safety, however, require reënforcements, every effort will be made to supply them.' I can add nothing to the explicitness of this language, which still applies to the existing status.

"The right to send forward reënforcements when, in the judgment of the President, the safety of the garrison requires them, rests on the same unquestionable foundation as the right to occupy the fortress itself. In the letter of Senator Davis and others to yourself, under date of the 15th ultimo, they say : ' We therefore think it especially due from South Carolina to our States —to say nothing of other slaveholding States—that she should, as far as she can consistently with her honor, avoid initiating hostilities between her and the United States or any other power ;' and you now yourself give to the President the gratifying assurance that 'South Carolina has every disposition to preserve the public peace;' and since he is himself sincerely animated by the same desire, it would seem that this common and patriotic object must be of certain attainment. It is difficult, however, to reconcile with this assurance the declaration on your part that 'it is a consideration of her [South Carolina's] own dignity as a sovereign, and the safety of her people, which prompts her to demand that this property should not longer be used as a military post by a government she no longer acknowledges,' and the thought you so constantly present, that this occupation must lead to a collision of arms and the prevalence of civil war. Fort Sumter is in itself a military post, and nothing else; and it would seem that not so much the fact as the purpose of its use should give to it a hostile or friendly character. This fortress is now held by the Government of the United States for the same objects for which it has been held from the completion of its construction. These are national and defensive; and were a public enemy now to attempt the capture of Charleston or the destruction of the commerce of its harbor, the whole force of the batteries of this fortress would be at once exerted for their protection. How the presence of a small garrison, actuated by such a spirit as this, can compromise the dignity or honor of South Carolina, or become a source of irritation to her people, the President is at a loss to understand. The attitude of that garrison, as has been often declared, is neither menacing, nor defiant, nor unfriendly. It is acting under orders to stand strictly on the defensive; and the government and people of South Carolina must well know that they can never receive aught but shelter from its guns, unless, in the absence of all provocation, they should assault it and seek its destruction. The intent with which this fortress is held by the President is truthfully stated by Senator Davis and others in their letter to yourself of the 15th January, in which they say: 'It is not held with any hostile or unfriendly purpose toward your State, but merely as property of the United States, which the President deems it his duty to protect and preserve.'

"If the announcement so repeatedly made of the President's pacific purposes in continuing the occupation of Fort Sumter until the question shall have been settled by competent authority, has failed to impress the government of South Carolina, the forbearing conduct of his administration for the last few months should be received as conclusive evidence of his sincerity. And if this forbearance, in view of the circumstances which have so severely tried it, be not accepted as a satisfactory pledge of the peaceful policy of this administration toward South Carolina, then it may be safely affirmed that neither language nor conduct can possibly furnish one. If, with all the multiplied proofs which exist of the President's anxiety for peace, and of the earnestness with which he has pursued it, the authorities of that State shall assault Fort Sumter, and peril the lives of the handful of brave and loyal men shut up within its walls, and thus plunge our common country into the horrors of civil war, then upon them and those they represent must rest the responsibility.

"Very respectfully, your obedient servant,

"J. HOLT,
"*Secretary of War.*

"Hon. I. W. HAYNE, *Attorney-General of the State of South Carolina.*

"P. S.—The President has not, as you have been informed, received a copy of the letter to yourself from the Senators, communicating that of Mr. Holt of the 22d January."

This letter of Mr. Holt, though firm and decided in character, is courteous and respectful, both in tone and in terms. It reviews the subject in an able and comprehensive manner, explaining and justifying the conduct of the President. Unlike the letters to which it is a response, it contains no menace. In conclusion it does no more than fix the responsibility of commencing a civil war on the authorities of South Carolina, should they assault Fort Sumter and imperil the lives of the brave and loyal men shut up within its walls. It does not contain a word or an expression calculated to afford just cause of offence; yet its statements and its arguments must have cut Colonel Hayne to the quick. To reply to them successfully was impossible. He, therefore, had no resort but to get angry. Following in the footsteps of his predecessors, on the 8th February he addressed an insulting answer not to Secretary Holt, as usage and common civility required, but directly to the President. He then suddenly left Washington, leaving his missile behind him to be delivered after his departure. From his conduct he evidently anticipated its fate. His letter was returned to him on the same day, directed to Charleston, with the following indorsement: " The character of this letter is such that it cannot be received. Col. Hayne having left the city before it was sent to the President, it is returned to him by the first mail." What has become of it we do not know. No copy was retained, nor have we ever heard of it since.

What effect this letter of Mr. Holt may have produced upon the truculent Governor of South Carolina we shall not attempt to decide. Certain it is, from whatever cause, no attack was made upon Fort Sumter until six weeks after the close of Mr. Buchanan's administration. The fort remained unmolested until South Carolina had been for some time a member of the Confederate States. It was reserved for Mr. Jefferson Davis, their President, to issue the order for its bombardment, and thus formally to commence the civil war. This he did with a full consciousness that such would be the fatal effect; because in the letter from him and other Southern Senators to Col. Hayne, of the 15th January, both he and they had warned Governor Pickens that an attack upon the fort would be "the instituting hostilities between her [South Carolina] and the United States."

Thus ended the second mission from South Carolina to the

President, and thus was he relieved from the truce concluded by Major Anderson. But in the mean time, before the termination of this truce, the action of the General Assembly of Virginia, instituting the Peace Convention, had interposed an insurmountable obstacle to the reënforcement of Fort Sumter, unless attacked or in immediate danger of attack, without entirely defeating this beneficent measure. Among their other proceedings they had passed a resolution "that ex-President John Tyler is hereby appointed by the concurrent vote of each branch of the General Assembly, a commissioner to the President of the United States; and Judge John Robertson is hereby appointed by a like vote, a commissioner to the State of South Carolina and the other States that have seceded or shall secede, with instructions respectfully to request the President of the United States and the authorities of such States to agree to abstain, pending the proceedings contemplated by the action of the General Assembly, from any and all acts calculated to produce a collision of arms between the States and the Government of the United States."

Mr. Tyler arrived in Washington on the 23d January, a fortnight before the departure of Col. Hayne, bearing with him a copy of the Virginia resolutions. These he presented to the President on the following day, assuring him that whilst the people of Virginia were almost universally inclined to peace and reconstruction, yet any efforts on her part to reconstruct or preserve the Union "depended for their success on her being permitted to conduct them undisturbed by outside collision."

This resolution, it will be observed, requested the President, and not Congress, to enter into the proposed agreement. Mr. Tyler, therefore, urged the President to become a party to it. This he refused, stating, according to Mr. Tyler's report to the Governor of Virginia, "that he had in no manner changed his views as presented in his annual message; that he could give no pledges; that it was his duty to enforce the laws, and the whole power rested with Congress." He promised, notwithstanding, that he would present the subject to that body. This was due both to its intrinsic importance and to the State of Virginia, which had manifested so strong a desire to restore and preserve the Union.

The President, accordingly, in his message of the 28th January, submitting the Virginia resolutions to Congress, observed in regard to this one, that "however strong may be my desire to enter into such an agreement, I am convinced that I do not possess the power. Congress, and Congress alone, under the war-making power, can exercise the discretion of agreeing to abstain 'from any and all acts calculated to produce a collision of arms' between this and any other Government. It would, therefore, be a usurpation for the Executive to attempt to restrain their hands by an agreement in regard to matters over which he has no constitutional control. If he were thus to act, they might pass laws which he should be bound to obey, though in conflict with his agreement. Under existing circumstances, my present actual power is confined within narrow limits. It is my duty at all times to defend and protect the public property within the seceding States, so far as this may be practicable, and especially to employ all constitutional means to protect the property of the United States, and to preserve the public peace at this the seat of the Federal Government. If the seceding States abstain 'from any and all acts calculated to produce a collision of arms,' then the danger so much to be deprecated will no longer exist. Defence, and not aggression, has been the policy of the administration from the beginning. But whilst I can enter into no engagement such as that proposed, I cordially commend to Congress, with much confidence that it will meet their approbation, to abstain from passing any law calculated to produce a collision of arms pending the proceedings contemplated by the action of the General Assembly of Virginia. I am one of those who will never despair of the Republic. I yet cherish the belief that the American people will perpetuate the union of the States on some terms just and honorable for all sections of the country. I trust that the mediation of Virginia may be the destined means, under Providence, of accomplishing this inestimable benefit. Glorious as are the memories of her past history, such an achievement, both in relation to her own fame and the welfare of the whole country, would surpass them all."

This noble and patriotic effort of Virginia met no favor from

Congress. Neither House referred these resolutions of her General Assembly to a committee, or even treated them with the common courtesy of ordering them to be printed. In the Senate no motion was made to refer them, and the question to print them with the accompanying message was debated from time to time until the 21st February,* when the Peace Convention had nearly completed its labors, and after this no further notice seems to have been taken of the subject. In the House the motion to refer and print the Virginia resolutions, made by Mr. Stanton, of Ohio, on the day they were received, was never afterwards noticed.† This mortifying neglect on the part of the Representatives of the States and of the people, made a deep and unfortunate impression on the citizens of Virginia.

* Con. Globe, pp. 590, 636. † H. J., p. 236. Con. Globe, p. 601.

CHAPTER XI.

Fort Sumter again—An expedition prepared to relieve it—The expedition abandoned on account of a despatch from Major Anderson—Mr. Holt's letter to President Lincoln—Fort Pickens in Florida—Its danger from the rebels—The *Brooklyn* ordered to its relief—The means by which it was saved from capture approved by General Scott and Messrs. Holt and Toucey, with the rest of the Cabinet—Refutation of the charge that arms had been stolen—Report of the Committee on Military Affairs and other documentary evidence—The Southern and Southwestern States received less than their quota of arms—The Pittsburg cannon—General Scott's unfounded claim to the credit of preventing their shipment to the South—Removal of old muskets—Their value—Opinion of Mr. Holt in regard to the manner in which President Buchanan conducted the administration.

It is now necessary to return to Fort Sumter. This was the point on which the anxious attention of the American people was then fixed. It was not known until some days after the termination of the truce, on the 6th February, that Governor Pickens had determined to respect the appeal from the General Assembly of Virginia, and refrain from attacking the fort during the session of the Peace Convention. It, therefore, became the duty of the administration in the mean time to be prepared, to the extent of the means at command, promptly to send succor to Major Anderson should he so request, or in the absence of such request, should they ascertain from any other quarter that the fort was in danger. From the tenor of the Major's despatches to the War Department, no doubt was entertained that he could hold out, in case of need, until the arrival of reenforcements. In this state of affairs, on the very day (30th January) on which the President received the demand for the surrender of the fort, he requested the Secretaries of War and the Navy, accompanied by General Scott, to meet him for the purpose of devising the best practicable means of instantly reënforcing Major Anderson, should this be required. After several consultations an expedition for this purpose was quietly prepared at New York, under the direction of Secretary Toucey, for the relief of Fort Sumter, the command of which was intrusted to his intimate friend, the late lamented Commander Ward of the navy. This gallant officer had been authorized to select his own officers and men, who were to rendezvous on board of the receiving-ship, of which he was then in command. The expedition consisted of a few small steamers, and it was arranged that on receiving a telegraphic despatch from the Secretary, whenever the emergency might require, he should in the course of the following night set sail for Charleston, entering the harbor in the night, and anchoring if possible under the guns of Fort Sumter.

It is due to the memory of this brave officer to state that he had sought the enterprise with the greatest enthusiasm, and was willing to sacrifice his life in the accomplishment of the object, should such be his fate, saying to Secretary Toucey this would be the best inheritance he could leave to his wife and children.

According to General Scott's version of this affair in his report to President Lincoln: " At this time, when this [the truce on the 6th February] had passed away, Secretaries Holt and Toucey, Captain Ward of the navy, and myself, with the knowledge of the President [Buchanan], settled upon the employment under the captain (who was eager for the expedition) of three or four small steamers belonging to the coast survey." But this expedition was kept back, according to the General; and for what reason? Not because the Peace Convention remained still in session, and the President would not break it up by sending reënforcements to Fort Sumter whilst the authorities of South Carolina continued to respect the appeal of the General Assembly of Virginia to avoid collision, and whilst Major Anderson at the point of danger had asked no reënforcements. The General, passing over these the true causes for the delay in issuing the order to Commander Ward to set sail, declares this was kept back " by something like a truce or armistice made here [in Washington] between President Buchanan and the principal seceders of South Carolina," etc., etc., the existence of which has never been pretended by any person except himself. It soon appeared that General Scott, as well as the President and Secretaries of War and the Navy, had been laboring under a great misapprehension in supposing, from the information received from Major Anderson, that this small expedition, under Commander Ward, might be able to relieve Fort Sumter. How inadequate this would have proved to accomplish the object, was soon afterwards demonstrated by a letter, with enclosures, from Major Anderson to the Secretary of War. This was read by Mr. Holt, greatly to his own surprise and that of every other member of the Cabinet, on the morning of the 4th March, at the moment when the Thirty-sixth Congress and Mr. Buchanan's administration were about to expire. In this the Major declares that he would not be willing to risk his reputation on an attempt to throw reënforcements into Charleston harbor with a force of less than twenty thousand good and well-disciplined men. Commander Ward's expedition, consisting of only a few small vessels, borrowed from the Treasury Department and the Coast Survey, with but two or three hundred men on board, was necessarily abandoned. On the next day (5th March) the Secretary of War transmitted Major Anderson's letter, with its enclosures, to President Lincoln. This he accompanied by a letter from himself reviewing the correspondence between the War Department and Major Anderson from the date of his removal to Fort Sumter. The following is a copy, which we submit without comment:

"WAR DEPARTMENT, *March 5th*, 1861.

"SIR: I have the honor to submit for your consideration several letters with enclosures received on yesterday from Major Anderson and Captain Foster, of the Corps of Engineers, which are of a most important and unexpected character. Why they were unexpected will appear from the following brief-statement:

"After transferring his forces to Fort Sumter, he (Major Anderson) addressed a letter to this Department, under date of the 31st December, 1860, in which he says: 'Thank God, we are now where the Government may send us additional troops *at its leisure.* To be sure the uncivil and uncourteous action of the Governor [of South Carolina], in preventing us from purchasing any thing in the city, will annoy and inconvenience us somewhat; *still we are safe.*' And after referring to some deficiency in his stores, in the articles of soap and candles, he adds: 'Still we can cheerfully put up with the inconvenience of doing without them for the satisfaction we feel in the knowledge that we can command this harbor *as long as our Government wishes to keep it.*' And again, on the 6th January, he wrote: 'My position will, should there be no treachery among the workmen whom we are compelled to retain for the present, enable me to hold this fort *against any force which can be brought against me;* and it would enable me, in the event of war, to annoy the South Carolinians by preventing them from throwing in supplies into their new posts, except by the aid of the Wash Channel through Stone River.'

"Before the receipt of this communication, the Government, being without information as to his condition, had despatched the *Star of the West* with troops and supplies for Fort Sumter; but the vessel having been fired on from a battery at the entrance to the harbor, returned without having reached her destination.

"On the 16th January, 1861, in replying to Major Anderson's letters of the 31st December and of 6th January, I said: 'Your late despatches, as well as the very intelligent statements of Lieutenant Talbot, have relieved the Government of the apprehensions previously entertained for your safety. In consequence it is not its purpose at present to reënforce you. The attempt to do so would no doubt be attended by a collision of arms and the effusion of blood—a national calamity, which the President is most anxious to avoid. You will, therefore, report frequently your condition, and the character and activity of the preparations, if any, which may be being made for an attack upon the fort, or for obstructing the Government in any endeavors it may make to strengthen your command. Should your despatches be of a nature too important to be intrusted to the mails, you will convey them by special messenger. Whenever, in your judgment, additional supplies or reënforcements are necessary for your safety or for a successful defence of the fort, you will at once communicate the fact to this Department, and a prompt and vigorous effort will be made to forward them.'

"Since the date of this letter Major Anderson has regularly and frequently reported the progress of the batteries being constructed around him, and which looked either to the defence of the harbor, or to an attack on his own position; but he has not suggested that these works compromised his safety, nor has he made any request that additional supplies or reënforcements should be sent to him. On the contrary, on the 30th January, 1861, in a letter to this Department, he uses this emphatic language: 'I do hope that no attempt will be made by our friends to throw supplies in; their doing so would do more harm than good.'

"On the 5th February, when referring to the batteries, etc., constructed in his vicinity, he said: 'Even in their present condition, they will make it impossible for any hostile force, other than a large and well-appointed one, to enter this harbor, and the chances are that it will then be at a great sacrifice of life;' and in a postscript he adds: 'Of course in speaking of forcing an entrance, I do not refer to the little stratagem of a small party slipping in.' This suggestion of a stratagem was well considered in connection with all the information that could be obtained bearing upon it; and in consequence of the vigilance and number of the guard-boats in and outside of the harbor, it was rejected as impracticable.

"In view of these very distinct declarations, and of the earnest desire to avoid a collision as long as possible, it was deemed entirely safe to adhere to the line of policy indicated in my letter of the 16th January, which has been already quoted. In that Major Anderson had been requested to report 'at once,' 'whenever, in his judgment, additional supplies or reënforcements were necessary for his safety or for a successful defence of the fort.' So long, therefore, as he remained silent upon this point, the Government felt that there was no ground for apprehension. Still, as the necessity for action might arise at any moment, an expedition has been quietly prepared and is ready to sail from New York on a few hours' notice for transporting troops and supplies to Fort Sumter. This step was taken under the supervision of General Scott, who arranged its details, and who regarded the reënforcements thus provided for as sufficient for the occasion. The expedition, however, is not upon a scale approaching the seemingly extravagant estimates of Major Anderson and Captain Foster, now offered for the first time, and for the disclosures of which the Government was wholly unprepared.

"The declaration now made by the Major that he would not be willing to risk his reputation on an attempt to throw reënforcements into Charleston harbor, and with a view of holding possession of the same, with a force of less than twenty thousand good and well-disciplined men, takes the Department by surprise, as his previous correspondence contained no such intimation.

"I have the honor to be,
"Very respectfully,
"Your obedient servant,
"J. HOLT.

"TO THE PRESIDENT."

Having pointed out the course pursued by President Buchanan in regard to Fort Sumter, we must now return to Fort Pickens, in Florida. This feeble State was the last from which a revolutionary outbreak could have reasonably been expected. Its numbers had not entitled it to admission into the Union, and a large amount of blood and treasure had been expended by the Government of the United States for the protection and defence of its inhabitants against the Seminole Indians. Nevertheless, weak as the State was, its troops, under the command of Colonel William H. Chase, formerly of the corps of engineers of the United States army, suddenly rose in rebellion, attacked the troops of the United States, and expelled them from Pensacola and the adjacent navy yard. Lieutenant Slemmer, of the artillery, and his brave little command, consisting of between seventy and eighty men, were thus forced to take refuge in Fort Pickens, where they were in imminent danger of being captured every moment by a greatly superior force.

From the interruption of regular communications with Washington, Secretary Holt did not receive information of these events until some days after their occurrence, and then only through a private channel. Reënforcements were despatched to Fort Pickens without a moment's unnecessary delay. The *Brooklyn*, after being superseded by the *Star of the West*, had fortunately remained at her old station, ready for any exigency. She immediately took on board a company of United States troops from Fortress Monroe, under the command of Captain Vogdes, of the artillery, and with provisions and military stores left Hampton Roads on the 24th January for Fort Pickens. The Secretary of the Navy had, with prudent precaution, withdrawn from foreign stations all the vessels of war which could possibly be spared with any regard to the protection of our foreign commerce, and had thus rendered the home squadron unusually large. Several of the vessels of which it was composed were at the time in the vicinity of Fort Pickens. These, united with the *Brooklyn*, were deemed sufficient for its defence. "The fleet," says the Secretary, "could have thrown six hundred men into the fort (seamen and marines), without including the company from Fortress Monroe." *

Four days after the *Brooklyn* had left Fortress Monroe, Senators Slidell, Hunter, and Bigler received a telegraphic despatch from Senator Mallory, of Florida, dated at Pensacola on the 28th January, with an urgent request that they would lay it before the President. This despatch expressed an ardent desire to preserve the peace, as well as the most positive assurance from himself and Colonel Chase, that no attack would be made on the fort if its present status should be suffered to remain. The President carefully considered this proposal. The *Brooklyn* might not arrive in time for the preservation of this important fort, and for the relief of Lieutenant Slemmer. Besides, a collision at that point between the opposing forces would prove fatal to the Peace Convention so earnestly urged by Virginia, and then about to assemble. But, on the other hand, the fort was greatly in need of provisions, and these must at every hazard be supplied. Mr. Mallory and Colonel Chase must be distinctly informed that our fleet in the vicinity would be always on the alert and ready to act at a moment's warning, not only in case the fort should be attacked, but whenever the offi-

---

* His testimony before the Hale Committee and the Court-Martial on Captain Armstrong. Report No. 37, pp. 58, 234.

cers in command should observe preparations for such an attack. No precaution must be omitted on their part necessary to hold the fort.

The conclusion at which the President arrived, with the approbation of every member of his Cabinet, will be seen in the joint order dated on the 29th January, immediately transmitted by telegraph from Secretaries Toucey and Holt to the commanders of the *Macedonian* and *Brooklyn*, and "other naval officers in command," and "to Lieutenant A. J. Slemmer, 1st artillery, commanding Fort Pickens, Pensacola, Florida." The following is a copy: "In consequence of the assurances received from Mr. Mallory in a telegram of yesterday to Messrs. Slidell, Hunter, and Bigler, with a request it should be laid before the President, that Fort Pickens would not be assaulted, and an offer of such assurance to the same effect from Colonel Chase, for the purpose of avoiding a hostile collision, upon receiving satisfactory assurances from Mr. Mallory and Colonel Chase that Fort Pickens will not be attacked, you are instructed not to land the company on board the *Brooklyn* unless said fort shall be attacked, or preparations shall be made for its attack. The provisions necessary for the supply of the fort you will land. The *Brooklyn* and the other vessels of war on the station will remain, and you will exercise the utmost vigilance and be prepared at a moment's warning to land the company at Fort Pickens, and you and they will instantly repel any attack on the fort. The President yesterday sent a special message to Congress communicating the Virginia resolutions of compromise. The commissioners of different States are to meet here on Monday, the 4th February, and it is important that during their session a collision of arms should be avoided, unless an attack should be made, or there should be preparations for such an attack. In either event the *Brooklyn* and the other vessels will act promptly. Your right, and that of the other officers in command at Pensacola, freely to communicate by special messenger [with the Government], and its right in the same manner to communicate with yourself and them, will remain intact, as the basis on which the present instruction is given."

On the arrival of this order at Pensacola the satisfactory

assurances which it required were given by Mr. Mallory and Colonel Chase to our naval and military commanders, and the result proved most fortunate. The *Brooklyn* had a long passage. Although she left Fortress Monroe on the 24th January, she did not arrive at Pensacola until the 6th February. In the mean time Fort Pickens, with Lieutenant Slemmer (whose conduct deserves high commendation) and his command, were, by virtue of this order, supplied with provisions and placed in perfect security, until an adequate force had arrived to defend it against any attack. The fort has ever since been in our possession.

General Scott, in his report to President Lincoln, speaks of this arrangement in the hostile spirit toward President Buchanan which pervades the whole document. He condemns it without qualification. He alleges "that the *Brooklyn*, with Captain Vogdes' company alone, left the Chesapeake for Fort Pickens about January the 22d, and on the 29th President Buchanan, having entered into a *quasi* armistice with certain leading seceders at Pensacola and elsewhere, caused Secretaries Holt and Toucey to instruct, in a joint note, the commanders of the war vessels off Pensacola, and Lieutenant Slemmer, commanding Fort Pickens, to commit no act of hostility, and not to land Captain Vogdes' company unless the fort should be attacked." He washes his hands of all knowledge of the transaction by declaring, "That joint note I never saw, but suppose the armistice was consequent upon the meeting of the Peace Convention at Washington, and was understood to terminate with it."

Will it be believed that General Scott himself had expressly approved this joint order before it was issued, which he presents to President Lincoln in such odious colors? President Buchanan had a distinct recollection that either the Secretary of War or of the Navy, or both, had at the time informed him of this fact. Still he would have hesitated to place himself before the public on an important question of veracity in direct opposition to a report to his successor by the Commanding General of the army. He was relieved from this embarrassment by finding among his papers a note from Secretary Holt to himself, dated on the 29th January, the day on which the joint order was issued. From this the following is an extract: "I have the satisfaction of saying that on submitting the paper to General Scott he expressed himself entirely satisfied with it, saying that there could be no objection to the arrangement in a military point of view or otherwise." How does General Scott, in November, 1862, attempt to escape from this dilemma? Whilst acknowledging that few persons are as little liable as Mr. Holt to make a misstatement, either by accident or design, he yet states that he has not the slightest recollection of any interview with him on the subject.* He proceeds to say that he does indeed remember that Mr. Holt, about this time, approached his bedside when he was suffering from an access of pain; leaving it to be inferred, though he does not directly say so, that this might account for his want of attention; and then he slides off, as is his wont, to another subject. But his subterfuge will not avail him. The testimony of Mr. Holt is conclusive that he not only expressed his satisfaction with the order, but expressly declared that there could be no objection to it in a military or any other point of view. It is impossible that Mr. Holt, on the very day of the interview, and without any conceivable motive, should have made a false report to the President of what had just occurred between himself and the General. Strange forgetfulness!

General Scott, also, in his report to President Lincoln, comments severely on the delay of the order for reënforcements to Fort Taylor, Key West, and Fort Jefferson, Tortugas Island, notwithstanding this had been issued so early as the 4th January, and though these reënforcements had arrived in sufficient time to render both forts perfectly secure. This the General admits; and there the matter ought to have ended. But not so. It was necessary to elicit from this simple transaction reasons for magnifying his own services and censuring President Buchanan. According to the report, he had experienced great difficulty in obtaining permission from the President to send these reënforcements; "and this," says he, "was only effected by the aid of Secretary Holt, a strong and loyal man." He then launches forth into the fearful consequences which might

* General Scott's rejoinder to ex-President Buchanan, "National Intelligencer," Nov. 12, 1862.

have followed but for his own vigilance and foresight. He even goes so far as to say that with the possession of these forts, "the rebels might have purchased an early recognition."

In opposition to these fanciful speculations, what is the simple statement of the fact? The administration were well aware of the importance of these forts to the commerce of the Gulf of Mexico. General Scott asked the attention of Secretary Floyd, then about to leave office, to the reënforcement of them by a note of the 28th December. Not receiving any response, he addressed a note on the 30th to the President on the same subject. The rupture with the first South Carolina commissioners occurred on the 2d January, and the time had then arrived when the President, acting on his established policy, deemed it necessary to send reënforcements not only to Fort Sumter, but also to Forts Taylor and Jefferson, and these were accordingly despatched to the two latter on the 4th January. The same course precisely would have been pursued had General Scott remained at his headquarters in New York.

But the most remarkable instance of General Scott's want of memory remains to be exposed. This is not contained in his report to President Lincoln, but is to be found in his letter of the 8th November, 1862, to the "National Intelligencer," in reply to that of ex-President Buchanan. Unable to controvert any of the material facts stated in this letter, the General deemed it wise to escape from his awkward position by repeating and indorsing the accusation against Secretary Floyd, in regard to what has been called "the stolen arms," although this had been condemned as unfounded more than eighteen months before, by the report of the Committee on Military Affairs of the House of Representatives. This was that the Secretary, in order to furnish aid to the approaching rebellion, had fraudulently sent public arms to the South for the use of the insurgents. This charge chimed in admirably with public prejudice at the moment. Although the committee, after full investigation, had so long before as January, 1861, proved it to be unfounded, yet it has continued, notwithstanding, to be repeated and extensively credited up till the present moment. Numerous respectable citizens still believe that the Confederate

States have been fighting us with cannon, rifles, and muskets thus treacherously placed in their possession. This delusion presents a striking illustration of the extent to which public prejudice may credit a falsehood not only without foundation, but against the clearest official evidence. Although the late President has not been implicated as an accessory to the alleged fraud, yet he has been charged with a want of vigilance in not detecting and defeating it.

The pretext on which General Scott seized to introduce this new subject of controversy at so late a period, is far-fetched and awkward. Mr. Buchanan, whilst repelling the charge in the General's report to President Lincoln, that he had acted under the influence of Secretary Floyd in refusing to garrison the Southern fortifications, declares that "all my Cabinet must bear me witness that I was the President myself, responsible for all the acts of the administration; and certain it is that during the last six months previous to the 29th December, 1860, the day on which he resigned his office, after my request, he exercised less influence in the administration than any other member of the Cabinet."* Whereupon the General, in order to weaken the force and impair the credibility of this declaration, makes the following insidious and sarcastic remarks: "Now, notwithstanding this broad assumption of responsibility, I should be sorry to believe that Mr. Buchanan specially consented to the removal, by Secretary Floyd, of 115,000 extra muskets and rifles, with all their implements and ammunition, from Northern repositories to Southern arsenals, so that on the breaking out of the maturing rebellion, they might be found without cost, except to the United States, in the most convenient positions for distribution among the insurgents. So, too, of the one hundred and twenty or one hundred and forty pieces of heavy artillery, which the same Secretary ordered from Pittsburg to Ship Island, in Lake Borgne, and Galveston, Texas, for forts not yet erected. Accidentally learning, early in March, that under this *posthumous* order the shipment of these guns had commenced, I communicated the fact to Secretary Holt (acting for Secretary Cameron) just in time to defeat the robbery."

* Letter to "National Intelligencer," 28th Oct., 1862.

Whilst writing this paragraph it would seem impossible that the General had ever read the report of the Committee on Military Affairs, and equally impossible that he, as Commanding General of the army, should have been ignorant of this important document, so essentially connected with his official duties.

But to proceed to the report of the committee, which effectually disproves the General's assertions. At the commencement of the session of 1860–'61, public rumor gave birth to this charge. It very justly and properly attracted the attention of the House of Representatives, and from its nature demanded a rigorous investigation. Accordingly, on the motion of Mr. Stanton, of Ohio, the chairman of the Committee on Military Affairs, the House adopted a resolution instructing the committee "to inquire and report to the House to whom and at what price the public arms, distributed since the 1st January, 1860, had been disposed of," etc., etc. The investigation was deemed of such paramount importance that the House authorized the committee not only to send for persons and papers, but also to report at any time in preference to all other business. From the nature of the charge it could not be difficult for the committee to establish either its truth or its falsehood. Arms could not be removed from one armory or arsenal to another by Secretary Floyd, without the knowledge and active participation of the officers and attachés of the Ordnance Bureau. At its head was Colonel Craig, an officer as loyal and faithful as any who belonged to the army. It was through his agency alone that the arms could have been removed, and it is certain that had he known or suspected treachery on the part of the Secretary, he would instantly have communicated this to the President, in order that it might be defeated.

The committee made their first report to the House on the 9th January, 1861.* With this they presented two tables (Nos. 2 and 3), communicated to them by Mr. Holt, then the Secretary of War, from the Ordnance Bureau, exhibiting "the number and description of arms distributed since 1st January, 1860, to the States and Territories, and at what price." Whoever

---

* "Congressional Globe," p. 294. House Journal, p. 156.

shall examine table No. 2 will discover that the Southern and Southwestern States received much less in the aggregate instead of more than the quota of arms to which they were justly entitled under the law for arming the militia. Indeed, it is a remarkable fact that neither Arkansas, Delaware, Kentucky, Louisiana, North Carolina, nor Texas received any portion of these arms, though they were army muskets of the very best quality. This arose simply from their own neglect, because the quota to which they were entitled would have been delivered to each of them on a simple application to the Ordnance Bureau. The whole number of muskets distributed among all the States, North and South, was just 8,423. Of these the Southern and Southwestern States received only 2,091, or less than one-fourth. Again, the whole number of long range rifles of the army calibre distributed among all the States in the year 1860, was 1,728. Of these, six of the Southern and Southwestern States, Kentucky, Louisiana, Mississippi, North Carolina, Tennessee, and Virginia received in the aggregate 758, and the remainder of these States did not receive any.

Thus it appears that the aggregate of rifles and muskets distributed in 1860 was 10,151, of which the Southern and Southwestern States received 2,849, or between one-third and one-fourth of the whole number. Such being the state of the facts, well might Mr. Stanton have observed in making this report, much to his credit for candor and fairness, that "there are a good deal of rumors, and speculations, and misapprehension as to the true state of facts in regard to this matter." * The report of the committee and the opinion expressed by its chairman before the House, it might have been supposed, would satisfy General Scott that none of these muskets or rifles had been purloined by Secretary Floyd. But not so. The ex-President had stated in his letter to the "National Intelligencer," of November 7th, 1862, that "the Southern States received in 1860 less instead of more than the quota of arms to which they were entitled by law." This statement was founded on the report of the committee, which had now been brought fully to his notice. He, notwithstanding, still persisted in his

* "Congressional Globe," 1860-'61, p. 294.

error, and in his letter to the "National Intelligencer" of the 2d December, 1862, he says: " This is most strange contrasted with information given to me last year, and a telegram just received from Washington and a high officer, not of the Ordnance Department, in these words and figures: 'Rhode Island, Delaware, and Texas had not drawn at the end of eighteen sixty (1860) their annual quotas of arms for that year, and Massachusetts, Tennessee, and Kentucky only in part. Virginia, South Carolina, Georgia, Florida, Alabama, Louisiana, Mississippi, and Kansas were by the order of the Secretary of War supplied with their quotas for eighteen sixty-one (1861) in advance, and Pennsylvania and Maryland in part.'" It is in vain that the General attempts to set up an anonymous telegram against the report of the committee. From what source did he derive the information given to him last year? And who was the author of the telegram? He does not say in either case. Surely before he gave this telegram to the world, under the sanction of his own name, he ought to have ascertained from the Ordnance Bureau whether it was true or false. This he might easily and speedily have done, had he been careful to present an authentic statement. There is a mysterious vagueness about this telegram, calculated if not intended to deceive the casual reader into the belief that a great number of these arms had been distributed among the enumerated States, embracing their quotas not only for 1860 but for 1861. From it no person could imagine that these eight States in the aggregate had received fewer muskets and rifles than would be required to arm two full regiments.

The next subject investigated by the committee was, had Secretary Floyd sent any cannon to the Southern States? This was a most important inquiry. Our columbiads and 32-pounders were at the time considered equal, if not superior, to any cannon in the world. It was easy to ascertain whether he had treacherously, or otherwise, sent any of these formidable weapons to the South. Had he done this, it would have been impossible to conceal the fact and escape detection. The size and ponderous weight of these cannon rendered it impracticable to remove them from the North to the South without the knowledge of many outside persons, in addition to those connected with the Ordnance Bureau. The committee reported on this subject on the 18th February, 1861. There was no evidence before them that any of these cannon had actually been transmitted to the South. Indeed, this was not even pretended. From their report, however, it does appear that Secretary Floyd had attempted to do this on one occasion a very short time before he left the department, but that he had failed in this attempt in consequence of a countermand of his order issued by Mr. Holt, his successor in the War Department.

It requires but a few words to explain the whole transaction. Secretary Floyd, on the 20th December, 1860, without the knowledge of the President, ordered Captain (now Colonel) Maynadier, of the Ordnance Bureau, to cause the guns necessary for the armament of the forts on Ship Island and at Galveston to be sent to those places. This order was given verbally and not in the usual form. It was not recorded, and the forts were far from being prepared to receive their armaments. The whole number of guns required for both forts, according to the statement of the Engineer Department to Captain Maynadier, was one hundred and thirteen columbiads and eleven 32-pounders. When, late in December, 1860, these were about to be shipped at Pittsburg for their destination on the steamer *Silver Wave*, a committee of gentlemen from that city first brought the facts to the notice of President Buchanan. The consequence was, that, in the language of the report of the committee: " Before the order of the late Secretary of War [Floyd] had been fully executed by the actual shipment of said guns from Pittsburg, it was countermanded by the present Secretary." This prompt proceeding elicited a vote of thanks, on the 4th January, 1861, from the Select and Common Councils of that city, " to the President, the Attorney-General [Black], and the acting Secretary of War [Holt]."

It is of this transaction, so clearly explained by the committee in February, 1861, that General Scott, so long after as the 8th November, 1862, speaks in the language which we again quote: " Accidentally learning, early in March, that under this *posthumous* order [of Secretary Floyd] the shipment of these guns had commenced, I communicated the fact to Secretary

Holt (acting for Secretary Cameron) just in time to defeat the robbery." This statement is plain and explicit. The period of the General's alleged communication to Secretary Holt is precisely fixed. It was in March, after the close of Mr. Buchanan's administration, and whilst Mr. Holt was acting for Secretary Cameron, who had not yet taken possession of the department. This was just in time to prevent the "*posthumous*" order of Secretary Floyd from being carried into execution. Why does the General italicize the word "*posthumous*"? Perhaps he did not understand its signification. If this word has any meaning as applicable to the subject, it is that Mr. Floyd had issued the order to Captain Maynadier after his office had expired. Be this as it may, the object is palpable. It was to show that Mr. Buchanan had suffered his administration to terminate leaving the "posthumous" order of Governor Floyd in full force until after Mr. Lincoln's accession, and that it would even then have been carried into execution but for the General's lucky interposition.

The General, in his letter to the "National Intelligencer" of 2d December, 1862, attempts to excuse this deplorable want of memory to the prejudice of Mr. Buchanan. Whilst acknowledging his error in having said that the countermand of Mr. Floyd's order was in March, instead of early in the previous January, he insists that this was an immaterial mistake, and still actually claims the credit of having prevented the shipment of the cannon. "An immaterial mistake!" Why, *time* was of the very essence of the charge against Mr. Buchanan. It was the alleged delay from January till March in countermanding the order, which afforded any pretext for an assault on his administration. After his glaring mistake had been exposed, simple justice, not to speak of magnanimity, would have required that he should retract his error in a very different spirit and manner from that which he has employed.

It is due to Colonel Maynadier to give his own explanation for having obeyed the order of Secretary Floyd. In his letter to the Potter Committee of the House of Representatives, dated 3d February, 1862, he says: "In truth it never entered my mind at this time (20th December, 1860), that there could be any improper motive or object in the order, for on the question of union and secession Mr. Floyd was then regarded throughout the country as a strong advocate of the Union and opponent of secession. He had recently published, over his own signature, in a Richmond paper, a letter on this subject, which gained him high credit at the North for his boldness in rebuking the pernicious views of many in his own State."

The committee, then, in the third place, extended back their inquiry into the circumstances under which Secretary Floyd had a year before, in December, 1859, ordered the removal of one-fifth of the old percussion and flint-lock muskets from the Springfield armory, where they had accumulated in inconvenient numbers, to five Southern arsenals. The committee, after examining Colonel Craig, Captain Maynadier, and other witnesses, merely reported to the House the testimony they had taken, without in the slightest degree implicating the conduct of Secretary Floyd. Indeed, this testimony is wholly inconsistent with the existence of any improper motive on his part. He issued the order to Colonel Craig (December 29th, 1859) almost a year before Mr. Lincoln's election, several months before his nomination at Chicago, and before the Democratic party had destroyed its prospects of success by breaking up the Charleston Convention. Besides, Secretary Floyd was at the time, as he had always been, an open and avowed opponent of secession. Indeed, long afterwards, when the question had assumed a more serious aspect, we are informed, as already stated by Captain Maynadier, that he had in a Richmond paper boldly rebuked the advocates of this pernicious doctrine. The order and all the proceedings under it were duly recorded. The arms were not to be removed in haste, but "from time to time as may be most suitable for economy and transportation," and they were to be distributed among the arsenals, "in proportion to their respective means of proper storage." All was openly transacted, and the order was carried into execution by the Ordnance Bureau according to the usual course of administration, without any reference to the President.

The United States had on hand 499,554, say 500,000 of these muskets. They were in every respect inferior to the new rifle muskets, with which the army had for some years been supplied. They were of the old calibre of $\frac{69}{100}$ of an inch, which had been changed in 1855 to that of $\frac{58}{100}$ in the new rifled muskets. It was 105,000 of these arms that Secretary Floyd ordered to be sent to the five Southern arsenals; "65,000 of them were percussion muskets of the calibre of $\frac{69}{100}$, and 40,000 of this calibre altered to percussion." By the same order 10,000 of the old percussion rifles of the calibre of $\frac{54}{100}$ were removed to these arsenals. These constitute the 115,000 extra muskets and rifles, with all their implements and ammunition, which, according to General Scott's allegation nearly three years thereafter, had been sent to the South to furnish arms to the future insurgents. We might suppose from this description, embracing "ammunition," powder and ball, though nowhere to be found except in his own imagination, that the secessionists were just ready to commence the civil war. His sagacity, long after the fact, puts to shame the dulness of the Military Committee. Whilst obliged to admit that the whole proceeding was officially recorded, he covers it with an air of suspicion by asserting that the transaction was "very quietly conducted." And yet it was openly conducted according to the prescribed forms, and must have been known at the time to a large number of persons, including the General himself, outside either of the War Department, the Springfield armory, or the Southern arsenals. In truth, there was not then the least motive for concealment, even had this been possible.

The General pronounces these muskets and rifles to have been of an "*extra*" quality. It may, therefore, be proper to state from the testimony what was their true character.

In 1857 proceedings had been instituted by the War Department, under the act of 3d March, 1825, "to authorize the sale of unserviceable ordnance, arms, and military stores."* The inspecting officers under the act condemned 190,000 of the old muskets, "as unsuitable for the public service," and recommended that they be sold. In the spring of 1859, 50,000 of them were offered at public sale. "The bids received," says Colonel Craig, "were very unsatisfactory, ranging from 10½

---

* 4 Stat. at Large, 127.

cents to $2.00, except one bid for a small lot for $3.50. In submitting them to the Secretary I recommended that none of them be accepted at less than $2.00." An effort was then made to dispose of them at private sale for the fixed price of $2.50. So low was the estimate in which they were held, that this price could not be obtained, except for 31,610 of them in parcels. It is a curious fact, that although the State of Louisiana had purchased 5,000 of them at $2.50, she refused to take more than 2,500. On the 5th July, 1859, Mr. H. G. Fant purchased a large lot of them at $2.50 each, payable in ninety days; but in the mean time he thought better of it, and like the State of Louisiana failed to comply with his contract. And Mr. Belnap, whose bid at $2.15 for 100,000 of them intended for the Sardinian Government had been accepted by the Secretary, under the impression it was $2.50, refused to take them at this price after the mistake had been corrected. Colonel Craig, in speaking of these muskets generally, both those which had and had not been condemned, testified that "It is certainly advisable to get rid of that kind of arms whenever we have a sufficient number of others to supply their places, and to have all our small arms of one calibre. The new gun is rifled. A great many of those guns [flint-locks], altered to percussion, are not strong enough to rifle, and therefore they are an inferior gun. They are of a different calibre from those now manufactured by the Government."

Had the cotton States at the time determined upon rebellion, what an opportunity they lost of supplying themselves with these condemned "extra muskets and rifles" of General Scott!

In opposition to the strictures of General Scott upon Mr. Buchanan's administration, it may be pardonable to state the estimate in which it was held by Mr. Holt, the Secretary of War. No man living had better opportunities than himself of forming a just judgment of its conduct, especially in regard to military matters. Besides, in respect to these, he had been in constant official communication with General Scott from the first of January, 1861, until the inauguration of President Lincoln. He had previously been Postmaster-General from the decease of his predecessor, Governor Brown, in March, 1859, until the last day of December, 1860, when he was appointed Secretary of War, at this period the most important and responsible position in the Cabinet. In this he continued until the end of the administration. In his customary letter of resignation addressed to Mr. Buchanan, immediately before the advent of the new administration, and now on file in the State Department, he did not confine himself to the usual routine in such cases, but has voluntarily added an expression of his opinion of the administration of which he had been so long a member. He says that—

"In thus terminating our official relations, I avail myself of the occasion to express to you my heartfelt gratitude for the confidence with which, in this and other high positions, you have honored me, and for the firm and generous support which you have constantly extended to me, amid the arduous and perplexing duties which I have been called to perform. In the full conviction that your labors will yet be crowned by the glory that belongs to an enlightened statesmanship and to an unsullied patriotism, and with sincerest wishes for your personal happiness, I remain most truly

"Your friend, "J. Holt."

It is fair to observe that the policy of President Lincoln toward the seven cotton States which had seceded before his inauguration, was, in the main, as conservative and forbearing as that of Mr. Buchanan. No fault can be justly found with his inaugural address, except that portion of it derogating from the authority of decisions of the Supreme Court. This was doubtless intended to shield the resolution of the Chicago platform, prohibiting slavery in Territories, from the Dred Scott decision. It cannot be denied that this had at the time an unhappy influence upon the border States, because it impaired the hope of any future compromise of this vital question.

President Lincoln specifies and illustrates the character of his inaugural in his subsequent message to Congress of the 4th July, 1861. He says: "The policy chosen looked to the exhaustion of all peaceable measures, before a resort to any stronger ones. It sought to hold the public places and property, not already wrested from the Government, and to collect the revenue, relying for the rest on time, discussion, and the ballot-box. It promised a continuance of the mails at Government expense to the very people who were resisting the Government, and it gave repeated pledges against any disturbance to any of the people or any of their rights. Of all that a President might constitutionally and justifiably do in such a case, every thing was forborne without which it was possible to keep the Government on foot."

The policy thus announced, whilst like that of Mr. Buchanan, was of a still more forbearing character. Nay, more; the administration of Mr. Lincoln deliberated, and at one time, it is believed, had resolved, on the advice of General Scott, to withdraw the troops under Major Anderson from the harbor of Charleston, although this had been repeatedly and peremptorily refused by the preceding administration. If sound policy had not enjoined this forbearing course, it would have been dictated by necessity, because Congress had adjourned after having deliberately refused to provide either men or means for a defensive, much less an aggressive movement.

The policy thus announced by Mr. Lincoln, under the circumstances, was the true policy. It was the only policy which could present a reasonable hope of preserving and confirming the border States in their allegiance to the Government. It was the only policy which could by possibility enable these States to bring back the seceded cotton States into the Union. It was the only policy which could cordially unite the Northern people in the suppression of rebellion, should they be compelled to resist force by force for the preservation of the Constitution and the Union. It was, however, rendered impossible to pursue this conservative policy any longer after the Government of the Confederate cotton States, on the 13th April, 1861, had commenced the civil war by the bombardment and capture of Fort Sumter. Its wisdom has been vindicated by the unanimous and enthusiastic uprising of the Northern people, without distinction of party, to suppress the rebellion which had thus been inaugurated.

CHAPTER XII.

The reduction of the expenses of the Government under Mr. Buchanan's administration—The expedition to Utah—The Covode Committee.

THE rancorous and persistent opposition to Mr. Buchanan's administration throughout its whole term, did not divert it from devoting its efforts to promote the various and important interests intrusted to its charge. Both its domestic and foreign policy proved eminently successful. This appears from the records of the country. We deem it necessary to refer only to a few of the most important particulars.

The administration succeeded by rigid economy in greatly reducing the expenditures of the Government. To this task Mr. Buchanan had pledged himself in his inaugural. It was no easy work. An overflowing treasury had produced habits of prodigality which it was difficult to correct. Over the contingent expenses of Congress, which had become far more extravagant than those of any other branch of the Government, the President could exercise no control. For these the two Houses were exclusively responsible, and they had so far transcended all reasonable limits, that their expenses, though in their nature they ought to have been purely incidental, had far exceeded the whole of the regular appropriation for their pay and mileage. Such was the extent of the abuse, that in the two fiscal years ending respectively on the 30th June, 1858 and 1859, whilst the regular pay and mileage of the members were less than $2,350,000, these contingencies amounted to more than three millions and a half. In the fiscal year ending on the 30th June, 1860, they were somewhat reduced, but still exceeded $1,000,000.

Notwithstanding this extravagance and the large outlay unavoidably incurred for the expedition to Utah, the President succeeded in gradually diminishing the annual expenditures until they were reduced to the sum of $55,402,465.46. We do not mention the cost of the expedition to Paraguay, because, through the careful management of the Secretary of the Navy, this amounted to very little more than the ordinary appropriation for the naval service. This aggregate embraces all the expenses of the Government, legislative, executive, and judicial, for the year ending 30th June, 1860, but not the interest on the public debt. If this, which was $3,177,314, be added, the whole would amount to $58,579,779.46. If to this we should make a liberal addition for appropriations recommended by the War and Navy Departments, as necessary for the defence of the country, but which were rejected by Congress, we shall be able to appreciate justly the correctness of the President's declaration in his annual message of December, 1860, "that the sum of $61,000,000, or, at the most, $62,000,000, is amply sufficient to administer the Government and to pay the interest on the public debt, unless contingent events should hereafter render extraordinary expenditures necessary." These statements, though made in the message, were never controverted by any member of either House in this hostile Congress. The expenditure was reduced to a much lower figure than the friends of the administration deemed possible. The result was the fruit of rigid economy and strict accountability. All public contracts, except in a very few cases where this was impracticable, were awarded, after advertisement, to the lowest bidder. And yet, in the face of all these facts, the administration of Mr. Buchanan has been charged with extravagance.

UTAH.

In addition to the troubles in Kansas, President Buchanan, at an early period of his administration, was confronted by an open resistance to the execution of the laws in the Territory of Utah. All the officers of the United States, judicial and executive, except two Indian agents, had found it necessary for their personal safety to escape from the Territory. There no longer remained in it any Government, except the Mormon despotism of Brigham Young. This being the condition of affairs, the President had no alternative but to adopt vigorous measures for restoring the supremacy of the Constitution and the laws. For this purpose he appointed a new Governor (Cumming) and other Federal officers, to take the place of Governor Young and of those who had been compelled to leave the Territory. To have sent these officers to Utah without a military force to protect them whilst performing their duties, would have only invited further aggression. He therefore ordered that a detachment of the army should accompany them to act as a *posse comitatus*, when required by the civil authority for the execution of the laws.

There was much reason to believe that Governor Young had long desired and intended to render himself independent. "He knows [says the President, in his annual message of December, 1857] that the continuance of his despotic power depends upon the exclusion of all settlers from the Territory, except those who will acknowledge his divine mission and implicitly obey his will; and that an enlightened public opinion would soon prostrate institutions at war with the laws both of God and man. He has, therefore, for several years, in order to maintain his independence, been industriously employed in collecting and fabricating arms and munitions of war, and in disciplining the Mormons for military service. As Superintendent of Indian Affairs, he has had an opportunity of tampering with the Indian tribes, and exciting their hostile feelings against the United States. This, according to our information, he has accomplished in regard to some of these tribes, while others have remained true to their allegiance, and have communicated his intrigues to our Indian agents."

"At the date of the President's instructions to Govenor Cumming, a hope was indulged that no necessity might exist for employing the military in restoring and maintaining the authority of the law, but this hope has now vanished. Governor Young has, by proclamation, declared his determination to maintain his power by force, and has already committed acts of hostility against the United States. Unless he should retrace his steps, the Territory of Utah will be in a state of open rebellion. He has committed these acts of hostility, notwithstanding Major Van Vliet, an officer of the army, sent to Utah by the Commanding General to purchase provisions for the troops, had given him the strongest assurances of the peaceful intentions of the Government, and that the troops would only be employed as a *posse comitatus* when called on by the civil authority to aid in the execution of the laws."

He not only refused to sell, or permit the Mormons to sell, any provisions for the subsistence of the troops, but he informed Major Van Vliet that he had laid in a store of provisions for three years, which in case of necessity he would conceal " and then take to the mountains, and bid defiance to all the powers of the Government."

The message proceeds to state that " a great part of all this may be idle boasting; but yet no wise government will lightly estimate the efforts which may be inspired by such frenzied fanaticism as exists among the Mormons in Utah. This is the first rebellion which has existed in our Territories; and humanity itself requires that we should put it down in such a manner that it shall be the last. To trifle with it would be to encourage it and to render it formidable."

It was not until the 29th of June, 1857, that the General in Chief (Scott) was enabled to issue orders, from his headquarters at New York, to Brigadier General Harney, for the conduct of the expedition.* (And here it may be proper to observe that Col. A. S. Johnston, of the 2d United States cavalry, was soon after substituted in the command for General Harney. This was done on the earnest request of Governor Walker, who believed that Harney's services in Kansas were indispensable.)

The season was now so far advanced, and Utah was so distant, that doubts were entertained whether the expedition ought not to be delayed until the next spring. But the necessity for a prompt movement to put down the resistance of Brigham Young to the execution of the laws, and to prevent the consequences of leaving him in undisturbed possession of supreme

---

* Senate Documents, 1857-'58, vol. iii., p. 21.

power for another year, were most fortunately sufficient to overcome these doubts. General Scott in his orders refers to these difficulties, and makes them the occasion of prescribing to the commander the great care and diligence he ought to employ. He says: "The lateness of the season, the dispersed condition of the troops, and the smallness of the numbers available, have seemed to present elements of difficulty, if not hazard, in this expedition. But it is believed that these may be compensated by unusual care in its outfit and great prudence in its conduct. All disposable recruits have been reserved for it. So well is the nature of this service appreciated, and so deeply are the honor and interests of the United States involved in its success, that I am authorized to say the Government will hesitate at no expense requisite to complete the efficiency of your little army, and to insure health and comfort to it, as far as attainable."

The happy result of this expedition we shall present in the language of the annual message of the 6th of December, 1858, as follows: "The present condition of the Territory of Utah, when contrasted with what it was one year ago, is a subject for congratulation. It was then in a state of open rebellion, and cost what it might, the character of the Government required that this rebellion should be suppressed, and the Mormons compelled to yield obedience to the Constitution and the laws. In order to accomplish this object, as I informed you in my last annual message, I appointed a new Governor instead of Brigham Young, and other Federal officers to take the place of those who, consulting their personal safety, had found it necessary to withdraw from the Territory. To protect these civil officers, and to aid them as a *posse comitatus* in the execution of the laws in case of need, I ordered a detachment of the army to accompany them to Utah. The necessity for adopting these measures is now demonstrated.

"On the 15th of September, 1857, Governor Young issued his proclamation, in the style of an independent sovereign, announcing his purpose to resist by force of arms the entry of the United States troops into our own Territory of Utah. By this he required all the forces in the Territory 'to hold themselves in readiness to march at a moment's notice to repel any and all such invasion,' and established martial law from its date throughout the Territory. These proved to be no idle threats. Forts Bridger and Supply were vacated and burnt down by the Mormons, to deprive our troops of a shelter after their long and fatiguing march. Orders were issued by Daniel H. Wells, styling himself 'Lieutenant-General, Nauvoo Legion,' to stampede the animals of the United States troops on their march, to set fire to their trains, to burn the grass and the whole country before them and on their flanks, to keep them from sleeping by night surprises, and to blockade the road by felling trees and destroying the fords of rivers, etc., etc., etc.

"These orders were promptly and effectually obeyed. On the 4th of October, 1857, the Mormons captured and burned, on Green River, three of our supply trains, consisting of seventy-five wagons loaded with provisions and tents for the army, and carried away several hundred animals. This diminished the supply of provisions so materially that General Johnston was obliged to reduce the ration, and even with this precaution there was only sufficient left to subsist the troops until the first of June.

"Our little army behaved admirably in their encampment at Fort Bridger under these trying privations. In the midst of the mountains, in a dreary, unsettled, and inhospitable region, more than a thousand miles from home, they passed the severe and inclement winter without a murmur. They looked forward with confidence for relief from their country in due season, and in this they were not disappointed.

"The Secretary of War employed all his energies to forward them the necessary supplies, and to muster and send such a military force to Utah as would render resistance on the part of the Mormons hopeless, and thus terminate the war without the effusion of blood. In his efforts he was efficiently sustained by Congress. They granted appropriations sufficient to cover the deficiency thus necessarily created, and also provided for raising two regiments of volunteers 'for the purpose of quelling disturbances in the Territory of Utah, for the protection of supply and emigrant trains, and the suppression of Indian hostilities on the frontiers.'* Happily, there was no occasion to call these regiments into service. If there had been, I should have felt serious embarrassment in selecting them, so great was the number of our brave and patriotic citizens anxious to serve their country in this distant and apparently dangerous expedition. Thus it has ever been, and thus may it ever be!

"The wisdom and economy of sending sufficient reënforcements to Utah are established not only by the event, but in the opinion of those who, from their position and opportunities, are the most capable of forming a correct judgment. General Johnston, the commander of the forces, in addressing the Secretary of War from Fort Bridger, under date of October 18th, 1857, expresses the opinion that 'unless a large force is sent here, from the nature of the country, a protracted war on their [the Mormons'] part is inevitable.' This he considered necessary, to terminate the war 'speedily and more economically than if attempted by insufficient means.'

"In the mean time it was my anxious desire that the Mormons should yield obedience to the Constitution and the laws, without rendering it necessary to resort to military force. To aid in accomplishing this object, I deemed it advisable, in April last, to despatch two distinguished citizens of the United States, Messrs. Powell and McCulloch, to Utah. They bore with them a proclamation addressed by myself to the inhabitants of Utah, dated on the 6th day of that month, warning them of their true condition, and how hopeless it was on their part to persist in rebellion against the United States, and offering all those who should submit to the laws a full pardon for their past seditions and treasons. At the same time I assured those who should persist in rebellion against the United States that they must expect no further lenity, but look to be rigorously dealt with, according to their deserts. The instructions to these agents, as well as a copy of the proclamation and their reports, are herewith submitted. It will be seen by their report of the 3d of July last, that they have fully confirmed the opinion expressed by General Johnston in the previous October as to the necessity of sending reënforcements to Utah. In this they state that they

---

* Act of 7th April, 1858, 11 Laws, p. 262.

'are firmly impressed with the belief that the presence of the army here, and the large additional force that had been ordered to this Territory, were the chief inducements that caused the Mormons to abandon the idea of resisting the authority of the United States. A less decisive policy would probably have resulted in a long, bloody, and expensive war.' These gentlemen conducted themselves to my entire satisfaction, and rendered useful services in executing the humane intentions of the Government.

"It also affords me great satisfaction to state that Governor Cumming has performed his duty in an able and conciliatory manner, and with the happiest effect. I cannot, in this connection, refrain from mentioning the valuable services of Colonel Thomas L. Kane, who, from motives of pure benevolence, and without any official character or pecuniary compensation, visited Utah during the last inclement winter for the purpose of contributing to the pacification of the Territory.

"I am happy to inform you that the Governor and other civil officers of Utah are now performing their appropriate functions without resistance. The authority of the Constitution and the laws has been fully restored, and peace prevails throughout the Territory. A portion of the troops sent to Utah are now encamped in Cedar Valley, forty-four miles southwest of Salt Lake City, and the remainder have been ordered to Oregon to suppress Indian hostilities.

"The march of the army to Salt Lake City, through the Indian Territory, has had a powerful effect in restraining the hostile feelings against the United States which existed among the Indians in that region, and in securing emigrants to the far west against their depredations. This will also be the means of establishing military posts and promoting settlements along the route.

"I recommend that the benefits of our land laws and preemption system be extended to the people of Utah, by the establishment of a land office in that Territory."

Nearly eight years after these events had passed into history, Mr. Buchanan was no little surprised to discover that General

Scott, in his autobiography, published in 1864,* asserts that he had protested against the Utah expedition, and that it was set on foot by Secretary Floyd, "to open a wide field for frauds and peculation." He does not even intimate that the expedition had been ordered by the President. The censure is cast upon Floyd, and upon Floyd alone. The President had, as a matter of course, left the military details of the movement to the Secretary of War and the Commanding General of the Army. From a reference to the instructions from the General to General Harney, the President could not have inferred the existence of any such protest. On the contrary, General Scott explicitly states the fact that they had been "prepared in concert with the War Department, and sanctioned by its authority wherever required." In these instructions General Scott, so far from intimating that he had protested against the expedition, states that "the community, and in part the civil Government of Utah Territory, are in a state of substantial rebellion against the laws and authority of the United States. A new civil Governor is about to be designated, and to be charged with the establishment and maintenance of law and order. Your able and energetic aid, with that of the troops to be placed under your command, is relied upon to secure the success of his mission." And the General, as we have already seen, expresses the belief that the honor and interest of the United States were deeply involved in the result. Most certainly Mr. Buchanan, until he read the autobiography, never learned that General Scott had protested against the Utah expedition.

THE COVODE COMMITTEE.

We have already more than once referred to the violent and persistent opposition manifested in Congress to President Buchanan's administration throughout its whole term. This was displayed in a signal manner by the creation and proceedings of the notorious Covode Committee, during the session immediately preceding the Presidential election. It was instituted, beyond doubt, to render the existing Democratic administration odious

* Vol. ii., p. 504.

in the eyes of the people, and thereby to promote the election of any Republican candidate who might be nominated. The manner in which this committee was raised, by stifling debate, plainly augured the character of its future action.

On the 5th March, 1860, Mr. John Covode, a Representative from Pennsylvania, moved to suspend the rules of the House so as to enable him to introduce the resolutions creating his committee.* The Speaker decided that this motion was not debatable. Several members endeavored to discuss the character of the resolutions, but they were soon called to order and silenced. Before Mr. Underwood was stopped he had got so far as to say: "I rise to a point of order. It is, that it is not in order, in this House, for any member to propose an investigation upon vague, loose, and indefinite charges, but it is his duty to state the grounds distinctly upon which he predicates his inquiry. If the gentleman who offered these resolutions will state to the House, upon his responsibility as a member, that he knows, or has been informed and believes, that offers have been made to bribe, as insinuated in that resolution, nobody will object. But I do object to charges against any officer of the Government by insinuation." Mr. Covode was silent to this appeal, but Mr. Bingham came to his relief by objecting to the debate as "all out of order."

Mr. Winslow afterwards (amidst loud and continued cries of "Order") said: "I feel some hesitation about my vote. These resolutions are very vague and indefinite, large in their terms, and framed like a French indictment, covering a deal of ground and abounding in a multitude of general charges. I have perfect confidence in the integrity of the President and his Cabinet. Let any specific charge be brought against him or them, and I will cheerfully yield the fullest investigation, and accord the promptest action. I will do nothing to hinder but every·thing to facilitate it. I cannot, however, vote for a committee on these sweeping charges." Mr. John Cochrane, of New York, had also got so far as to say: "Because no charges have been made on which an investigation can be founded," when "Mr. Grow and others called the gentleman to order."

* House Journal, p. 450; "Congressional Globe," pp. 997, 998.

The motion to suspend the rules was passed, and the resolutions were then before the House for consideration and discussion, when Mr. Covode instantly rose before any other member could obtain the floor, and called for the previous question on the adoption of the resolutions, which if sustained would cut off all amendment and debate.

Mr. NOELL. "I desire to offer an amendment, and ask that it may be read for information."

Mr. COVODE. "I cannot yield for that purpose."

Mr. NOELL. "I ask to have the amendment read for information."

Mr. BINGHAM. "I object."

"The previous question was seconded and the main question ordered to be put, and under the operation thereof the resolutions were adopted."

On the 9th March, 1860, Mr. Speaker Pennington appointed Mr. Covode of Pennsylvania, Mr. Olin of New York, Mr. Winslow of North Carolina, Mr. Train of Massachusetts, and Mr. James C. Robinson of Illinois, members of the committee.* The Covode Committee was thus ushered into existence in ominous silence, its authors having predetermined not to utter a word themselves, nor to suffer its opponents to utter a word, on the occasion of its birth. The President could not remain silent in the face of these high-handed and unexampled proceedings. He felt it to be his imperative duty to protest against them as a dangerous invasion by the House of the rights and powers of the Presidential office under the Constitution of the United States. Accordingly he transmitted to the House, on the 28th March, 1860, the following message : †

"To the House of Representatives:

"After a delay which has afforded me ample time for reflection, and after much and careful deliberation, I find myself constrained by an imperious sense of duty, as a coördinate branch of the Federal Government, to protest against the first two clauses of the first resolution adopted by the House of Representatives on the 5th instant, and published in the "Congres-

---

* House Journal, p. 484.   † Ibid., p. 618.

sional Globe" on the succeeding day. These clauses are in the following words: '*Resolved*, That a committee of five members be appointed by the Speaker, for the purpose, 1st, of investigating whether the President of the United States, or any other officer of the Government, has, by money, patronage, or other improper means, sought to influence the action of Congress, or any committee thereof, for or against the passage of any law appertaining to the rights of any State or Territory; and 2d, also to inquire into and investigate whether any officer or officers of the Government have, by combination or otherwise, prevented or defeated, or attempted to prevent or defeat, the execution of any law or laws now upon the statute book, and whether the President has failed or refused to compel the execution of any law thereof.'

"I confine myself exclusively to these two branches of the resolution, because the portions of it which follow relate to alleged abuses in post-offices, navy-yards, public buildings, and other public works of the United States. In such cases inquiries are highly proper in themselves, and belong equally to the Senate and the House as incident to their legislative duties, and being necessary to enable them to discover and to provide the appropriate legislative remedies for any abuses which may be ascertained. Although the terms of the latter portion of the resolution are extremely vague and general, yet my sole purpose in adverting to them at present is to mark the broad line of distinction between the accusatory and the remedial clauses of this resolution. The House of Representatives possess no power under the Constitution over the first or accusatory portion of the resolution, except as an impeaching body; whilst over the last, in common with the Senate, their authority as a legislative body is fully and cheerfully admitted.

"It is solely in reference to the first or impeaching power that I propose to make a few observations. Except in this single case, the Constitution has invested the House of Representatives with no power, no jurisdiction, no supremacy whatever over the President. In all other respects he is quite as independent of them as they are of him. As a coördinate branch of the Government he is their equal. Indeed, he is the only direct representative on earth of the people of all and each of the sovereign States. To them, and to them alone, is he responsible whilst acting within the sphere of his constitutional duty, and not in any manner to the House of Representatives. The people have thought proper to invest him with the most honorable, responsible, and dignified office in the world, and the individual, however unworthy, now holding this exalted position, will take care, so far as in him lies, that their rights and prerogatives shall never be violated in his person, but shall pass to his successors unimpaired by the adoption of a dangerous precedent. He will defend them to the last extremity against any unconstitutional attempt, come from what quarter it may, to abridge the constitutional rights of the Executive, and render him subservient to any human power except themselves.

"The people have not confined the President to the exercise of executive duties. They have also conferred upon him a large measure of legislative discretion. No bill can become a law without his approval, as representing the people of the United States, unless it shall pass after his veto by a majority of two-thirds of both Houses. In his legislative capacity he might, in common with the Senate and the House, institute an inquiry to ascertain any facts which ought to influence his judgment in approving or vetoing any bill. This participation in the performance of legislative duties between the coördinate branches of the Government ought to inspire the conduct of all of them, in their relations toward each other, with mutual forbearance and respect. At least each has a right to demand justice from the other. The cause of complaint is, that the constitutional rights and immunities of the Executive have been violated in the person of the President.

"The trial of an impeachment of the President before the Senate on charges preferred and prosecuted against him by the House of Representatives, would be an imposing spectacle for the world. In the result, not only his removal from the Presidential office would be involved, but, what is of infinitely greater importance to himself, his character, both in the eyes of the present and of future generations, might possibly be tarnished. The disgrace cast upon him would in some degree be reflected upon the character of the American people who elected him. Hence the precautions adopted by the Constitution to secure a fair trial. On such a trial it declares that 'the Chief Justice shall preside.' This was doubtless because the framers of the Constitution believed it to be possible that the Vice-President might be biassed by the fact that 'in case of the removal of the President from office' 'the same shall devolve on the Vice-President.'

"The preliminary proceedings in the House in the case of charges which may involve impeachment, have been well and wisely settled by long practice upon principles of equal justice both to the accused and to the people. The precedent established in the case of Judge Peck, of Missouri, in 1831, after a careful review of all former precedents, will, I venture to predict, stand the test of time. In that case, Luke Edward Lawless, the accuser, presented a petition to the House, in which he set forth minutely and specifically his causes of complaint. He prayed 'that the conduct and proceedings in this behalf of said Judge Peck may be inquired into by your honorable body, and such decision made thereon as to your wisdom and justice shall seem proper.' This petition was referred to the Judiciary Committee; such has ever been deemed the appropriate committee to make similar investigations. It is a standing committee, supposed to be appointed without reference to any special case, and at all times is presumed to be composed of the most eminent lawyers in the House from different portions of the Union, whose acquaintance with judicial proceedings, and whose habits of investigation, qualify them peculiarly for the task. No tribunal, from their position and character, could in the nature of things be more impartial. In the case of Judge Peck the witnesses were selected by the committee itself, with a view to ascertain the truth of the charge. They were cross-examined by him, and every thing was conducted in such a manner as to afford him no reasonable cause of complaint. In view of this precedent, and, what is of far greater importance, in view of the Constitution and the principles of eternal justice, in what manner has the President of the United States been treated by the House of Representatives? Mr. John Covode, a representative from Pennsylvania, is the accuser of the President. Instead of following the wise precedents of former times, and especially that in the case of Judge Peck, and referring the accusation to the Committee on the Judiciary, the House have made my accuser one of my judges.

"To make the accuser the judge is a violation of the principles of universal justice, and is condemned by the practice of all civilized nations. Every freeman must revolt at such a spectacle. I am to appear before Mr. Covode, either personally or by a substitute, to cross-examine the witnesses which he may produce before himself to sustain his own accusations against me, and perhaps even this poor boon may be denied to the President.

"And what is the nature of the investigation which his resolution proposes to institute? It is as vague and general as the English language affords words in which to make it. The committee is to inquire, not into any specific charge or charges, but whether the President has, 'by money, patronage, or other improper means, sought to influence,' not the action of any individual member or members of Congress, but 'the action' of the entire body 'of Congress' itself, 'or any committee thereof.' The President might have had some glimmering of the nature of the offence to be investigated, had his accuser pointed to the act or acts of Congress which he sought to pass or to defeat by the employment of 'money, patronage, or other improper means.' But the accusation is bounded by no such limits. It extends to the whole circle of legislation; to interference 'for or against the passage of any law appertaining to the rights of any State or Territory.' And what law does not appertain to the rights of some State or Territory? And what law or laws has the President failed to execute? These might easily have been pointed out had any such existed.

"Had Mr. Lawless asked an inquiry to be made by the House whether Judge Peck, in general terms, had not violated his judicial duties, without the specification of any particular act, I do not believe there would have been a single vote in that body in favor of the inquiry. Since the time of the Star Chamber and of general warrants, there has been no such proceeding in England.

"The House of Representatives, the high impeaching power of the country, without consenting to hear a word of explanation, have indorsed this accusation against the President, and made it their own act. They even refused to permit a member to inquire of the President's accuser what were the specific charges against him. Thus, in this preliminary accusation of 'high crimes and misdemeanors' against a coördinate branch of the Government, under the impeaching power, the House refused to hear a single suggestion even in regard to the correct mode of proceeding, but, without a moment's delay, passed the accusatory resolutions under the pressure of the previous question. In the institution of a prosecution for any offence against the most humble citizen—and I claim for myself no greater rights than he enjoys—the Constitution of the United States, and of the several States, require that he shall be informed, in the very beginning, of the nature and cause of the accusation against him, in order to enable him to prepare for his defence. There are other principles which I might enumerate, not less sacred, presenting an impenetrable shield to protect every citizen falsely charged with a criminal offence. These have been violated in the prosecution instituted by the House of Representatives against the executive branch of the Government. Shall the President alone be deprived of the protection of these great principles, which prevail in every land where a ray of liberty penetrates the gloom of despotism? Shall the Executive alone be deprived of rights which all his fellow-citizens enjoy? The whole proceeding against him justifies the fears of those wise and great men who, before the Constitution was adopted by the States, apprehended that the tendency of the Government was to the aggrandizement of the legislative at the expense of the executive and judicial departments.

"I again declare, emphatically, that I make this protest for no reason personal to myself; and I do it with perfect respect for the House of Representatives, in which I had the honor of serving as a member for five successive terms. I have lived long in this goodly land, and have enjoyed all the offices and honors which my country could bestow. Amid all the political storms through which I have passed, the present is the first attempt which has ever been made, to my knowledge, to assail my personal or official integrity; and this as the time is approaching when I shall voluntarily retire from the service of my country. I feel proudly conscious that there is no public act of my life which will not bear the strictest scrutiny. I defy all investigation. Nothing but the basest perjury can sully my good name. I do not fear even this, because I cherish an humble confidence that the Gracious Being who has hitherto defended and protected me against the shafts of falsehood and malice will not desert me now, when I have become 'old and gray-headed.' I can declare, before God and my country, that no human being (with an exception scarcely worthy of notice) has, at any period of my life, dared to approach me with a corrupt or dishonorable proposition; and, until recent developments, it had never entered into my imagination that any person, even in the storm of exasperated political excitement, would charge me, in the most remote degree, with having made such a proposition to any human being. I may now, however, exclaim, in the language of complaint employed by my first and greatest predecessor, that I have been abused 'in such exaggerated and indecent terms as could scarcely be applied to a Nero, to a notorious defaulter, or even to a common pickpocket.'

"I do, therefore, for the reasons stated, and in the name of the people of the several States, solemnly protest against these proceedings of the House of Representatives, because they are in violation of the rights of the coördinate executive branch of the Government, and subversive of its constitutional independence; because they are calculated to foster a band of interested parasites and informers, ever ready, for their own advantage, to swear before *ex parte* committees to pretended private conversations between the President and themselves, incapable, from their nature, of being disproved, thus furnishing material for harassing him, degrading him in the eyes of the country, and eventually, should he be a weak or a timid man, rendering him subservient to improper influences, in order to avoid such persecutions and annoyances; because they tend to destroy that harmonious action for the common good which ought to be maintained, and which I sincerely desire to cherish between coördinate branches of the Government; and, finally, because, if unresisted, they would establish a precedent dangerous and embarrassing to all my successors, to whatever political party they might be attached.

"JAMES BUCHANAN.

"WASHINGTON, *March 28th*, 1860."

The principles maintained in this message found no favor with the majority in the House. It was referred to the Committee on the Judiciary, of which Mr. Hickman, of Pennsylvania, was chairman.* On the 9th of April, 1861, he reported resolutions from the majority of the committee in opposition to its doctrines, whilst these were sustained by the minority. The majority resolutions were adopted by the House on the 8th of June following.†

Meanwhile the Covode Committee continued to pursue its secret inquisitorial examinations until the 16th of June, 1860, when Mr. Train, one of its members, and not Mr. Covode the chairman, made a report from the majority, accompanied by the mass of all sorts of testimony which it had collected.‡ The views of the minority were presented by Mr. Winslow of North Carolina, now no more—a man possessing every estimable quality both of head and of heart, and one who had enjoyed the highest honors which his own State could confer.

The committee, though it had been engaged for three months with vindictive zeal and perseverance in hunting up all sorts of testimony against the President and members of his Cabinet, yet finally shrunk from the responsibility of reporting a single resolution accusing or censuring any one of them. In the boundless field it had explored, it failed to discover a single point on which it could venture to rest any such resolution. This surely was a triumphant result for the President.

We refrain from now portraying the proceedings of the committee in their true light, because this has already been sufficiently done by the message of the President to the House of the 28th June, 1860, of which we insert a copy from the Journal. §

* House Journal, pp. 622, 699.   † Ibid., p. 1014.
‡ Ibid., p. 1114.   § Ibid., p. 1218.

"To the House of Representatives:

"In my message to the House of Representatives of the 28th March last, I solemnly protested against the creation of a committee, at the head of which was placed my accuser, for the purpose of investigating whether the President had 'by money, patronage, or other improper means, sought to influence the action of Congress, or any committee thereof, for or against the passage of any law appertaining to the rights of any State or Territory.' I protested against this because it was destitute of any specification; because it referred to no particular act to enable the President to prepare for his defence; because it deprived him of the constitutional guards which, in common with every citizen of the United States, he possesses for his protection; and because it assailed his constitutional independence as a coördinate branch of the Government. There is an enlightened justice, as well as a beautiful symmetry, in every part of the Constitution. This is conspicuously manifested in regard to impeachments. The House of Representatives possesses 'the sole power of impeachment;' the Senate 'the sole power to try all impeachments;' and the impeachable offences are 'treason, bribery, or other high crimes or misdemeanors.' The practice of the House, from the earliest times, had been in accordance with its own dignity, the rights of the accused, and the demands of justice. At the commencement of each judicial investigation which might lead to an impeachment, specific charges were always preferred; the accused had an opportunity of cross-examining the witnesses, and he was placed in full possession of the precise nature of the offence which he had to meet. An impartial and elevated standing committee was charged with this investigation, upon which no member inspired with the ancient sense of honor and justice would have served, had he ever expressed an opinion against the accused. Until the present occasion it was never deemed proper to transform the accuser into the judge, and to confer upon him the selection of his own committee.

"The charges made against me, in vague and general terms, were of such a false and atrocious character that I did not entertain a moment's apprehension for the result. They were abhorrent to every principle instilled into me from my youth, and every practice of my life, and I did not believe it possible that the man existed who would so basely perjure himself as to swear to the truth of any such accusations. In this conviction I am informed I have not been mistaken. In my former protest, therefore, I truly and emphatically declared that it was made for no reason personal to myself, but because the proceedings of the House were in violation of the rights of the coördinate executive branch of the Government, subversive of its constitutional independence, and, if unresisted, would establish a precedent dangerous and embarrassing to all my successors. Notwithstanding all this, if the committee had not transcended the authority conferred upon it by the resolution of the House of Representatives, broad and general as this was, I should have remained silent upon the subject. What I now charge is, that they have acted as tho ughthey possessed unlimited power, and, without any warrant whatever in the resolution under which they were appointed, have pursued a course not merely at war with the constitutional rights of the Executive, but tending to degrade the presidential office itself to such a degree as to render it unworthy of the acceptance of any man of honor or principle.

"The resolution of the House, so far as it is accusatory of the President, is confined to an inquiry whether he had used corrupt or improper means to influence the action of Congress or any of its committees on legislative measures pending before them. Nothing more, nothing less. I have not learned through the newspapers, or in any other mode, that the committee have touched the other accusatory branch of the resolution, charging the President with a violation of duty in failing to execute some law or laws. This branch of the resolution is therefore out of the question. By what authority, then, have the committee undertaken to investigate the course of the President in regard to the Convention which framed the Lecompton Constitution ? By what authority have they undertaken to pry into our foreign relations, for the purpose of assailing him on account of the instructions given by the Secretary of State to our Minister in Mexico, relative to the Tehuantepec route ? By what authority have they inquired into the causes of removal from office, and this from the parties themselves removed, with a view to prejudice his character, notwithstanding this power of removal belongs exclusively to the President under the Constitution, was so decided by the first Congress in the year 1789, and has accordingly ever since been exercised? There is in the resolution no pretext of authority for the committee to investigate the question of the printing of the post-office blanks, nor is it to be supposed that the House, if asked, would have granted such an authority, because this question had been previously committed to two other committees—one in the Senate and the other in the House. Notwithstanding this absolute want of power, the committee rushed into this investigation in advance of all other subjects.

"The committee proceeded for months, from March 22d, 1860, to examine *ex parte*, and without any notice to myself, into every subject which could possibly affect my character. Interested and vindictive witnesses were summoned and examined before them; and the first and only information of their testimony which, in almost every instance, I received, was obtained from the publication of such portions of it as could injuriously affect myself, in the New York journals. It mattered not that these statements were, so far as I have learned, disproved by the most respectable witnesses who happened to be on the spot. The telegraph was silent respecting these contradictions. It was a secret committee in regard to the testimony in my defence, but it was public in regard to all the testimony which could by possibility reflect on my character. The poison was left to produce its effect upon the public mind, whilst the antidote was carefully withheld.

"In their examinations the committee violated the most sacred and honorable confidences existing among men. Private correspondence, which a truly honorable man would never even entertain a distant thought of divulging, was dragged to light. Different persons in official and confidential relations with myself, and with whom it was supposed I might have held conversations, the revelation of which would do me injury, were examined. Even members of the Senate and members of my own

Cabinet, both my constitutional advisers, were called upon to testify, for the purpose of discovering something, if possible, to my discredit.

"The distribution of the patronage of the Government is by far the most disagreeable duty of the President. Applicants are so numerous, and their applications are pressed with such eagerness by their friends both in and out of Congress, that the selection of one for any desirable office gives offence to many. Disappointed applicants, removed officers, and those who for any cause, real or imaginary, had become hostile to the administration, presented themselves, or were invited by a summons to appear before the committee. These are the most dangerous witnesses. Even with the best intentions, they are so influenced by prejudice and disappointment, that they almost inevitably discolor truth. They swear to their own version of private conversations with the President without the possibility of contradiction. His lips are sealed and he is left at their mercy. He cannot, as a coördinate branch of the Government, appear before a committee of investigation to contradict the oaths of such witnesses. Every coward knows that he can employ insulting language against the President with impunity, and every false or prejudiced witness can attempt to swear away his character before such a committee without the fear of contradiction.

"Thus for months, whilst doing my best at one end of the avenue to perform my high and responsible duties to the country, has there been a committee of the House of Representatives in session at the other end of the avenue, spreading a drag-net, without the shadow of authority from the House, over the whole Union, to catch any disappointed man willing to malign my character, and all this in secret conclave. The lion's mouth at Venice, into which secret denunciations were dropped, is an apt illustration of the Covode Committee. The Star Chamber, tyrannical and odious as it was, never proceeded in such a manner. For centuries there has been nothing like it in any civilized country, except the revolutionary tribunal of France, in the days of Robespierre. Now, I undertake to state and to prove that should the proceedings of the committee be sanctioned by the House, and become a precedent for future times, the balance of the Constitution will be entirely upset, and there will no longer remain the three coördinate and independent branches of the Government—legislative, executive, and judicial. The worst fears of the patriots and statesmen who framed the Constitution in regard to the usurpations of the legislative on the executive and judicial branches will then be realized. In the language of Mr. Madison, speaking on this very subject, in the forty-eighth number of the 'Federalist:' 'In a representative republic, where the executive magistracy is carefully limited both in the extent and duration of its power, and where the legislative power is exercised by an assembly which is inspired, by a supposed influence over the people, with an intrepid confidence in its own strength, which is sufficiently numerous to feel all the passions which actuate a multitude, yet not so numerous as to be incapable of pursuing the objects of its passions by means which reason prescribes, it is against the enterprising ambition of this department that the people ought to indulge all their jealousy and exhaust all their precautions.' And in the expressive and pointed language of Mr. Jefferson, when speaking of the tendency of the legislative branch of Government to usurp the rights of the weaker branches: 'The concentrating these in the same hands is precisely the definition of despotic government. It will be no alleviation that these powers will be exercised by a plurality of hands, and not by a single one. One hundred and seventy-three despots would surely be as oppressive as one. Let those who doubt it turn their eyes on the Republic of Venice. As little will it avail us that they are chosen by ourselves. An elective despotism was not the government we fought for, but one which should not only be founded on free principles, but in which the powers of government should be so divided and balanced among several bodies of magistracy, as that no one could transcend their legal limits without being effectually checked and controlled by the others.'

"Should the proceedings of the Covode Committee become a precedent, both the letter and spirit of the Constitution will be violated. One of the three massive columns on which the whole superstructure rests will be broken down. Instead of the executive being a coördinate, it will become a subordinate branch of the Government. The presidential office will be dragged into the dust. The House of Representatives will then have rendered the Executive almost necessarily subservient to its wishes, instead of being independent. How is it possible that two powers in the State can be coördinate and independent of each other, if the one claims and exercises the power to reprove and to censure all the official acts and all the private conversations of the other, and this upon *ex parte* testimony before a secret inquisitorial committee—in short, to assume a general censorship over the others? The idea is as absurd in public as it would be in private life. Should the President attempt to assert and maintain his own independence, future Covode Committees may dragoon him into submission by collecting the hosts of disappointed office-hunters, removed officers, and those who desire to live upon the public treasury, which must follow in the wake of every administration, and they, in secret conclave, will swear away his reputation. Under such circumstances, he must be a very bold man should he not surrender at discretion and consent to exercise his authority according to the will of those invested with this terrific power. The sovereign people of the several States have elected him to the highest and most honorable office in the world. He is their only direct representative in the Government. By their Constitution they have made him commander-in-chief of their army and navy. He represents them in their intercourse with foreign nations. Clothed with their dignity and authority, he occupies a proud position before all nations, civilized and savage. With the consent of the Senate, he appoints all the important officers of the Government. He exercises the veto power, and to that extent controls the legislation of Congress. For the performance of these high duties he is responsible to the people of the several States, and not in any degree to the House of Representatives.

"Shall he surrender these high powers, conferred upon him as the representative of the American people, for their benefit, to the House, to be exercised under their overshadowing influence and control? Shall he alone of all the citizens of the United States be denied a fair trial? Shall he alone not be 'informed of the nature and cause of the accusation' against him? Shall he alone not 'be confronted with the witnesses' against him? Shall the House of Representatives, usurping the powers of the Senate, proceed to try the President, through the agency of a secret committee of the body where it is impossible he can make any defence, and then, without affording him an opportunity of being heard, pronounce a judgment of censure against him? The very same rule might be applied, for the very same reason, to every judge of every court of the United States. From what part of the Constitution is this terrible secret inquisitorial power derived? No such express power exists. From which of the enumerated powers can it be inferred? It is true the House cannot pronounce the formal judgment against him of 'removal from office,' but they can, by their judgment of censure, asperse his reputation, and thus, to the extent of their influence, render the office contemptible. An example is at hand of the reckless manner in which this power of censure can be employed in high party times. The House, on a recent occasion, have attempted to degrade the President by adopting the resolution of Mr. John Sherman, declaring that he, in conjunction with the Secretary of the Navy, 'by receiving and considering the party relations of bidders for contracts, and the effect of awarding contracts upon pending elections, have set an example dangerous to the public safety, and deserving the reproof of this House.'

"It will scarcely be credited that the sole pretext for this vote of censure was the simple fact that in disposing of the numerous letters of every imaginable character which I daily receive, I had, in the usual course of business, referred a letter from Colonel Patterson, of Philadelphia, in relation to a contract, to the attention of the Secretary of the Navy, the head of the appropriate department, without expressing or intimating any opinion whatever on the subject; and to make the matter, if possible, still plainer, the Secretary had informed the committee that '*the President did not in any manner interfere in this case, nor has he in any other case of contract since I have been in the department.*' The absence of all proof to sustain this attempt to degrade the President, whilst it manifests the venom of the shaft aimed at him, has destroyed the vigor of the bow.

" To return, after this digression. Should the House, by the institution of Covode committees, votes of censure, and other devices to harass the President, reduce him to subservience to their will, and render him their creature, then the well-balanced Government which our fathers framed will be annihilated. This conflict has already been commenced in earnest by the House against the Executive. A bad precedent rarely if ever dies. It will, I fear, be pursued in the time of my successors, no matter what may be their political character. Should secret committees be appointed with unlimited authority to range over all the words and actions, and, if possible, the very thoughts of the President, with a view to discover something in his past life prejudicial to his character, from parasites and informers, this would be an ordeal which scarcely any mere man since the fall could endure. It would be to subject him to a reign of terror from which the stoutest and purest heart might shrink. I have passed triumphantly through this ordeal. My vindication is complete. The committee have reported no resolution looking to an impeachment against me; no resolution of censure; not even a resolution pointing out any abuses in any of the executive departments of the Government to be corrected by legislation. This is the highest commendation which could be bestowed on the heads of these departments. The sovereign people of the States will, however, I trust, save my successors, whoever they may be, from any such ordeal. They are frank, bold, and honest. They detest delators and informers. I therefore, in the name and as the representative of this great people, and standing upon the ramparts of the Constitution which they 'have ordained and established,' do solemnly protest against these unprecedented and unconstitutional proceedings.

" There was still another committee raised by the House on the 6th March last, on motion of Mr. Hoard, to which I had not the slightest objection. The resolution creating it was confined to specific charges, which I have ever since been ready and willing to meet. I have at all times invited and defied fair investigation upon constitutional principles. I have received no notice that this committee have ever proceeded to the investigation.

"Why should the House of Representatives desire to encroach on the other departments of the Government? Their rightful powers are ample for every legitimate purpose. They are the impeaching body. In their legislative capacity it is their most wise and wholesome prerogative to institute rigid examinations into the manner in which all departments of the Government are conducted, with a view to reform abuses, to promote economy, and to improve every branch of administration. Should they find reason to believe, in the course of their examinations, that any grave offence had been committed by the President or any officer of the Government, rendering it proper, in their judgment, to resort to impeachment, their course would be plain. They would then transfer the question from their legislative to their accusatory jurisdiction, and take care that in all the preliminary judicial proceedings, preparatory to the vote of articles of impeachment, the accused should enjoy the benefit of cross-examining the witnesses, and all the other safeguards with which the Constitution surrounds every American citizen.

"If, in a legislative investigation, it should appear that the public interest required the removal of any officer of the Government, no President has ever existed who, after giving him a fair hearing, would hesitate to apply the remedy. This I take to be the ancient and well-established practice. An adherence to it will best promote the harmony and the dignity of the intercourse between the coördinate branches of the Government, and render us all more respectable both in the eyes of our own countrymen and of foreign nations.

"JAMES BUCHANAN.

"WASHINGTON, June 22, 1860."

On the reading of this message it was, on motion of Mr. Benjamin Stanton, of Ohio, referred to a select committee, consisting of himself, Mr. Curry, Mr. Charles F. Adams, Mr. Sedgwick, and Mr. Pryor, which was instructed to report to the House at the next session. No report was ever made. Thus ended the Covode Committee.

CHAPTER XIII.

The successful foreign policy of the administration with Spain, Great Britain, China, and Paraguay—Condition of the Mexican Republic; and the recommendations to Congress thereupon not regarded, and the effect—The origin, history, and nature of the "Monroe Doctrine"—The treaty with Mexico not ratified by the Senate, and the consequences.

THE administration of Mr. Buchanan, in conducting our foreign affairs, met with great and uncommon success.

SPAIN.

Our relations with Spain were in a very unsatisfactory condition on his accession to power. Our flag had been insulted, and numerous injuries had been inflicted on the persons and property of American citizens by Spanish officials acting under the direct control of the Captain General of Cuba. These gave rise to many but unavailing reclamations for redress and indemnity against the Spanish Government. Our successive ministers at Madrid had for years ably presented and enforced these claims, but all without effect. Their efforts were continually baffled on different pretexts. There was a class of these claims called the "Cuban claims," of a nature so plainly just that they could not be gainsayed. In these more than one hundred of our citizens were directly interested. In 1844 duties had been illegally exacted from their vessels at different custom houses in Cuba, and they appealed to their Government to have these duties refunded. Their amount could be easily ascertained by the Cuban officials themselves, who were in possession of all the necessary documents. The validity of these claims was eventually recognized by Spain, but not until after a delay of ten years. The amount due was fixed, according to her own statement, with which the claimants were satisfied, at the sum of $128,635.54. Just at the moment when the claimants were expecting to receive this amount without further delay, the Spanish Government proposed to pay, not the whole, but only one-third of it, and this provided we should accept it in full satisfaction of the entire claim. They added that this offer was made, not in strict justice, but as a special favor.

Under these circumstances, the time had arrived when the President deemed it his duty to employ strong and vigorous remonstrances to bring all our claims against Spain to a satisfactory conclusion. In this he succeeded in a manner gratifying to himself, and it is believed to all the claimants, but unfortunately not to the Senate of the United States. A convention was concluded at Madrid on the 5th March, 1860, establishing a joint commission for the final adjudication and payment of all the claims of the respective parties. By this the validity and amount of the Cuban claims were expressly admitted, and their speedy payment was placed beyond question. The convention was transmitted to the Senate for their constitutional action on the 3d May, 1860, but on the 27th June they determined, greatly to the surprise of the President, and the disappointment of the claimants, that they would " not advise and consent " to its ratification.

The reason for this decision, because made in executive session, cannot be positively known. This, as stated and believed at the time, was because the convention had authorized the Spanish Government to present its Amistad claim, like any other claim, before the Board of Commissioners for decision. This claim, it will be recollected, was for the payment to the Spanish owners of the value of certain slaves, for which the Spanish Government held the United States to be responsible under the treaty with Spain of the 27th October, 1795. Such was the evidence in its favor, that three Presidents of the United States had recommended to Congress to make an appropriation for its payment, and a bill for this purpose had passed the Senate. The validity of the claim, it is proper to observe, was not recognized by the convention. In this respect it was placed on the same footing with all the other claims of the parties, with the exception of the Cuban claims. All the Spanish Government obtained for it was simply a hearing before the Board, and this could not be denied with any show of impartiality. Besides, it is quite certain that no convention could have been concluded without such a provision.

It was most probably the extreme views of the Senate at the time against slavery, and their reluctance to recognize it even so far as to permit a foreign claimant, although under the sanction of a treaty, to raise a question before the Board which might involve its existence, that caused the rejection of the convention. Under the impulse of such sentiments, the claims of our fellow-citizens have been postponed if not finally defeated. Indeed, the Cuban claimants, learning that the objections in the Senate arose from the Amistad claim, made a formal offer to remove the difficulty by deducting its amount from the sum due to them, but this of course could not be accepted.

GREAT BRITAIN.

With Great Britain our relations were in a most unsatisfactory condition at the commencement of Mr. Buchanan's administration. Two irritating and dangerous questions were pending between them, either of which might at any moment have involved them in war. The first arose out of her claim to a protectorate over the Mosquito Coast, and her establishment of a colonial government over the Bay Islands, which territories belonged respectively to the feeble Central American Republics of Nicaragua and Honduras. These acts of usurpation on the part of the British Government were in direct violation of the Monroe doctrine, which has been so wisely and strenuously maintained by our Government ever since it was announced. It was believed that the Clayton and Bulwer treaty, concluded in April, 1850, under the administration of General Taylor, had settled these questions in favor of the United States, and that Great Britain would withdraw from the territories of Nicaragua and Honduras. But not so. She still persisted in holding them. She even contended that the treaty only prohibited her from making future acquisitions in Central America, and by inference admitted the right to hold all her then existing possessions. The true construction of this treaty was the subject of a prolonged correspondence between Mr. Buchanan while Minister in London and the British Government. This produced no effect at the time. After he became President, however, the question was amicably and honorably settled, under his advice and approbation, by treaties between Great Britain and the two Central American States, in accordance with our construction of the Clayton and Bulwer treaty.

Great Britain, both before and after the war of 1812, had persistently claimed the right of search. Her exercise of this right in the spring of 1858 had nearly involved the two countries in war. The American people have ever been peculiarly sensitive against any attempt, from whatever power, to invade the freedom of the seas. This their whole history attests from the days of the Revolution. The question was now brought to direct issue by the British Government, from which there could be no escape. At this period she despatched a number of small armed vessels, which had been employed in the Crimean war, to the coast of Cuba and the Gulf of Mexico, with instructions to search American merchantmen whom they might suspect as slave-traders. These waters are traversed by a large portion of our navigation, and their free and uninterrupted use is essential to the security of our coastwise trade between the different States. This was all placed at the mercy of the junior officers in command of these small vessels. They proceeded at once to execute their orders. They forcibly boarded and searched numerous American vessels, and this often, as might have been expected, in a rude and offensive manner. Day after day reports of these violent proceedings succeeded each other, and produced general indignation throughout the country. The call of the people was loud for immediate redress. The President remonstrated to the British Government against these deliberate violations of our national sovereignty, but judging from the experience of the past, this would have proved unavailing. It had become necessary to resist force by force.

Without awaiting the action of Congress, he assumed this responsibility, which he thought the exigency demanded and would justify. He accordingly ordered every ship of war within reach to the Gulf, with instructions from the Secretary of the Navy "to protect all vessels of the United States on the high seas from search or detention by the vessels of war of any other nation." This decisive measure received the unqualified and enthusiastic approbation of the American people, and the Senate, though somewhat tardily, approved it by an unanimous vote.* Had an attempt been afterwards made to search any of our vessels, this would have been resisted by force; a collision between the armed vessels of the two powers, acting under the authority of each, would have occurred, and this would have been the commencement of hostilities.

But fortunately no collision took place. The British Government became sensible they were in the wrong, and at once recalled the orders under which their commanders had acted. They did far more. They abandoned their claim to the right of search, for which they had so long contended, and recognized the validity of the principle of international law in favor of the freedom of the seas, always maintained by our own Government. Thus have vessels of the United States been forever secured from visitation and search by British cruisers, in time of peace, under any circumstances whatever.

In this satisfactory manner was the long controversy between the two Governments finally settled. We deem it proper here to insert an extract from the annual report of the Secretary of the Navy (Mr. Toucey), to the President, of the 6th December, 1858,† in which he states the action of his Department in carrying into effect the instructions of the President. The Secretary says: "The force sent into the neighborhood of Cuba to resist the exercise of the right of search by British cruisers, consisted of the steam frigates Wabash and Colorado; the sloops of war Macedonian, Constellation, Jamestown, Saratoga, and Plymouth; the steamers Water Witch, Arctic, Fulton, and Despatch, and the brig Dolphin comprising the Mediterranean squadron under Flag Officer Lavallette, the home squadron

* Congressional Globe, p. 3061.   † Senate Documents, vol. iv., p. 3.

under Flag Officer McIntosh, and such other vessels as were sent out specially for the purpose. They were all deemed effective for the object for which they were sent, because in the execution of their mission no one of them would have hesitated to resist a ship of the largest class. They were instructed to protect all vessels of the United States against the exercise of the right of search on the high seas, in time of peace, by the armed vessels of any other power. These instructions have been often repeated, and are now regarded as standing instructions to the navy of the United States wherever employed. They put the deck of an American vessel on the same footing with American soil, the invasion of which under foreign authority is to be as strenuously resisted in the one case as in the other. They regard such invasion as in the highest degree offensive to the United States, incompatible with their sovereignty and with the freedom of the seas, and to be met and resisted by the whole power of the country. It was your policy promptly and decisively to embrace the opportunity to bring this question of right, upon which we had gone through one war and half a century of negotiation, to final issue, by placing all other nations in a posture where they must either fight for it or abandon it. The result has proved the wisdom of the measure."

CHINA.

The same success attended our negotiations with China.* The treaty of July, 1844, with that empire, had provided for its own revision and amendment at the expiration of twelve years from its date, should experience render this necessary. Changes in its provisions had now become indispensable for the security and extension of our commerce. Besides, our merchants had just claims against the Chinese Government, for injuries sustained in violation of the treaty. To effect these changes, and to obtain indemnity for these injuries, the Hon. William B. Reed was sent as Minister to China. His position proved to be one of great delicacy. England and France were engaged in war against China, and urged the United States to become a

---

* Message, 8th December, 1857, p. 14.

party to it. They alleged that it had been undertaken to accomplish objects in which we had a common interest with themselves. This was the fact; but the President did not believe that our grievances, although serious, would justify a resort to hostilities. Whilst Mr. Reed was, therefore, directed to preserve a strict neutrality between the belligerents, he was instructed to coöperate cordially with the Ministers of England and France in all peaceful measures to secure by treaty those just concessions to commerce which the civilized nations of the world had a right to expect from China. The Russian Government, also, pursued the same line of policy.

The difficulty, then, was to obtain for our country, whilst remaining at peace, the same commercial advantages which England and France might acquire by war. This task our Minister performed with tact, ability, and success, by the conclusion of the treaty of Tientsin of the 18th June, 1858, and the two supplemental conventions of Shanghae of the 8th November following.* These have placed our commercial relations with China on the same satisfactory footing with those of England and France, and have resulted in the actual payment of the full amount of all the just claims of our citizens, leaving a surplus to the credit of the Treasury. This object has been accomplished, whilst our friendly relations with the Chinese Government were never for a moment interrupted, but on the contrary have been greatly strengthened.

PARAGUAY.

The hostile attitude of the Government of Paraguay toward the United States early commanded the attention of the President. That Government had, upon frivolous and even insulting pretexts, refused to ratify the treaty of friendship, commerce, and navigation, concluded with it on the 4th March, 1853, as amended by the Senate, though this only in mere matters of form.† It had seized and appropriated the property of American citizens residing in Paraguay, in a violent and arbitrary

---

* Pamphlet Laws, 1861-'62, p. 177, appendix.
† Senate Documents, 1857-'58, vol. ii., p. 35, etc., etc.

manner; and finally, by order of President Lopez, it had fired upon the United States steamer *Water Witch* (1st February, 1855), under Commander Thomas J. Page of the navy, and killed the sailor at the helm, whilst she was peacefully employed in surveying the Parana river, to ascertain its fitness for steam navigation. The honor, as well as the interest of the country, demanded satisfaction.

The President brought the subject to the notice of Congress in his first annual message (8th December, 1857). In this he informed them that he would make a demand for redress on the Government of Paraguay, in a firm but conciliatory manner, but at the same time observed, that "this will the more probably be granted, if the Executive shall have authority to use other means in the event of a refusal. This is accordingly recommended." Congress responded favorably to this recommendation. On the 2d June, 1858,* they passed a joint resolution authorizing the President "to adopt such measures, and use such force as, in his judgment, may be necessary and advisable, in the event of a refusal of just satisfaction by the Government of Paraguay," "in connection with the attack on the United States steamer *Water Witch*, and with other matters referred to in the annual message."† They also made an appropriation to defray the expenses of a commissioner to Paraguay, should he deem it proper to appoint one, "for the adjustment of difficulties" with that Republic.

Paraguay is situated far in the interior of South America, and its capital, the city of Asuncion, on the left bank of the river Paraguay, is more than a thousand miles from the mouth of the La Plata.

The stern policy of Dr. Francia, formerly the Dictator of Paraguay, had been to exclude all the rest of the world from his dominions, and in this he had succeeded by the most severe and arbitrary measures. His successor, President Lopez, found it necessary, in some degree, to relax this jealous policy; but, animated by the same spirit, he imposed harsh restrictions in his intercourse with foreigners. Protected by his remote and secluded position, he but little apprehended that a navy from our

* U. S. Stat. at Large, vol. xi., p. 370. † Ibid., p. 319.

far distant country could ascend the La Plata, the Parana, and the Paraguay, and reach his capital. This was doubtless the reason why he had ventured to place us at defiance. Under these circumstances the President deemed it advisable to send with our commissioner to Paraguay, Hon. James B. Bowlin, a naval force sufficient to exact justice should negotiation fail.* This consisted of nineteen armed vessels, great and small, carrying two hundred guns and twenty-five hundred sailors and marines, all under the command of the veteran and gallant Shubrick. Soon after the arrival of the expedition at Montevideo, Commissioner Bowlin and Commodore Shubrick proceeded (30th December, 1858) to ascend the rivers to Asuncion in the steamer *Fulton*, accompanied by the *Water Witch*. Meanwhile the remaining vessels rendezvoused in the Parana, near Rosario, a position from which they could act promptly, in case of need.

The commissioner arrived at Asuncion on the 25th January, 1859, and left it on the 10th February. Within this brief period he had ably and successfully accomplished all the objects of his mission. In addition to ample apologies, he obtained from President Lopez the payment of $10,000 for the family of the seaman (Chaney) who had been killed in the attack on the *Water Witch*, and also concluded satisfactory treaties of indemnity and of navigation and commerce with the Paraguayan Government.† Thus the President was enabled to announce to Congress, in his annual message (December, 1859), that " all our difficulties with Paraguay had been satisfactorily adjusted."

Even in this brief summary it would be unjust to withhold from Secretary Toucey a commendation for the economy and efficiency he displayed in fitting out this expedition.‡ It is a remarkable fact in our history, that its entire expenses were defrayed out of the ordinary appropriations for the naval service. Not a dollar was appropriated by Congress for this purpose, unless we may except the sum of $289,000 for the purchase of seven small steamers of light draft, worth more than their cost,

---

* Message 19th Dec., 1859.
† United States Pamphlet Laws, 1859–'60, p. 119, appendix.
‡ Report of Sec. Toucey, 2d Dec., 1859; Sen. Doc. 1859–'60, vol. iii., p. 1137.

and which were afterwards usefully employed in the ordinary naval service.*

It may be remarked that the President, in his message already referred to, justly observes, "that the appearance of so large a force, fitted out in such a prompt manner, in the far distant waters of the La Plata, and the admirable conduct of the officers and men employed in it, have had a happy effect in favor of our country throughout all that remote portion of the world."

THE MEXICAN REPUBLIC AND THE MONROE DOCTRINE.

The relations of the United States with Mexico on the accession of Mr. Buchanan to the Presidency in March, 1857, were of an unfriendly and almost hostile character. That Republic had been in a state of constant revolution ever since it achieved its independence from Spain. The various constitutions adopted from time to time had been set at naught almost as soon as proclaimed; and one military leader after another, in rapid succession, had usurped the government. This fine country, blessed with a benign climate, a fertile soil, and vast mineral resources, was reduced by civil war and brigandage to a condition of almost hopeless anarchy. Meanwhile, our treaties with the Republic were incessantly violated. Our citizens were imprisoned, expelled from the country, and in some instances murdered. Their vessels, merchandise, and other property were seized and confiscated. While the central Government at the capital were acting in this manner, such was the general lawlessness prevailing, that different parties claiming and exercising local authority in several districts were committing similar outrages on our citizens. Our treaties had become a dead letter, and our commerce with the Republic was almost entirely destroyed. The claims of American citizens filed in the State Department, for which they asked the interposition of their own Government with that of Mexico to obtain redress and indemnity, exceeded $10,000,000. Although this amount may have

---

* Letter of Sec. Toucey, May 11, 1860, to Committee on Naval Expenditures, vol. vi., No. 86 Miscellaneous Doc. of H. R.

been exaggerated by the claimants, still their actual losses must have been very large.*

In all these cases as they occurred our successive ministers demanded redress; but their demands were only followed by new injuries. Their testimony was uniform and emphatic in reference to the only remedy which in their judgments would prove effectual. "Nothing but a manifestation of the power of the Government of the United States," wrote Mr. John Forsyth, our Minister in 1856, "and of its purpose to punish these wrongs, will avail. I assure you that the universal belief here is, that there is nothing to be apprehended from the Government of the United States, and that local Mexican officials can commit these outrages upon American citizens with absolute impunity."

In the year 1857 a favorable change occurred in the affairs of the Republic, inspiring better hopes for the future. A constituent Congress, elected by the people of the different States for this purpose, had framed and adopted a republican Constitution. It adjourned on the 17th February, 1857, having provided for a popular election to be held in July for a President and members of Congress. At this election General Comonfort was chosen President almost without opposition. His term of office was to commence on the 1st of December, 1857, and to continue for four years. In case his office should become vacant, the Constitution had provided that the Chief Justice of Mexico, then General Juarez, should become President, until the end of the term. On the 1st December, 1857, General Comonfort appeared before the Congress then in session, took the oath to support the Constitution, and was duly inaugurated.

But the hopes thus inspired for the establishment of a regular constitutional Government soon proved delusive. President Comonfort, within one brief month, was driven from the capital and the Republic by a military rebellion headed by General Zuloaga; and General Juarez consequently became the constitutional President of Mexico until the 1st day of December, 1861. General Zuloaga instantly assumed the name of

* List of Claims, Senate Executive Documents, p. 18, 2d session 35th Congress, President's Message.

President with indefinite powers; and the entire diplomatic corps, including the minister from the United States, made haste to recognize the authority of the usurper without awaiting instructions from their respective Governments. But Zuloaga was speedily expelled from power. Having encountered the resistance of the people in many parts of the Republic, and a large portion of the army in the capital having "pronounced" against him, he was in turn compelled to relinquish the Presidency. The field was now cleared for the elevation of General Miramon. He had from the beginning been the favorite of the so-called "Church party," and was ready to become their willing instrument in maintaining the vast estates and prerogatives of the Church, and in suppressing the Liberal Constitution. An assembly of his partisans, called together without even the semblance of authority, elected him President; but he warily refused to accept the office at their hands. He then resorted to another but scarcely more plausible expedient to place himself in power. This was to identify himself with General Zuloaga, who had just been deposed, and to bring him again upon the stage as President. Zuloaga accordingly reappeared in this character; but his only act was to appoint Miramon "President Substitute," when he again retired. It is under this title that Miramon has since exercised military authority in the city of Mexico, expecting by this stratagem to appropriate to himself the recognition of the foreign ministers which had been granted to Zuloaga. He succeeded. The ministers continued their relations with him as "President Substitute" in the same manner as if Zuloaga had still remained in power. It was by this farce, for it deserves no better name, that Miramon succeeded in grasping the Presidency. The idea that the chief of a nation at his own discretion may transfer to whomsoever he may please the trust of governing delegated to him for the benefit of the people, is too absurd to receive a moment's countenance. But when we reflect that Zuloaga, from whom Miramon derived his title, was himself a military usurper, having expelled the constitutional President (Comonfort) from office, it would have been a lasting disgrace to the Mexican people had they tamely submitted to the yoke. To such an imputation a large majority proved themselves not to be justly exposed. Although, on former occasions, a seizure of the capital and the usurpation of power by a military chieftain had been generally followed, at least for a brief season, by an acquiescence of the Mexican people, yet they now rose boldly and independently to defend their rights.

President Juarez, after having been driven from the city of Mexico by Zuloaga, proceeded to form a constitutional Government at Guanájuato. From thence he removed to Vera Cruz, where he put his administration in successful operation. The people in many portions of the Republic rallied in its support and flew to arms. A civil war thus began between the friends of the Constitution and the partisans of Miramon. In this conflict it was not possible for the American people to remain indifferent spectators. They naturally favored the cause of President Juarez, and expressed ardent wishes for his success. Meanwhile Mr. Forsyth, the American Minister, still continued at the city of Mexico in the discharge of his official duties until June, 1858, when he suspended his diplomatic relations with the Miramon Government, until he should ascertain the decision of the President. Its outrages toward American citizens and its personal indignities toward himself, without hope of amendment or redress, rendered his condition no longer tolerable. Our relations, bad as they had been under former governments, had now become still worse under that of Miramon. President Buchanan approved the step which Mr. Forsyth had taken. He was consequently directed to demand his passports, to deposit the archives of the legation with Mr. Black, our consul at the city of Mexico, and to proceed to Vera Cruz, where an armed steamer would be in readiness to convey himself and family to the Unted States.*

Thus was all diplomatic intercourse finally terminated with the Government of Miramon; whilst none had been organized with that of Juarez. The President entertained some hope that this rupture of diplomatic relations might cause Miramon to reflect seriously on the danger of war with the

---

* Letter of General Cass to Mr. Forsyth, July 15th, 1858. Senate Documents, 1858-'59, vol. i., p. 48.

United States, and might at least arrest future outrages on our citizens. Instead of this, however, he persisted in his course of violence against the few American citizens who had the courage to remain under his power. The President in his message of December, 1859,* informs Congress that "murders of a still more atrocious character have been committed in the very heart of Mexico, under the authority of Miramon's Government, during the present year. Some of these were worthy only of a barbarous age, and if they had not been clearly proven, would have seemed impossible in a country which claims to be civilized." And in that of December, 1860, he says: "To cap the climax, after the battle of Tacubaya, in April, 1859, General Marquez ordered three citizens of the United States, two of them physicians, to be seized in the hospital at that place, taken out and shot, without crime, and without trial. This was done, notwithstanding our unfortunate countrymen were at the moment engaged in the holy cause of affording relief to the soldiers of both parties who had been wounded in the battle, without making any distinction between them."

"Little less shocking was the recent fate of Ormond Chase, who was shot in Tepic on the 7th August by order of the same Mexican general, not only without a trial, but without any conjecture by his friends of the cause of his arrest." He was represented to have been a young man of good character and intelligence, who had made numerous friends in Tepic, and his unexpected execution shocked the whole community. "Other outrages," the President states, "might be enumerated; but these are sufficient to illustrate the wretched state of the country and the unprotected condition of the persons and property of our citizens in Mexico."

"The wrongs which we have suffered from Mexico are before the world, and must deeply impress every American citizen. A Government which is either unable or unwilling to redress such wrongs, is derelict to its highest duties."

Meanwhile the civil war between the parties was conducted with various success; but the scale preponderated in favor of the Constitutional cause. Ere long the Government of

* House Journal, p. 207.

Juarez extended its authority and was acknowledged in all the important ports and throughout the sea-coasts and external territory of the Republic; whilst the power of Miramon was confined to the city of Mexico and the surrounding States.

The final triumph of Juarez became so probable, that President Buchanan deemed it his duty to inquire and ascertain whether, according to our constant usage in such cases, he might not recognize the Constitutional Government. For the purpose of obtaining reliable information on this point, he sent a confidential agent to Mexico to examine and report the actual condition and prospects of the belligerents. In consequence of his report, as well as of intelligence from other sources, he felt justified in appointing a new minister to the Mexican Republic. For this office Mr. Robert M. McLane, a distinguished citizen of Maryland, was selected. He proceeded on his mission on the 8th March, 1859, invested "with discretionary authority to recognize the Government of President Juarez, if on his arrival in Mexico he should find it entitled to such recognition, according to the established practice of the United States." In consequence, on the 7th of April Mr. McLane recognized the Constitutional Government by presenting his credentials to President Juarez, having no hesitation, as he said, "in pronouncing the Government of Juarez to be the only existing Government of the Republic." He was cordially received by the authorities at Vera Cruz, who have ever since manifested the most friendly disposition toward the United States.

Unhapily, however, the Constitutional Government, though supported by a large majority both of the people and of the several Mexican States, had not been able to expel Miramon from the capital. In the opinion of the President, it had now become the imperative duty of Congress to act without further delay, and to enforce redress from the Government of Miramon for the wrongs it had committed in violation of the faith of treaties against citizens of the United States.

Toward no other Government would we have manifested so long and so patient a forbearance. This arose from our warm sympathies for a neighboring Republic. The territory under the sway of Miramon around the capital was not accessible to our forces without passing through the States under the jurisdiction of the Constitutional Government. But this from the beginning had always manifested the warmest desire to cultivate the most friendly relations with our country. No doubt was therefore entertained that it would cheerfully grant us the right of passage. Moreover, it well knew that the expulsion of Miramon would result in the triumph of the Constitutional Government and its establishment over the whole territory of Mexico. What was, also, deemed of great importance by the President, this would remove from us the danger of a foreign war in support of the Monroe doctrine against any European nation which might be tempted, by the distracted condition of the Republic, to interfere forcibly in its internal affairs under the pretext of restoring peace and order.

Such is the outline of the President's policy. Had it been sanctioned by Congress, it is beyond question that we should not at this day witness the transformation of the Republic into a monarchy.

Accordingly, in his message to Congress of the 19th of December, 1859, he says: "We may in vain apply to the Constitutional Government at Vera Cruz, although it is well disposed to do us justice, for adequate redress. Whilst its authority is acknowledged in all the important ports and throughout the sea-coasts of the Republic, its power does not extend to the city of Mexico and the States in its vicinity, where nearly all the recent outrages have been committed on American citizens. We must penetrate into the interior before we can reach the offenders, and this can only be done by passing through the territory in the occupation of the Constitutional Government. The most acceptable and least difficult mode of accomplishing the object will be to act in concert with that Government. Their consent and their aid might, I believe, be obtained; but if not, our obligation to protect our own citizens in their just rights secured by treaty would not be the less imperative. For these reasons I recommend to Congress to pass a law authorizing the President, under such conditions as they may deem expedient, to employ a sufficient military force to enter Mexico for the purpose of obtaining indemnity for the past and security for the future. I purposely refrain from any suggestion as to whether this force shall consist of regular troops or volunteers, or both. This question may be most appropriately left to the decision of Congress. I would merely observe that, should volunteers be selected, such a force could be easily raised in this country among those who sympathize with the sufferings of our unfortunate fellow-citizens in Mexico, and with the unhappy condition of that Republic. Such an accession to the forces of the Constitutional Government would enable it soon to reach the city of Mexico, and extend its power over the whole Republic. In that event, there is no reason to doubt that the just claims of our citizens would be satisfied, and adequate redress obtained for the injuries inflicted upon them. The Constitutional Government have ever evinced a strong desire to do justice, and this might be secured in advance by a preliminary treaty.

"It may be said that these measures will, at least indirectly, be inconsistent with our wise and settled policy not to interfere in the domestic concerns of foreign nations. But does not the present case fairly constitute an exception? An adjoining republic is in a state of anarchy and confusion from which she has proved wholly unable to extricate herself. She is entirely destitute of the power to maintain peace upon her borders, or to prevent the incursions of banditti into our territory. In her fate and in her fortune—in her power to establish and maintain a settled government—we have a far deeper interest, socially, commercially, and politically, than any other nation. She is now a wreck upon the ocean, drifting about as she is impelled by different factions. As a good neighbor, shall we not extend to her a helping hand to save her? *If we do not, it would not be surprising should some other nation undertake the task, and thus force us to interfere at last, under circumstances of increased difficulty, for the maintenance of our established policy.*"

These recommendations of the President were wholly disregarded by Congress during the session of 1859–1860. Indeed, they were not even noticed in any of its proceedings. The members of both parties were too exclusively occupied in discussing the slavery question, and in giving their attention to the approaching Presidential election, to devote any portion of their time to the important Mexican question.

The President again brought the subject before Congress in his next annual message of December, 1860; but with no better effect. In recurring to his recommendations at the previous session for the employment of a military force, and the consequences which had already resulted and would afterwards follow from the neglect with which it had been treated, he observes: "No other alternative was left, except the entire abandonment of our fellow-citizens who had gone to Mexico under the faith of treaties, to the systematic injustice, cruelty, and oppression of Miramon's Government. Besides, it is almost certain that the simple authority to employ this force would of itself have accomplished all our objects, without striking a single blow. The Constitutional Government would, then, ere this have been established at the city of Mexico, and would have been ready and willing, to the extent of its ability, to do us justice.

"*In addition, and I deem this a most important consideration, European Governments would have been deprived of all pretext to interfere in the territorial and domestic concerns of Mexico. We should thus have been relieved from the obligation of resisting, even by force, should this become necessary, any attempt by these Governments to deprive our neighboring Republic of portions of her territory, a duty from which we could not shrink without abandoning the traditional and established policy of the American people.*"

He adds: "I am happy to observe that, firmly relying upon the justice and good faith of these Governments, there is no *present* danger that such a contingency will happen."

This was inserted in the message, because Mr. McLane at the time had received informal though only verbal assurances to this effect in his intercourse with European diplomatists in Mexico. And indeed there was no danger of foreign interference so long as the question of a military expedition to Mexico had not been decided by Congress.

The President did not apprehend interference in Mexico from any European sovereign except the Emperor of the French. It was his known policy to seek new colonies for France; and his minister exercised great influence over Miramon. Besides, he had previously directed his attention in a special manner to Central America. The President, therefore, watched his proceedings with constant vigilance, under the conviction that should he attempt to colonize the whole or any portion of Mexico, this would almost necessarily involve the United States in a war with France in vindication of the Monroe doctrine.

THE ORIGIN, HISTORY, AND NATURE OF "THE MONROE DOCTRINE."

The allied powers of Europe had triumphed over Napoleon, and had restored the elder branch of the Bourbons, in the person of Louis XVIII., to the throne of France. Emboldened by this success, Russia, Austria, and Prussia, in 1815, formed the Holy Alliance. To this France, and nearly all the other continental powers, soon afterwards acceded. Great Britain, however, stood aloof and refused to become a party to it. The object of the allies was to abolish liberal Governments on the continent of Europe, and to maintain the divine right of sovereigns to rule according to their own discretion—in short, to roll back the tide of progress toward free institutions, and to restore the old despotisms as they had existed before the French Revolution. Accordingly France was deputed to destroy, by force of arms, the liberal Government of the Cortes in Spain, and to restore the implacable and bigoted Ferdinand VII. to absolute power. In 1823 a French army, commanded by the Duke d'Angoulême, invaded Spain, and in a single campaign accomplished these objects.

In the year before the date of this expedition, the Government of the United States had formally acknowledged the independence of the different southern Republics, formerly Spanish colonies; and an appropriation of one hundred thousand dollars had been made (May 4, 1822)* by Congress to defray

* 3 United States Statutes, 678.

the expense of missions to these "independent nations on the American continent."

Whilst the French invasion was in successful progress, the British Government became satisfied that the allies, after crushing the Spanish liberals, intended to employ their arms in assisting Ferdinand VII. to resubjugate what they termed his rebellious colonies on this side of the Atlantic. To such an enterprise Great Britain was strenuously opposed, and she resolved to resist it. If successful, this would prove to be a severe blow to her trade in that quarter of the world—an interest to which she has ever been sensitively alive.

To avert the impending danger Mr. Canning, then the British Minister for Foreign Affairs, in August, 1823, proposed to Mr. Rush, the American Minister in London, that the two Governments should immediately unite in publishing "a joint declaration before Europe," manifesting their opposition to the policy and purposes of the alliance in regard to this continent. This expressed the opinion that the recovery of the colonies by Spain was hopeless; that their recognition as independent States was one of time and circumstances; that the two powers were not disposed, however, to interpose obstacles in the way to any arrangements by amicable negotiations between the colonies and Spain; but that whilst they aimed at the acquisition of no portion of these colonies for themselves, they would not see the transfer of any of them to a third power with indifference. Mr. Canning also observed that in his opinion such a joint declaration by Great Britain and the United States would alone prove sufficient to prevent the allies from any forcible interference against the former Spanish colonies. For these reasons he earnestly urged Mr. Rush to become a party to it on behalf of his Government. Although Mr. Rush had no direct instructions to warrant him in such an act, and this he had communicated to Mr. Canning, yet he wisely agreed to assume the responsibility, but upon one express condition. This was, that the British Government should first acknowledge the independence of the new American Republics, as the United States had already done. Mr. Canning, though resolved on defeating the projects of the alliance against these Republics, was not prepared at the time to take this decisive step, and therefore the joint declaration was never made.

Mr. Rush, in his despatch of September 19, 1823, to Mr. John Quincy Adams, then Secretary of State,* communicated to him a lucid statement of these negotiations, with explanatory documents. After these had been considered by President Monroe, he sent them, with his own views on the subject, to Mr. Jefferson, and asked his advice as to the course which ought to be pursued by the Government to ward off the threatened danger.

Mr. Jefferson's answer is dated at Monticello, on the 24th October, 1823. It is earnest, enthusiastic, and eloquent, displaying in old age the statesmanlike sagacity and ardent patriotism of the author of the Declaration of Independence. It foreshadows and recommends the "Monroe Doctrine" to the fullest extent. From its importance we quote it entire from Randall's Life of Jefferson, vol. iii., p. 491. Mr. Jefferson says: "The question presented by the letters you have sent me is the most momentous which has ever been offered to my contemplation since that of independence. That made us a nation; this sets our compass and points the course which we are to steer through the ocean of time opening on us; and never could we embark on it under circumstances more auspicious. Our first and fundamental maxim should be, never to entangle ourselves in the broils of Europe. Our second, never to suffer Europe to intermeddle with cis-Atlantic affairs. America, North and South, has a set of interests distinct from those of Europe, and peculiarly her own. She should, therefore, have a system of her own, separate and apart from that of Europe. While the last is laboring to become the domicile of despotism, our endeavor should surely be to make our hemisphere that of freedom. One nation, most of all, could disturb us in this pursuit; she now offers to lead, aid, and accompany us in it. By acceding to her proposition, we detach her from the band of despots, bring her mighty weight into the scale of free government, and emancipate a continent at one stroke, which might otherwise linger long in doubt and difficulty. Great Britain is the nation which can do us the most harm of any one, or all on

---

* Rush's "Residence at the Court of London," p. 429.

earth; and with her on our side, we need not fear the whole world. With her, then, we should most sedulously cherish a cordial friendship; and nothing would tend more to knit our affections than to be fighting once more, side by side, in the same cause. Not that I would purchase even her amity at the price of taking part in her wars. But the war in which the present proposition might engage us, should that be its consequence, is not her war, but ours. Its object is to introduce and establish the American system of keeping out of our land all foreign powers, of never permitting those of Europe to intermeddle with the affairs of our nations. It is to maintain our own principle, not to depart from it; and if, to facilitate this, we can effect a division in the body of the European powers, and draw over to our side its most powerful member, surely we should do it. But I am clearly of Mr. Canning's opinion, that it will prevent instead of provoking war. With Great Britain withdrawn from their scale and shifted into that of our two continents, all Europe combined would not undertake such a war. For how would they propose to get at either enemy without superior fleets? Nor is the occasion to be slighted which this proposition offers, of declaring our protest against the atrocious violations of the rights of nations, by the interference of any one in the internal affairs of another, so flagitiously begun by Bonaparte, and now continued by the equally lawless alliance calling itself holy.

"But we have first to ask ourselves a question: Do we wish to acquire to our own confederacy any one or more of the Spanish provinces? I candidly confess that I have ever looked on Cuba as the most interesting addition which could ever be made to our system of States. The control which, with Florida point, this island would give us over the Gulf of Mexico, and the countries and isthmus bordering on it, as well as all those whose waters flow into it, would fill up the measure of our political well-being. Yet as I am sensible that this can never be obtained, even with her own consent, but by war; and its independence, which is our second interest (and especially its independence of England), can be secured without it, I have no hesitation in abandoning my first wish to future chances, and accepting its independence, with peace and the friendship of England, rather than its association at the expense of war and her enmity.

"I could honestly, therefore, join in the declaration proposed, that we aim not at the acquisition of any of those possessions, that we will not stand in the way of any amicable arrangement between them and the mother country; but that we will oppose, with all our means, the forcible interposition of any other power, as auxiliary, stipendiary, or under any other form or pretext, and most especially their transfer to any power by conquest, cession, or acquisition in any other way. I should think it, therefore, advisable that the Executive should encourage the British Government to a continuance in the dispositions expressed in these letters, by an assurance of his concurrence with them as far as his authority goes; and that, as it may lead to war, the declaration of which requires an act of Congress, the case shall be laid before them for consideration, at their first meeting, and under the reasonable aspect in which it is seen by himself.

"I have been so long weaned from political subjects, and have so long ceased to take any interest in them, that I am sensible I am not qualified to offer opinions on them worthy of any attention. But the question now proposed involves consequences so lasting, and effects so decisive of our future destinies, as to rekindle all the interest I have heretofore felt on such occasions, and to induce me to the hazard of opinions which will prove only my wish to contribute still my mite toward any thing which may be useful to our country. And praying you to accept it at only what it is worth, I add the assurance of my constant and affectionate friendship and respect."

President Monroe, thus fortified by the support of Mr. Jefferson, proceeded to announce, in his seventh annual message to Congress, of December 2, 1823, the now celebrated "Monroe Doctrine." This is summed up in his assertion, "as a principle in which the rights and interests of the United States are involved, that the American continents, by the free and independent condition they have assumed and maintained, are henceforth not to be considered as subjects for future colonization by any European powers."

The word "*henceforth*" is employed because Great Britain and France, at the date of the message, not to speak of the Portuguese Empire of Brazil, possessed colonies on this continent, and these are exempted from its terms. It applies to the future and not to the past. This is more specifically stated afterwards in the declaration, that "with the existing colonies or dependencies of any European power we have not interfered and shall not interfere."

The reader has perceived that the recommendations of Mr. Jefferson went beyond the "joint declaration" which had been proposed by Mr. Canning. This was confined to the Spanish American colonies, but the Monroe doctrine extends the protection of the United States to every other portion of the continent.

In a subsequent portion of the message Mr. Monroe proceeds to discuss and condemn, in a clear and able manner, the projects of the alliance against the southern Republics, and to warn them of the consequences. In this, however, he never loses sight of the more comprehensive doctrine he had first announced against European colonization in any portion of America, employing such language as the following: "We owe it therefore to candor, and to the amicable relations existing between the United States and those [European] powers, to declare that we should consider any attempt on their part to extend their system *to any portion of this hemisphere* as dangerous to our peace and safety." And again, after stating that our established policy was not to interfere in the internal concerns of any European power, to consider the Government *de facto* as the legitimate Government, and to cultivate friendly relations with it, he says: "But in regard to these continents circumstances are eminently and conspicuously different. It is impossible that the allied powers should extend their political system *to any portion of either continent* without endangering our peace and happiness, nor can any one believe that our southern brethren, if left to themselves, would adopt it of their own accord. It is equally impossible, therefore, that we should behold such interposition, in any form, with indifference."

Such is the Monroe doctrine. It is in opposition to future European colonization on any part of the American continent; it is in opposition to the introduction of European despotic or monarchical institutions in any part of the American continent; and is in opposition to any attempt of European sovereigns to subjugate the North American Republic of Mexico, or any of the South American Republics. In regard to those Republics, he emphatically says: "But with the Governments who have declared their independence and maintained it, and whose independence we have, on great consideration and on just principles, acknowleged we could not view any interposition for the purpose of oppressing them, or controlling in any other manner their destiny, by any European power, in any other light than as the manifestation of an unfriendly disposition toward the United States." It was eminently wise that the United States, the most ancient and by far the most powerful Republic on this continent, should have interposed such a shield to defend their weaker sisters against the assaults of European despotism.

"When President Monroe's message arrived in London [we are informed by Mr. Rush],* the whole document excited great attention. It was upon all tongues; the press was full of it; the Spanish American deputies were overjoyed; Spanish American securities rose in the stock market, and the safety of the new States from all European coercion was considered as no longer doubtful." The allies soon after abandoned their hostile purposes against the new Republics, and their independence was secured.

That portion of the message for the protection of the new Republics, being in accordance with the avowed policy of Great Britain, was received with favor by the British Government; but not so the portion of it against future European colonization. This encountered their decided opposition.† "The Monroe doctrine," nevertheless, soon became a canon of political faith for the American people, and they placed it side by side

---

* Rush, p. 458.   † Ibid., pp. 458, 471.

with their hostility to the impressment of American seamen, and to the search of American vessels on the high seas.

The authors and friends of the Monroe doctrine entertained no doubt of its wisdom and policy. With the established independence of the Republic of Mexico and the Republics south of it, there arose two distinct and opposing forms of government on the opposite sides of the Atlantic; the one republican, the other monarchical; the one devoted to free institutions, the other to despotic rule. The nations of Europe having determined to resist any change in their monarchical forms, it was but just and reasonable that those of America in self-protection should equally resist all attempts from the other side of the Atlantic to change their free institutions. To repeat the language of Mr. Jefferson, "America, North and South, has a set of interests distinct from those of Europe, and peculiarly her own; she should, therefore, have a system of her own, separate and apart from that of Europe. While the last is laboring to become the domicile of despotism, our endeavor should surely be to make our hemisphere that of freedom." Governments so radically opposed in principle could not be intermingled in adjoining territories without dangerous disputes and collisions. The contrast between them would be a perennial source of jealousy. Each would necessarily endeavor to propagate its own principles among the neighboring people of the other. In the interests of peace and friendship between the European monarchies and the American Republics, a wise foresight would forbid the former from establishing colonies within the territories or in the vicinity of the latter. Should the United States interpose forcibly to establish republican institutions on any part of the European continent, it is certain that all its sovereigns would combine to resist such an interference as dangerous to their monarchical system. Shall we, then, abandoning the Monroe doctrine, patiently suffer any of these sovereigns to extend their dominion, equally dangerous to our free forms of government, on this side of the Atlantic? No human sagacity could, twenty years ago, have foreseen the day when a foreign potentate, not even confining himself to the planting of colonies on American soil, should by invasion and force of arms convert the whole Republic of Mexico into a European monarchy. The idea, if suggested at that time, would have been treated as absurd, more especially when we reflect that this is the richest and most populous of the Republics which more than fifty years ago had been saved from European domination by our Government, and that its territories extend for a thousand miles along our own frontiers.

During the administration of President Polk, it became necessary that he should reaffirm the Monroe doctrine, in view of the designs of Great Britain to establish a protectorate over the Mosquito coast in the Republics of Nicaragua and Honduras. This he did, in decided terms, in his first annual message to Congress (2d December, 1845.) *

Great Britain, as we have already seen, through the interposition of the Government of the United States, eventually withdrew from the Mosquito protectorate, as well as from the colony of the Bay Islands, which she had afterwards established on the coast of Honduras. At the close of Mr. Buchanan's administration no European colony existed on the American continent, except such as had been established before the Monroe doctrine was announced, or had been formed out of territory then belonging to a European power.

The President, having failed in obtaining authority from Congress to employ a military force in Mexico, as a last resort adopted the policy of concluding a treaty with the Constitutional Government. By this means he thought something might be accomplished, both to satisfy the long deferred claims of American citizens, and to prevent foreign interference with the internal government of Mexico. Accordingly Mr. McLane, on the 14th day of December, 1859, signed a "Treaty of Transits and Commerce" with the Mexican Republic, and also a "Convention to enforce treaty stipulations, and to maintain order and security in the Territory of the Republics of Mexico and the United States." These treaties secured peculiar and highly valuable advantages to our trade and commerce, especially in articles the production of our agriculture and manu-

* 3 Statesman's Manual, p. 1458.

factures. They also guaranteed to us the secure possession and enjoyment of the Tehuantepec route, and of several other transit routes for our commerce, free from duty, across the territories of the Republic, on its way to California, and our other possessions on the Northwest coast, as well as to the independent Republics on the Pacific and to Eastern Asia.

In consideration of these advantages, " and in compensation for the revenue surrendered by Mexico on the goods and merchandise transported free of duty through the territory of that Republic, the Government of the United States agreed to pay to the Government of Mexico the sum of four millions of dollars." Of this sum two millions were to be paid immediately to Mexico, and the remaining two millions were to be retained by our Government " for the payment of the claims of citizens of the United States against the Government of the Republic of Mexico for injuries already inflicted, and which may be proven to be just according to the law and usage of nations and the principles of equity." It was believed that these stipulations, whilst providing two millions toward the payment of the claims of our citizens, would enable President Juarez with the remaining two millions to expel the usurping Government of Miramon from the capital, and place the Constitutional Government in possession of the whole territory of the Republic. This, we need not say, would have greatly promoted the interests of the United States. Besides, what was vastly important, these treaties, by vesting in the United States territorial and commercial rights which we would be bound to defend, might for this reason have prevented any European Government from attempting to acquire dominion over the territories of Mexico, and thus the Monroe doctrine would probably have remained inviolate. With this view Mr. McLane was seriously impressed: In his despatch of December 14th, 1859, to the Secretary of State, communicating the treaties, he expresses the apprehension that should they not be ratified, further anarchy would prevail in Mexico until it should be terminated by direct interference from some other quarter.

On the 4th January, 1860, the President submitted to the Senate the treaty and the convention with a view to their ratification, together with the despatch of Mr. McLane. These, on the same day, were referred to the Committee on Foreign Relations. Whether any or what other proceedings were had in relation to them we are unable to state, the injunction of secresy having never been removed by the Senate. Mr. McLane, who was then in Washington, had a conference with the committee, and received the impression that comparative unanimity existed in favor of the principal provisions of the treaty; but in regard to the convention the contingency of its possible abuse was referred to as constituting an objection to its ratification. Certain it is that neither the one nor the other was ever approved by the Senate, and consequently both became a dead letter. The Republic of Mexico was thus left to its fate, and has since become an empire under the dominion of a scion of the House of Hapsburg, protected by the Emperor of the French. The righteous claims of American citizens have therefore been indefinitely postponed.

APPENDIX.

GENERAL SCOTT'S "VIEWS" OF THE 29TH AND 30TH OF OCTOBER, 1860, PUBLISHED BY HIS AUTHORITY IN THE "NATIONAL INTELLIGENCER" OF THE 18TH OF JANUARY, 1861.

Views suggested by the imminent danger (October 29, 1860) of a disruption of the Union by the Secession of one or more of the Southern States.

To save time the right of secession may be conceded, and instantly balanced by the correlative right, on the part of the Federal Government, against an *interior* State or States, to reëstablish by force, if necessary, its former continuity of territory—*Paley's Moral and Political Philosophy, last chapter.*

But break this glorious Union by whatever line or lines that political madness may contrive, and there would be no hope of reuniting the fragments except by the laceration and despotism of the sword. To effect such result the intestine wars of our Mexican neighbors would, in comparison with ours, sink into mere child's play.

A smaller evil would be to allow the fragments of the great Republic to form themselves into new Confederacies, probably four.

All the lines of demarcation between the new Unions cannot be accurately drawn in advance, but many of them approximately may. Thus, looking to natural boundaries and commercial affinities, some of the following frontiers, after many waverings and conflicts, might perhaps become acknowledged and fixed:

1. The Potomac River and the Chesapeake Bay to the Atlantic.
2. From Maryland, along the crest of the Alleghany (perhaps the

Blue Ridge) range of mountains, to some point on the coast of Florida. 3. The line from say the head of the Potomac to the west or northwest, which it will be most difficult to settle. 4. The crest of the Rocky Mountains.

The Southeast Confederacy would, in all human probability, in less than five years after the rupture, find itself bounded by the first and second lines indicated above, the Atlantic, and the Gulf of Mexico, with its capital at say Columbia, South Carolina. The country between the second, third, and fourth of those lines would, beyond a doubt, in about the same time, constitute another Confederacy, with its capital at probably Alton or Quincy, Illinois. The boundaries of the Pacific Union are the most definite of all, and the remaining States would constitute the Northeast Confederacy, with its capital at Albany.

It, at the first thought, will be considered strange that seven slaveholding States and parts of Virginia and Florida should be placed (above) in a new Confederacy with Ohio, Indiana, Illinois, etc. But when the overwhelming weight of the great Northwest is taken in connection with the laws of trade, contiguity of territory, and the comparative indifference to free soil doctrines on the part of Western Virginia, Kentucky, Tennessee, and Missouri, it is evident that but little if any coercion, beyond moral force, would be needed to embrace them; and I have omitted the temptation of the unwasted public lands which would fall entire to this Confederacy—an apanage (well husbanded) sufficient for many generations. As to Missouri, Arkansas, and Mississippi, they would not stand out a month. Louisiana would coalesce without much solicitation, and Alabama, with West Florida, would be conquered the first winter from the absolute need of Pensacola for a naval depot.

If I might presume to address the South, and particularly dear Virginia—being "native here and to the manor born"—I would affectionately ask, Will not your slaves be less secure and their labor less profitable under the new order of things than under the old? Could you employ profitably two hundred slaves in all Nebraska, or five hundred in all New Mexico? The right, then, to take them thither would be a barren right. And is it not wise to

> "Rather bear the ills we have
> Than fly to others that we know not of?"

The Declaration of Independence proclaims and consecrates the same maxim: "Prudence, indeed, will dictate that Governments long established should not be changed for light and transient causes."

And Paley, too, lays down as a fundamental maxim of statesmanship, "never to pursue national *honor* as distinct from national *interest;*" but adds: "This rule acknowledges that it is often necessary to assert the honor of a nation for the sake of its interests."

The excitement that threatens secession is caused by the near prospect of a Republican's election to the Presidency. From a sense of propriety, as a soldier, I have taken no part in the pending canvass, and, as always heretofore, mean to stay away from the polls. My sympathies, however, are with the Bell and Everett ticket. With Mr. Lincoln I have had no communication whatever, direct or indirect, and have no recollection of ever having seen his person; but cannot believe any unconstitutional violence, or breach of law, is to be apprehended from his administration of the Federal Government.

From a knowledge of our Southern population it is my solemn conviction that there is some danger of an early act of rashness preliminary to secession, viz., the seizure of some or all of the following posts: Forts Jackson and St. Philip, in the Mississippi, below New Orleans, both without garrisons; Fort Morgan, below Mobile, without a garrison; Forts Pickens and McRee, Pensacola harbor, with an insufficient garrison for one; Fort Pulaski, below Savannah, without a garrison; Forts Moultrie and Sumter, Charleston harbor, the former with an insufficient garrison, and the latter without any; and Fort Monroe, Hampton Roads, without a sufficient garrison. In my opinion all these works should be immediately so garrisoned as to make any attempt to take any one of them, by surprise or *coup de main*, ridiculous.

With the army faithful to its allegiance, and the navy probably equally so, and with a Federal Executive, for the next twelve months, of firmness and moderation, which the country has a right to expect —*moderation* being an element of power not less than *firmness*—there is good reason to hope that the danger of secession may be made to pass away without one conflict of arms, one execution, or one arrest for treason.

In the mean time it is suggested that exports should remain as free as at present; all duties, however, on imports, collected (outside of the cities*) as such receipts would be needed for the national debt, invalid pensions, &c., and only articles contraband of war be refused

---

* In forts or on board ships-of-war. The great aim and object of this plan was to gain time—say eight or ten months—to await expected measures of conciliation on the part of the North, and the subsidence of angry feelings in the opposite quarter.

admittance. But even this refusal would be unnecessary, as the foregoing views eschew the idea of invading a seceded State.

WINFIELD SCOTT.

October 29th, 1860.

Lieut.-General Scott's respects to the Secretary of War to say—

That a copy of his " Views, &c." was despatched to the President yesterday, in great haste; but the copy intended for the Secretary, better transcribed (herewith), was not in time for the mail. General Scott would be happy if the latter could be substituted for the former.

It will be seen that the " Views " only apply to a case of secession that makes a *gap* in the present Union. The falling off (say) of Texas, or of all the Atlantic States, from the Potomac south, was not within the scope of General Scott's provisional remedies.

It is his opinion that instructions should be given, at once, to the commanders of the Barancas, Forts Moultrie and Monroe, to be on their guard against surprises and *coups de main*. As to *regular approaches* nothing can be said or done, at this time, without volunteers.

There is one (regular) company at Boston, one here (at the Narrows), one at Pittsburg, one at Augusta, Ga., and one at Baton Rouge—in all five companies only, within reach, to garrison or reënforce the forts mentioned in the " Views."

General Scott is all solicitude for the safety of the Union. He is, however, not without hope that all dangers and difficulties will pass away without leaving a scar or painful recollection behind.

The Secretary's most obedient servant,

WINFIELD SCOTT.

October 30th, 1860.

MESSAGE OF THE PRESIDENT OF THE UNITED STATES, OF THE 8TH OF JANUARY, 1861.

January 9, 1861.—Read and referred, with instructions, to a Select Committee of five, and ordered to be printed.

To the Senate and House of Representatives:

At the opening of your present session I called your attention to the dangers which threatened the existence of the Union. I expressed my opinion freely concerning the original causes of those dangers, and recommended such measures as I believed would have the effect of tranquillizing the country and saving it from the peril in which it had been needlessly and most unfortunately involved. Those opinions and recommendations I do not propose now to repeat. My own convictions upon the whole subject remain unchanged.

The fact that a great calamity was impending over the nation was even at that time acknowledged by every intelligent citizen. It had already made itself felt throughout the length and breadth of the land. The necessary consequences of the alarm thus produced were most deplorable. The imports fell off with a rapidity never known before, except in time of war, in the history of our foreign commerce; the Treasury was unexpectedly left without the means which it had reasonably counted upon to meet the public engagements; trade was paralyzed; manufactures were stopped; the best public securities suddenly sunk in the market; every species of property depreciated more or less; and thousands of poor men, who depended upon their daily labor for their daily bread, were turned out of employment.

I deeply regret that I am not able to give you any information upon the state of the Union which is more satisfactory than what I was then obliged to communicate. On the contrary, matters are still worse at present than they then were. When Congress met, a strong hope pervaded the whole public mind that some amicable adjustment of the subject would speedily be made by the representatives of the States and of the people, which might restore peace between the conflicting sections of the country. That hope has been diminished by every hour of delay; and as the prospect of a bloodless settlement fades away, the public distress becomes more and more aggravated. As evidence of this, it is only necessary to say that the treasury notes authorized by the act of 17th December last were advertised, according to the law, and that no responsible bidder offered to take any considerable sum at par at a lower rate of interest than twelve per cent. From these facts it appears that, in a government organized like ours, domestic strife, or even a well-grounded fear of civil hostilities, is more destructive to our public and private interests than the most formidable foreign war.

In my annual message I expressed the conviction, which I have long deliberately held, and which recent reflection has only tended to deepen and confirm, that no State has a right by its own act to secede from the Union, or throw off its Federal obligations at pleasure. I also declared my opinion to be that, even if that right existed and should be exercised by any State of the confederacy, the executive department of this government had no authority under the Constitution to recognize its validity by acknowledging the independence of such State. This left me no alternative, as the chief executive officer under the Constitution of the United States, but to collect the public revenues and to protect the public property so far as this might be practicable under existing laws. This is still my purpose. My province is to execute, and not to make the laws. It belongs to Congress, exclusively, to repeal, to modify, or to enlarge their provisions, to meet exigencies as they may occur. I possess no dispensing power.

I certainly had no right to make aggressive war upon any State, and I am perfectly satisfied that the Constitution has wisely withheld that power even from Congress. But the right and the duty to use military force defensively against those who resist the Federal officers in the execution of their legal functions, and against those who assail the property of the Federal government, is clear and undeniable.

But the dangerous and hostile attitude of the States toward each other has already far transcended and cast in the shade the ordinary executive duties already provided for by law, and has assumed such vast and alarming proportions as to place the subject entirely above and beyond executive control. The fact cannot be disguised that we are in the midst of a great revolution. In all its various bearings, therefore, I commend the question to Congress, as the only human tribunal, under Providence, possessing the power to meet the existing emergency. To them, exclusively, belongs the power to declare war, or to authorize the employment of military force in all cases contemplated by the Constitution; and they alone possess the power to remove grievances which might lead to war, and to secure peace and union to this distracted country. On them, and on them alone, rests the responsibility.

The Union is a sacred trust left by our revolutionary fathers to their descendants; and never did any other people inherit so rich a legacy. It has rendered us prosperous in peace and triumphant in war. The National flag has floated in glory over every sea. Under its shadow American citizens have found protection and respect in all lands beneath the sun. If we descend to considerations of purely material interest, when, in the history of all time, has a confederacy been bound together by such strong ties of mutual interest? Each portion of it is dependent on all, and all upon each portion, for prosperity and domestic security. Free trade throughout the whole supplies the wants of one portion from the productions of another, and scatters wealth everywhere. The great planting and farming States require the aid of the commercial and navigating States to send their productions to domestic and foreign markets, and to furnish the naval power to render their transportation secure against all hostile attacks.

Should the Union perish in the midst of the present excitement, we have already had a sad foretaste of the universal suffering which would result from its destruction. The calamity would be severe in every portion of the Union, and would be quite as great, to say the least, in the Southern as in the Northern States. The greatest aggravation of the evil, and that which would place us in the most unfavorable light both before the world and posterity, is, as I am firmly convinced, that the secession movement has been chiefly based upon a misapprehension at the South of the sentiments of the majority in several of the Northern States. Let the question be transferred from political assemblies to the ballot-box, and the people themselves would speedily redress the serious grievances which the South have suffered. But, in Heaven's name, let the trial be made before we plunge into armed conflict upon the mere assumption that there is no other alternative. Time is a great conservative power. Let us pause at this momentous point and afford the people, both North and South, an opportunity for reflection. Would that South Carolina had been convinced of this truth before her precipitate action! I, therefore, appeal through you to the people of the country to declare in their might that the Union must and shall be preserved by all constitutional means. I most earnestly recommend that you devote yourselves exclusively to the question how this can be accomplished in peace. All other questions, when compared with this, sink into insignificance. The present is no time for palliatives; action, prompt action, is required. A delay in Congress to prescribe or to recommend a distinct and practical proposition for conciliation may drive us to a point from which it will be almost impossible to recede.

A common ground on which conciliation and harmony can be produced is surely not unattainable. The proposition to compromise by letting the North have exclusive control of the territory above a certain line, and to give Southern institutions protection below that line, ought to receive universal approbation. In itself, indeed, it may not be entirely satisfactory; but when the alternative is between a reasonable concession on both sides and a destruction of the Union, it is an imputation upon the patriotism of Congress to assert that its members will hesitate for a moment.

Even now the danger is upon us. In several of the States which have not yet seceded, the forts, arsenals, and magazines of the United States have been seized. This is by far the most serious step which has been taken since the commencement of the troubles. This public property has long been left without garrisons and troops for its protection, because no person doubted its security under the flag of the country in any State of the Union. Besides, our small army has scarcely been sufficient to guard our remote frontiers against Indian incursions. The seizure of this property, from all appearances, has been purely aggressive, and not in resistance to any attempt to coerce a State or States to remain in the Union.

At the beginning of these unhappy troubles I determined that no act of mine should increase the excitement in either section of the country. If the political conflict were to end in a civil war, it was my determined purpose not to commence it, nor even to furnish an excuse for it by an act of this government. My opinion remains unchanged, that justice as well as sound policy requires us still to seek a peaceful solution of the questions at issue between the North and the South. Entertaining this conviction, I refrained even from sending reënforcements to Major Anderson, who commanded the forts in Charleston harbor, until an absolute necessity for doing so should make itself apparent, lest it might unjustly be regarded as a menace of military coercion, and thus furnish, if not a provocation, a pretext for an outbreak on the part of South Carolina. No necessity for these reënforcements seemed to exist. I was assured by distinguished and upright gentlemen of South Carolina * that no attack upon Major Anderson was intended, but that, on the contrary, it was the desire of the State authorities, as much as it was my own, to avoid the fatal consequences which must eventually follow a military collision.

And here I deem it proper to submit, for your information, copies of a communication, dated December 28, 1860, addressed to me by R. W. Barnwell, J. H. Adams, and J. L. Orr, "Commissioners" from South Carolina, with the accompanying documents, and copies of my answer thereto, dated December 31.

In further explanation of Major Anderson's removal from Fort Moultrie to Fort Sumter, it is proper to state that, after my answer to the South Carolina "Commissioners," the War Department received a letter from that gallant officer, dated December 27, 1860, the day after this movement, from which the following is an extract:

"I will add, as my opinion, that many things convinced me that the authorities of the State designed to proceed to a hostile act" [evidently referring to the orders dated December 11, of the late Secretary of War]. "Under this impression, I could not hesitate that it was my solemn duty to move my command from a fort which we could not probably have held longer than forty-eight or sixty hours to this one, where my power of resistance is increased to a very great degree." It will be recollected that the concluding part of these orders was in the following terms: "The smallness of your force will not permit you, perhaps, to occupy more than one of the three forts; but an attack on, or attempt to take possession of either one of them, will be regarded as an act of hostility, and you may then put your command into either of them which you may deem most proper to increase its power of resistance. You are also authorized to take similar defensive steps whenever you have tangible evidence of a design to proceed to a hostile act."

It is said that serious apprehensions are, to some extent, entertained, in which I do not share, that the peace of this District may be disturbed before the 4th of March next. In any event, it will be my duty to preserve it, and this duty shall be performed.

In conclusion, it may be permitted to me to remark that I have often warned my countrymen of the dangers which now surround us.

---

* Messrs McQueen, Miles, Bonham, Boyce, and Keitt, members of the House of Representatives from South Carolina, on the 8th of December, 1860.

This may be the last time I shall refer to the subject officially. I feel that my duty has been faithfully, though it may be imperfectly, performed; and whatever the result may be, I shall carry to my grave the consciousness that I at least meant well for my country.

JAMES BUCHANAN.

WASHINGTON CITY, *Jan.* 8, 1861.

THE END.

www.ingramcontent.com/pod-product-compliance
Lightning Source LLC
Chambersburg PA
CBHW032053220426
43664CB00008B/983